Copyright © 2011, 2012 by Tyler A. Tayrien

All rights reserved

ISBN-13: 978-1502359698

Arena: King of the Flat Tracks

Printed in the United States of America

Sam Arena Introduction

Sam Arena was, without a doubt, the top Northern California half-mile racer of the 1940s. He became a motorcycle racing legend from his undefeated seasons and by setting numerous flat rack records in the 1930s and 1940s, and later earned six National Hill Climb Championships throughout the 1940s and 1950s.

After a career of racing throughout the Western United States, Florida, New Zealand, and England, Sam retired from flat track racing in 1947 to focus on motorcycle hill climbs. From where Sam left off, local riders such as Al Rudy, Larry Headrick, and Joe Leonard (collectively known as the San Jose Bunch), began dominating in their sport under the watchful eye of Tom Sifton. In 1953, after working for famed innovator Sifton for 20 years, Sam became owner of the San Jose Harley Davidson dealership which was the center of Northern California racing throughout the 1950s during the golden age of motorcycle racing.

Set against the excitement of motorcycle racing, "ARENA: King of the Flat Tracks" takes you on a thrill ride through 25 years in the life of the great Sam Arena, and these modern day pony express riders who risked life and limb on Friday nights and Sunday afternoons to cross the finish line first.

Table of Contents

"The Great Arena" 3
Cocktail Hour 3
Chapter 1 / Sam's Youth 9
    Borrowing Joe's Motorcycle 11
    Teenage Years 14
    The Kid Party 16
    First Hill Climb 20
    Skating Rink 22
    The Flat Track 25
Chapter 2 / The New Boss 29
    Meeting the Parents 31
    Finnegan Spear's Bike 33
    Learning Experience 36
    Wall of Death 38
    Fresno Fairgrounds 41
    San Jose Motorcycle Club 43
Chapter 3 / Florida Racing 44
    Smokin' Joe Petrali 47
    Miami Hospitality 49
    Florida 200 Miler 53
    Florida Girl 55
Chapter 4 / Overseas Racing 61
    Sailing for Australia 64
    Getting Married 68
    Racing in England 71
    San Jose MC 76

Watsonville Dealership 77

　　　Oakland Speedway 78

　　　Daytona 200 80

　　　Nevada Speed Race 83

Chapter 5 / Oakland Victory 85

　　　Back to Daytona 86

　　　1939 Oakland 200 88

　　　Endurance Run 90

　　　Lake Port Crash 92

　　　Last Oakland Race 94

　　　World War 2 96

　　　Racing Resumes 101

Chapter 6 / Friant Dam 102

　　　Stockton Half Mile 103

　　　Tin Hat Derby 106

　　　Covo Hill Climb 111

　　　Hollister Invasion 114

　　　Retiring from Flat Tracks 117

On the Back Deck 119

"The Great Arena"

Cocktail Hour

As I got out of the car with my grocery bag, I checked my watch and it's just a couple of minutes after four o'clock, perfect timing. It's a beautiful Saturday afternoon and I'm ready to relax and enjoy myself for a while after a long week. My friend Sam and his wife Myrt have an open invitation for neighbors and friends to drop by their house after 4 o'clock on Saturdays for a little wine. These get-togethers had started out a few years before I met Sam, and it was mainly a way to drink his homemade wine with a couple of neighbors and it grew from there. On any given Saturday afternoon it might be just Sam by himself, or a half dozen people could come by to socialize.

Sam and Myrt's house is along a ridge on the Almaden Hills near the old quicksilver mines, and their property is situated a couple hundred feet higher than the surrounding areas, so from their deck the whole Santa Clara valley ringed by mountain ranges opens up. We are in midsummer, so the valley hills are golden brown, and Mount Hamilton with its observatory is easy to spot out high on the eastern hills. I walked over to the left of their house and let myself in through the side gate. As I came around I can see Sam sitting on the back deck with his little radio, so he must be listening to a San Francisco Giants game.

Sam is in his late 70's, tall and lanky with slicked back gray hair that's been thinning since he was probably in his 30s. I've seen pictures of Sam from the mid-1930s, and he was a handsome devil back in the day with his thick head of black hair. Sam has a certain regal quality to him, like someone who isn't fazed by life's ups and downs as he moves along at his own pace. Compared to some of the stories I've heard from his youth, he's mellowed with age, but he's still quite the character and fun to be around.

Today Sam is wearing gray tennis shoes with Velcro straps, tan corduroy pants, and a red and brown plaid shirt. You can see a silver necklace hanging around his neck every so often which holds a Saint Christopher medal that Myrt gave him for his birthday many years ago. Saint Christopher is the patron saint that protects travelers, so that must also include motorcycle racers which is what Sam used to be years ago.

During the hot summers, the deck is partially shaded by the apple and peach tree branches hanging overhead which helps keep things cool. Near the fruit trees on the slope leading up to the neighbor's property, Sam has a small gold fish pond that might hold 30 gallons of water just behind the retaining wall which is waist-high. A water pump in the pond cycles water into a small stream that comes from higher on the hill that flows over a waterwheel which revolves by the water's motion as it drops back into the pond. The nearby hills have raccoons that come out at night, so Sam must put a flat screen of chicken wire over the pond each evening so the coons don't have a gold fish dinner at Sam's expense. He's forgotten once or twice to cover the pond and found it empty the next morning.

On the large back deck is a low round table between two metal chairs, one chair is exclusively for Sam and the other is for whoever comes first. After that, anyone else must use one of the nearby plastic chairs to get close to the table. Sam's chair doesn't have the best scenery by the way it's angled, but the other metal chair provides a full valley view. That's the reason I get to Sam's house as close to 4:00 as possible, before anyone else shows up to get the best seat. Sam likes his chair because he can keep an eye on the back slider for when people drop by, or when Myrt brings out food, which is a top priority for Sam.

"Hey," I shouted as I came around the side and stepped up on the deck.

"What's happening Sam?"

"The Giants are losing again, bunch of bums" he replies as he turns off the radio.

I start bringing out things from my grocery bag and setting them on the table.

"What do you have there?"

"Just some goodies."

First out is a bottle of red wine, then a wedge of asiago cheese, and finally a sour dough baguette. Already sitting on the table are some partially full bottles of wine, probably from last weekend, a cutting block with a couple pieces of cheese, and wine glasses that are set out. Sam also has some of his unopened wine bottles out that have label's printed with the type of wine like Arena Red and Private Reserve Chardonnay.

Something else on the table is a tasty concoction that Myrt makes for guests. In a small bowl, she combines olive oil and white wine vinegar, olives, chopped garlic (elephant garlic, if possible), and a little dried oregano. She usually makes it a couple hours ahead of happy hour so that the flavors have time to blend together. The combination of a little garlic scooped up with a piece of bread, followed by some nice asiago cheese plopped into the mouth, takes the taste buds into overdrive. Wash it down with a little red wine, and it's a slice of heaven! But don't eat too much garlic, because besides cleaning all of the bugs out of you, the smell of garlic will start seeping out of your pores and it won't go away for a day or so.

For a little background on Sam, he is the fifth of seven children born into the Arena family. His parents came over from Trabia, Sicily, arriving at Ellis Island in 1906 when his oldest brother Danny was close to three years old. The Arena family originally settled in Syracuse, New York, where a large number of Italians were living, but after the first snow, which they never had experienced before, it was time to move on.

They came to the West Coast and lived in San Francisco for a couple years before they finally settled in San Jose, largely because the weather in San Jose has a Mediterranean feel very similar to Sicily.

When Sam was a kid in the early 1920s, San Jose had only about forty thousand people compared to nearly a million people today. The Arena family first got indoor plumbing in 1924 after they moved to a house on First Street when Sam was 12 years old. Like many people in those days, they only had an outhouse, but during the nighttime when nature called, they would use chamber pots which were slid under the bed. Back then, cars still had to share the road with the horses and buggies, and airplanes were so uncommon that when one flew overhead, the kids would stop whatever they were doing to watch it fly by.

Their house on First Street didn't have electricity, but their neighbor's did, so one afternoon Sam's dad grabbed a long electrical cord, plugged it into the neighbor's power socket and ran the wire from the neighbor's house in through one of the windows of their house. When they screwed a bulb into the light socket on the cord and flipped on the power, Sam couldn't believe how bright it was and it seemed as if the sun had been turned on inside the house.

After I popped the cork on the bottle that I brought, I said to Sam, "I'm going to go inside and say hi to Myrt." I opened the back door (glass slider) and walked into the kitchen, and since their house is a split level, I could see down to the living room where Myrt was sitting on the couch, eating a bowl of soup, and watching Bonanza. She's wearing black slacks with fuzzy white slippers, a light pink shirt, and a white button-up sweater. Myrt is thin as a rail, probably weighs less than 100 pounds soaking wet, and she's often wearing a sweater to keep warm.

With her gray hair piled high up on her head, she looks like a typical grandmother, but she's tough as a boot. I really like Myrt; she is a wonderful person and always a pleasure to talk with.

"Hello Myrt, what's going on?"

"I'm just having a little chicken noodle soup."

"Are you going to come out and join us?" I already knew the answer to that question. She has only sat outside with us a couple times in the few dozen times that I've been over.

"Probably not" she says smiling.

After chatting with Myrt for a while, I wanted to take a look out in the garage. I like going out there to see the posters on the walls of Sam from his old racing days. I've seen those dozens of times, but I still get a kick out of looking at them. One poster has Sam wearing his old leather football helmet, which seems ancient today, but this picture is from 50 years ago and that's what everyone wore.

There are also two shelves running the length of the garage which are lined with dusty trophies. Many of them have been damaged once or twice over the decades by earthquakes, especially from the Loma Prieta earthquake in 1989, so they've seen better days.

Over on another wall is a poster from a hill climb in 1949 that gave Sam a third National Championship. The poster describes the event held in Dubuque, Iowa, on September 25, 1949: "Sam Arena, the old maestro, fairly flew up the grade to win the 80-cubic-inch expert championship and posted the fastest time of the day, going the 329 feet in 9.62 seconds, all on his first try. Sam's main hill-climb rival, Windy Lindstrom, took first in the 45-cubic-inch division at the Dubuque National." Nearby is my favorite poster which is from Sam's spectacular win at the 1938 Oakland 200, but I will tell you about that poster later.

This time I went out to the garage to check on a motorcycle that he is building. Sam kept a spaghetti-style chrome-molly frame from a record-breaking hill climb win he had at Friant Dam 40 years ago, and he is slowly piecing it back together. After his big win, the motorcycle sat at the Arena Harley Davidson dealership, and over the years it got picked apart until all that was left was the jackshaft and clutch.

One day he decided that he would try to return the bike to its former glory, and the first step was putting a motor together. Recently he went to "45's Forever" in San Jose, which specializes in Harley parts and motors from the 1930s through the 1970s, and picked out a 45-cubic-inch motor for the project. Sam told them what he wanted, and they said that they would call in a few weeks with the current status.

Now the frame is up on his workbench in his garage waiting for the other pieces to come in. Sam has sanded the frame and shot gray primer over it, but he's still deciding on what color to paint it.

You never know what you might come across in Sam's garage. One time I found a small stack of stickers that Sam used to put on every motorcycle sold at his dealership. Each sticker has a small picture of a guy riding an airborne motorcycle and the words "Ol' 79" which was Sam's racing number back in the day. He didn't think much about the stickers when I mentioned finding them, but I was like a kid finding a neat toy in the bottom of a cereal box.

Back outside, Sam and I are relaxing with a little wine and enjoying the view. A little wine helps get Sam talking and he has hundreds of stories from his racing days and growing up as a kid when they called this area "Valley of Hearts Delight," and orchards covered most of the surrounding land. I always enjoy coming by to hear Sam's stories, so after we've gotten past how the San Francisco Giants are doing, and weather-related information, I asked Sam to tell me about his earliest memories of growing up in San Jose.

Chapter 1 / Sam's Youth

When I was a young boy, my brothers and all of my friends would play out in the orchards, or when the temperature warmed up, we would go to the swimming hole in Coyote Creek off of 17th and Williams. A bend in the river created an area wide and deep enough to get a running jump off the bank without any worries, or you can swing out on the tree rope and splash into the water. One bad thing is that the watering hole is also a favorite place for the truant officer, Mr. Lake, to find kids playing hooky from school. Everyone is afraid of Mr. Lake, and if someone sees him coming, everyone gets warned and we quickly scatter.

One warm summer day I'm coming home from the swimming hole with my brothers Joe and Danny, and the road had been oiled a couple days before and you could see the heat rising off of the blacktop. We are all barefoot and as we're walking along my feet just couldn't take it. I tried to walk in the dirt closer to the orchards, but then I couldn't keep up with my brothers. So I had to go back on the level ground close to the road and out of the soft dirt, but my feet started burning again from the oiled gravel. I'm on the verge of tears because my feet hurt so much, when Joe picked me up and sat me on his shoulders as he kept walking. I don't know how he can walk barefoot and I couldn't, but he's six years older and somehow his feet are tough enough to take the heat.

As we are going along and I'm sitting on Joe's shoulders, we watched a guy on a shiny blue motorcycle go by. Danny said that it looked like a new Henderson Deluxe. To me the guy seemed like he didn't have a care in the world as he rode off into the distance.

I said, "I'm going to have a motorcycle before long and then no more walking for me."

Danny replied, "It's not like you're walking right now anyway."

"You know what I mean!"

I've been saving money for several months from my paper route and I eventually had put together enough to buy a Smith Motor Wheel. The Smith Motor Wheel is a small gas powered motor that is mounted to the frame of a bicycle. A leather belt connects from the pulley on the motor to the rear wheel of the bicycle and as the pedals are cranked, the momentum builds up energy and after loosening the belt, the bike is put down and when the belt is tightened it propels the bike forward. A small tank hangs off of the frame that holds enough gas for over an hour of riding.

Now that my bicycle is motorized, I can make my paper route in record time, even fast enough that I can pick up another route and still do it in less time than riding a bicycle on just the one.

One day as I'm riding through the neighborhood, the local kids saw me having fun and they wanted rides. Baby Tony said, "Hey Sam, let me take your bike for a little ride."

I wasn't going to, but I thought for a second and said, "It will cost you a nickel."

Baby Tony dug into his pocket and pulled out a nickel and handed it to me.

I said, "If you crash it will cost you a quarter!"

"I ain't gonna crash."

He rode around the block and came back all excited, then another kid handed over a nickel. Before long I had made 20 cents, and no one crashed my bike, so I was really happy about it. From then on, whenever someone wanted to ride, I'd charge them a nickel to go around the block on my motorized bicycle. So, on top of the money I make from my paper route, I'm making a little coin on the side by charging for rides.

***** ***** *****

On Saturday, Danny and I went to the wooden track over on San Carlos Street to see the motorcycle races. Although the wooden track has seen its better days, when a track is newly built and the wood is sanded and polished, it's really nice. But as a track ages over time, splinters came into play, and if a rider goes down on a wooded track, he might get stuck like a pincushion. They say that racers might be pulling splinters out of their bodies for months, If not years, after crashing on a run-down wooden track.

The track bikes have small thin tires, big motors, and not much else. Once the first race begins, six guys are battling during the four-lap heat trying to qualify for the main event. It's exciting to watch the racers zoom around the track, but as they go by it hurts my ears because the motorcycles are so loud. As the riders go along the high-banked corners moving close to 50 mph (miles per hour), they are practically horizontal to the track with their faces just a couple feet off of the wooden planks.

These riders must be fearless or crazy to race those two-wheel rockets, but watching them gets my heart racing and I'm thinking that maybe I might want to try this someday. During the next heat, I saw local guy Phil Stosser shoot over the top of one of the high-banked corners and go out of sight. Maybe I didn't want to try this after all.

Borrowing Joe's Motorcycle

Although I still have the Smith Motor Wheel, I've been riding my brother's motorcycle a lot lately. Joe has an Indian Power Plus with a 61-cubic-inch motor, complete with a wooden eight-ball on the hand shift against the gas tank. When I'm riding Joe's Indian around, it makes my motorized bicycle seem like I'm still pedaling.

If Joe isn't using it, the bike is usually sitting out in the garage. So before he got home from school and I'd take it out for short rides around town. One day when I knew that he wouldn't be home until the evening, I took the Indian out for a little ride. I pushed the bike out of our driveway and down the sidewalk a few houses, then I jump-started it and took off down the street.

It's a nice warm day and the bike is running good, so I'm enjoying every minute of it. As I'm riding down Almaden Road and taking a turn onto Phelan Avenue, I hit a small gravel patch going into the corner and as the tires lost traction the bike slid out as I went down going about 20 mph. The Indian has a left-handed throttle, and with the bike falling on its left side, the throttle got stuck wide open. As the back tire is spinning I'm trying to shut off the motor, but as the motor redlined, the top of the cylinder blew off. From that small explosion, the spark plug shot upward into the gas tank piercing the metal, but the problem is that the plug is still sparking and a trickle of gas is coming down by it. Quicker than you could snap your fingers, the Indian Power Plus erupted into a small bonfire.

I'm desperately grabbing dirt from the side of the road and throwing it onto the bike trying to extinguish the fire just as a dump truck loaded with sand is driving by. The truck driver saw what is going on, stopped and backed up, then he used the lift to raise the bed and dump sand on the bike to put the fire out. Although he only used a small part of the load, a couple hundred pounds of cone shaped sand is covering my brother's bike.

The driver came down out of the truck and ambled back to where I was standing.

"Guess it got put out," the truck driver said without a hint of irony.

The air is filled with a combination of burning gas, paint, and metal from the still smoking sand pile. After some struggling, and trying not to get burned by the hot metal, I pulled the bike from the sand, and it didn't look too good at all. Parts of the bike are melted, most of the red paint and the Indian logo on the gas tank has burned off down to the metal, even the leather seat didn't escape unharmed.

I said out loud, "Not much here that's not ruined."

The truck driver nodded, "That's pretty safe to say."

I have got to get back home soon, and since the truck driver isn't going in my direction, I thanked him for his help and started pushing the bike with its melted tires the five miles home. The whole time that I am pushing my brother's bike, I'm thinking about which method he is going to use to kill me. After a couple hours, I made it home and pushed the bike behind the garage. No one had seen me so far, now I just need to find a good time to break the news.

That evening after the family had dinner I told Joe, "I was out riding your motorcycle earlier and had a little problem."

"What kind of problem?"

"I probably need to show you."

As we walked outside towards the garage, I stayed a couple steps away from Joe so I could start running if needed.

"I'll pay you back for any damages" I said as we walked. I don't think that I sounded very believable, but I hoped to keep the pounding he would inflict on me to a minimum. Once he saw what used to be his motorcycle, he yelled "What the hell happened?"

I retold the story, and although I completely destroyed his bike, for some reason Joe didn't beat me to a pulp like he had every right to. Even though I had borrowed his bike without permission, he knew that it was an accident. But Joe made it perfectly clear that borrowing anything from him without permission wasn't going to happen anymore.

After torching Joe's motorcycle, I had to get serious about getting my own motorcycle. It took several months, but with the money that I've been saving from my paper route, and some dough that Joe and Danny chipped in, I was able to find a 37-cubic-inch Indian Scout for cheap. The motorcycle needed some work like new piston rings, and the carburetor needed a rebuild, but I can do that myself. The first time I rode down the street on my very own motorcycle, it felt like I was on a cloud.

Teenage Years

When high school is out for the summer, I work at Biscelia Brothers Cannery, and during canning season, I usually run the peach-peeling machine on a 7-day, 10-hour shift. The process is mainly a combination of hot water and lye dissolving the skins on the peaches, and then cool water is sprayed on the fruit to clean it as it traveled along the conveyor belt. After that, the peaches go into another room where they are sliced and put into cans, then a header seals on the tops and the cans are sent on to the warehouse.

I'm earning $16 per week which is pretty good money for a teenager. That supplies me with gas for my motorcycle and helped me save enough money to buy my brother Danny's Ford Model T. The Ford isn't in very good shape, the folding canvas top is ripped and torn, and two of the four tires are bald, but it is still a vehicle that I can fix up. After Danny and I exchanged money, I went to work removing the doors and covers to the motor bay, and since it didn't have a front seat at the moment, only a wooden box, I built a wood bench to sit on while driving.

I usually have money in my pocket, but I don't like spending it, so I run out of gas every week or three and then I have to push the car to the nearest gas station and part with a dime. Because I enjoy working on motorcycles and the Model T, I enrolled in auto mechanics during my senior year at San Jose High. I figured that after graduation I can go by the Harley Davidson dealership and try to land a job. If that doesn't work out, I'll go to Adolph Lamagrie's Indian dealership over on the Alameda, or I could talk to my friend Mike Spadaford who is the local Excelsior dealer. Although I like Harley Davidson's the best, any mechanic job might have to do.

A few years ago this store only sold bicycles, then one day the place had new owners and a banner went up in front that read, "Powell Brothers, San Jose Harley Davidson." The place isn't very big, maybe six to eight motorcycles are lined up in parallel on the wooden showroom floor, and it has a small work area out in the back through the double doors.

The Powell brothers seem like good guys, but they have some shady characters hanging around the shop. Some are like the

Guillianie brothers, Jimmy and Fats, who frequent the place but I've never seen them on motorcycles. The word is that Jimmy ran moonshine during prohibition driving a Ford Roadster with a built motor out of a Cadillac, and if the Feds were after Jimmy, his roadster would leave them in the dust. Fats is more of a card player, they say that he always carries a roll of bills on him in case a card game came around. Another guy that hung around the dealership is Joey Lang who did time for a botched life insurance scheme. So while the Powell brothers might be selling Harleys, other things not related to motorcycles are probably going on at the dealership too.

One morning they found Fats Guillianie in a car behind the shop with a bullet in his head. Before long the cops showed up and started asking questions about the kind of people that frequent the dealership. Soon the Harley Davidson headquarters in Milwaukee got wind of things, and before long, the Powell brother's franchise rights were revoked and the factory put Fred Merlow in charge of the dealership.

As things blew over, the dealership got back to focusing on selling motorcycles and being a place for motorcycle enthusiasts to socialize. Soon after taking over, Mr. Merlow moved the shop from 580 First Street up the street to 465 South First Street, and not long after the move I came in to talk to him about getting a job.

"Hello Mr. Merlow, my name is Sam Arena."

"Sure Sam, I know you. What can I do for you?"

"I'm taking auto mechanics in school and I'll graduate in a month, I wanted to see if there's any chance you could use a mechanic?"

"The way it looks, we might have an opening if business keeps up. Come back in a couple weeks and I will know for sure."

So three weeks later I went back to talk with Mr. Merlow and he offered me a job. So after graduating, I started working as a mechanic for the Fred J. Merlow Harley Davidson dealership. I'm enjoying my work at the shop and Jerry Raye, who is one of the other shop mechanics, is showing me the ropes.

The Kid Party

One evening during the early summer, one of my friends is having one of those goofy house parties where everyone comes dressed up as kids and I'm going with my girlfriend Lillian. Although Lillian and I are dating, we aren't really an item, although she looks fine in a tight blouse. I just graduated from San Jose High and, if nothing else, this might be a good way to meet some new girls.

I picked up Lillian in my Model T and we drove over to the house party. I came dressed in cut-off jeans, no shoes and a white untucked shirt with a bow tie, while Lillian wore a light blue shirt and a white skirt with white tap shoes. The party is at a big house on Hicks Avenue and it's surrounded by cherry orchards that are in full bloom. I saw dozens of people dressed up like little kids, and some other people were just driving by to see what all the excitement was about.

Once we got inside, Lillian and I walked around to say hello to some of our friends and looking around the crowd, I recognized a few of the neighborhood kids and some from my old school. I went over to talk to a buddy, and that's when I saw from across the room a thin-framed girl with wavy dark hair. She is a doll wearing a white short-sleeve shirt and a little yellow skirt that puffed out. She also had on little white socks and black tappers and looked like a girl of 9 or 10 ready to go to church.

When I saw her, I said to myself, that's the one for me. But since I'm already here with someone, I'm in a bit of a jam. I needed to find a way to brush off my date for a little while so I can try to meet this mystery girl.

My buddy Jimmy is at the party and he didn't bring a date, so I went over to talk to him.

"I need you to do me a favor, I want to go talk to someone for a few minutes but I don't need Lillian coming to find me, so can you entertain her for a while?"

I knew he liked Lillian anyway, so I figured it wouldn't be a problem.

"Anything for a friend" he replied as he looked around for Lillian.

I said while pointing, "Last time I saw Lillian, she was talking with some of her girlfriends in one of the rooms over there." He smiled and started walking in that direction.

I headed the opposite direction to where I saw the mystery girl earlier and spotted her standing with two other girls. I watched her for a minute or two, but I knew that I didn't have a lot of time to spare, so it's now or never. I walked up to her, smiled, stuck out my hand and said,
"Hi, my name is Sam."

She looked at me and smiled as she held out her hand. "I'm Myrt."

Her girlfriends just kind of stood there, trying to figure out who I was.

"Do you mind if I talked to you for a minute?" They all kind of looked at each other for a moment, Myrt nodded to them, and then her two friends drifted off.

I said, "That's a great outfit you're wearing." I thought she looked like a million bucks.

"Thanks. My Mom and I made it for the party."

"How did you get that skirt so puffy?"

"You don't like it?"

"No, no, I think it's great."

She just smiled. Wow, what a pretty smile. We were standing there for a few awkward moments when Myrt said, "Everyone looks so funny."

"I know. I can't believe that I'm wearing this get-up."

"Ah, you look cute," she said as she smiled afterwards.

"Great, that's the look that I was after" I said laughing.

When I asked her who she had come with, she said that she had been set up on a blind date with someone named Kenny. "I thought my date was going to be with a Kenny I know from down the street, but instead he turned out to be another Kenny who I can't stand." Well I thought, at least she doesn't have a steady boyfriend. So far things were going well for two people who just met out of the blue.

I asked her, "So where do you go to school?"

"I just graduated from Theodore Roosevelt Junior High and I'm getting ready to go to the San Jose High to earn a domestic degree." Her just graduating from junior high means that she is three or four years younger than me.

I said, "I can't say that I've seen you around. Do you live around here?"

"I live over on North 9th Street."

I replied, "I'm over on 1st, so we live about eight or so blocks from each other."

Then she asked, "Where do you go to school?"

"I just graduated from San Jose Technical in auto mechanics."

As those words came out of my mouth, I hoped she didn't think I'm some creepy old guy. So to keep off the subject of how old I was I asked, "Do you have any brothers and sisters?"

"I have a brother Eugene and three sisters, Eleanor, Camille, and Eva. I am the youngest in the family. How about you?" she asked.

"Three brothers and three sisters: Danny, Joe, Annie, Josie, me, Angelo (Babe) and Sally (Celeste) who is the youngest. My oldest brother used to be Gaetano until a schoolteacher asked him his name, and when he said Gaetano, she called him Danny to Americanize him, and he's been called Danny ever since."

She looked a little confused. "He was born in Sicily before my parents came here."

She asked, "So you are really a Sam?"

"Actually, I'm Santo."

"Pleased to meet you Santo." She has a sense of humor, I like that.

I looked around for any sign of Lillian, and then I asked Myrt, "Do you want to dance."

"I don't know." I could tell that she is really bashful. "Maybe just one dance."

Out on the dance floor we talked about her school and hobbies, and she said that roller skating is one of her favorite things to do. The funny thing is when we were out on the dance floor, even with everyone around, it felt to me like it was just the two of us.

As the song ended and we came off the dance floor she said, "That was fun, but I need to go find my friends." I figured that I better say something good because I might not see her again. "I'm sure glad I got to meet you. Do you think that sometime we can see each other again?"

She paused and said, "How about your girlfriend?"

I was shocked that she knew I came here with someone. "She's just a friend," I said.

"Okay, maybe." Then she walked off to find her friends.

I was still at the party with Lillian, but it wasn't the same after meeting Myrt. I saw Myrt once more that night from across the room, and I wasn't sure if she saw me or not, but I'm hooked. I couldn't help thinking about her for the rest of the evening. When I got home later in the evening, Mama asked me how the dance was, "Great, I met a dream tonight."

First Hill Climb

At the Harley dealership, Mr. Merlow and I had been talking in the past few days about building a hill climber, and we finally decided to get serious. Fred had an old JH model in the back that had been picked over for parts, and it didn't have a front rim and tire, but other than missing one of the heads, it had a complete 61-cubic-inch motor, so it's a good place to start.

Mr. Merlow and I took out the motor and stripped the bike down to the bare bones. Starting with the motor, we put in new pistons and rings, valves, and found a matching head that we cleaned and ported like the other. After that we bolted the motor back in the frame and put in a lower gear into the transmission. Fred had to machine an oversized rear sprocket that would fit on the bike while I built a chain guard. After adding a front rim and tire, it didn't take long before we could fire up the motor and ride the bike around to see if everything worked.

With the big rear sprocket, it probably wouldn't go any faster than 20 mph, but we needed low-end power for the hills. I test-rode the Harley down the alley, but I didn't gun the throttle very much, as I was afraid that the front end would lift and flip the bike over before I could stop it. Everything seemed to be working fine on the bike, and the final step would be to weld together a set of hill-climb chains. The chain runs on either side of the tire holding the chains in place, while short chains cross the rear tire and are spaced out eight to ten times. We used worn out junk chains that we had around the shop and, after an hour or so, we had a set made and now we're ready for business. We circled the calendar for a tournament two weeks later that's up near Oakland.

On the morning of the hill-climb, Mr. Merlow and I loaded the bike into the back of his delivery truck and headed to Oakland. The event was busy with over 40 riders separated into four divisions, 45- and 80-cubic-inch, novice and professional. I paid my entrance fee, got a number, and after the stewards looked over my bike, I'm ready for the contest to begin.

As it got closer to my turn, I could see that the hill is pretty chewed up and getting traction might be difficult. Going up a steep hill like this isn't so much of a straight line; it's more of a weaving "S" as the rear tire is spinning to get traction. I've seen guys at hill climbs before using a jump-and-churn method when the dirt is so chopped up, and that seemed to work pretty well, so I figured that's something I might have to do today.

When it came for my turn, I lined up my black-primered bike at the bottom of the hill just in front of the short wooden guard wall that stops dirt from flying back 50 feet into the parking lot. From this view, the hill looked like it went straight up. I made sure that my helmet strap is tight and that my wrist band is secure. All hill climbers use a cable-tethered wristband that triggers the kill switch when someone gets knocked off their bike. At the end of the cable is a piece of leather that goes between two metal connectors, and when the leather is pulled out and the metal touches, the motor shuts off.

Once they gave me the sign that I was clear to go, I pulled in the clutch and dropped it into gear, and after I revved the motor a couple times, I let out the clutch and twisted the throttle. The bike roared and the front lifted slightly as I gained speed and the incline quickly increased. My speed is dropping as the angle of the hill gets steeper and the further up the hill I went, the more the ground is churned up and harder for the tire's chains to grip, but the bike still has power.

When I felt that the bike is close to getting bogged down in the dirt, I started jumping on the foot pegs trying to get the chains to dig in. I continued to do it, jumping the bike in short bursts, leap-frogging my way upwards until I crested the hill. In my excitement I went nearly 10 feet past the finish line because I wasn't 100% sure that I actually made it. A few guys slapped me on the back after I stopped, congratulating me for making it to the top. I ended up winning the first place trophy in the novice division on my very first hill climb.

Skating Rink

When Myrt and I were out on the dance floor at the kid party, she mentioned that she often went roller-skating on Sundays. On a Sunday afternoon two weeks after the night I met her, I drove the Model T over on the Alameda to the roller rink where she said that she goes to. I'm hoping that she is here and didn't skip this Sunday for some reason. Also, if she is here, I hope that she is not with a guy because that would really be a downer. On the other side of the coin, if she is here, maybe she doesn't want me around, but I'm sure I'll figure that out pretty quickly.

Within a minute of arriving, I saw Myrt out on the rink floor and my heart did an odd thump. She looked just as pretty as I remember, if not better. As I watched, it didn't look like she was with anyone, which is a good thing. After a few minutes, I walked up to the short wall going around the roller rink, and as she came around to my side, she saw me and looked surprised. When she stopped in front of where I was standing, she smiled.

"What are you doing here?"

"I thought that since I had some free time, I would drop by and do a little skating."

"Really?" She didn't sound very convinced.

She looked towards my empty hands and said, "Where are your skates?"

"I haven't grabbed them yet. I'm just making sure that it's not too crowded out on the floor. It doesn't look too bad out there." There were only about 40 people rolling around inside a place that could probably hold 240. "Let me go grab a pair of skates, and I'll be right back."

So I went over to the counter and threw down my nickel for a pair of skates. I started having second thoughts about showing up because I haven't been on skates since I was a kid. I sure hope that I don't fall on my ass in front of her, that would be tough to live down.

I skated out on the rink while she is just heading to the other side so I have a few seconds to warm up, but she's moving pretty quickly around the rink which isn't giving me much time to work on my skating skills.

She rolled up beside me. "Hello, stranger."

"Hey, you're pretty good on skates." She is a really good skater, and not just compared to me.

"I've been skating since I was a little girl. I've even won a couple of trophies."

"Impressive." I said smiling.

We skated and talked at the skating rink for little over an hour and by that time, I'd had enough.

"How about we walk over to the malt shop around the corner?"

"Okay, just as long as I'm home by four o'clock."

I figured walking would be better than taking my Model T so we could talk easier, then maybe I can drive her home afterwards.

When we got to the malt shop, we found a booth and sat down. As I look across the table at her, she has the most wonderful brown eyes, sort of like chocolate.

The boy came over to take our orders.

"What would you like, Myrt?"

"Strawberry malt."

"Make that two."

Once he walked away, Myrt said, "It's funny you showing up at the rink."

"It was just a coincidence" I replied. I'm sure she knows that I was only there to see her.

"You were pretty rusty when you started out there."

I smiled and said, "I don't know how you could tell."

"I was thinking that you said before that your folks are from Sicily, where in Sicily?"

"They are from the town of Trabia, which isn't too far from Palermo."

"What did you parents do when they lived in Trabia?"

"In the old country, my dad was a cooper, which is a barrel maker. He was known as one of the best coopers in all of Sicily. Now he mainly builds houses around San Jose."

When our malts showed up, we relaxed as each of us enjoyed our drinks.

I said, "You know everything about me, what does your Dad do?"

"He's a brick mason. He's working on the new Post Office at Market and Santa Clara."

"Second question, you know we're Sicilian, what nationality are your folks?"

"Well, my father is Scottish and my mother is of Spanish descent, her maiden name is Barrera." "So the Spanish side is where you get that sultry look."

She gave me a little sly smile over that comment.

After a few minutes of chit-chat, when our malts were about half way done, I wanted to ask her out on an actual date, not just me showing up unannounced.

"I was wondering, maybe we can go out next Saturday, catch a movie or something."

"Sure, a movie would be fun." she replied.

That was a relief. "I guess it's a date then."

I felt pretty good about how the afternoon turned out. We walked back to my car, and I took the long way as I drove her home.

Once we got to her house, I made sure to walk her up to her front porch steps.

I said, "I'll see you Saturday at 6:00."

"See you then."

As I drove home, I hoped that the week would go by fast.

The Flat Track

I went to the Emeryville fairgrounds to watch some flat track races, and it happens that Sprouts Elder is racing that day. Sprout's is a legend and he's practically unstoppable on both tracks and hills. I'm standing by the outer fence watching the racers and here comes Sprouts on his Douglas motorcycle sliding gracefully through the corners. To me, the sound and the speed are exciting as hell, and watching the racers battle it out gives me goose bumps. I've often thought that these guys are like modern day pony express riders, just on a different kind of horse. That night I knew that I had to try it myself, I just had to figure out how to find a motorcycle that I could use. My old Indian would blow up before I finished a race.

The following day I went by to see my friend Mike Spadaford who is the local Excelsior dealer.

"Hey, Mike."

"Sam, how's things?"

"Not too shabby."

"What brings you in today?"

"Well, I've got a favor to ask. I'd like to try my hand at flat track racing but I don't have a decent bike. Any chance you might have something lying around that I can use."

"I might have something out back, follow me." We walked out back of the shop, and he showed me a used Excelsior road model that was in decent condition.

"You don't mind me using it? It might not come back in this condition, or maybe not at all."

"I'm not worried about it."

"Thanks Mike, I appreciate it."

My brother helped me bring the Excelsior home, and I worked on it out in the family garage. I took off anything that wasn't needed like the head light and tail light, replaced the heavy full-size seat for a small bicycle seat that I welded on, removed the heavy front fender, and cut down the exhaust pipes.

I remember someone saying that you can practice spinning the rear tire on gravel to simulate what a dirt track feels like, so that week I took the Excelsior out to a gravel parking lot a few times to screw around. I did figure 8's on the gravel and broke the rear tire loose to learn how to handle the sliding. I laid the bike down twice and tore the hell out of my knee, but I felt better about the basics of sliding. The only thing left is to get out on a dirt oval track and see if I know anything about racing.

***** ***** *****

When I went to pick up Myrt on Saturday for our very first official date, I rode over to her parent's house on my motorcycle. My old Indian has a small buddy seat on the rear fender and with her slim frame, she didn't need any more than that. When I had mentioned at the malt shop that I might pick her up on my motorcycle, she said it was fine by her. Some girls won't get on a motorcycle at all, so I was happy to hear that she didn't mind. When I pulled up in front of her house, she is sitting on the steps talking with a girlfriend.

I shut off the bike and asked, "Are you ready to go?"

"Yep." Then Myrt said to her friend, "I'll talk to you later Ella."

Once I started my motorcycle, she didn't hesitate at all and hopped on.

"You okay back there?"

"I'm fine."

Then we took off for the movie theater to see a double feature of Laurel and Hardy.

After I bought popcorn and sodas, we walked into the theater and found a place closer to the back to sit. While we waited for the movie to begin, to break the ice I said, "You know we used to own a movie theatre."

"You did? Which one was that?"

"It was the Royal Theater over on 1st Street."

"You family doesn't own it anymore?"

"No. Things didn't turn out too good."

"Why is that?"

"Well, Dad didn't really check things over before he bought the place and once the theater opened, he found out the sound system was awful. Then, San Jose had several 100-degree days and the giant fans we used to try and cool down the place were worthless. My Dad never could get out from behind the eight ball, so after eight months, Papa sold the theater."

"That's too bad that it didn't work out."

I said, "Papa is a jack-of-all-trades. He used to have a card room over on Alma Street. It was a good place, and things went pretty well for the four years he owned it. Each year around Christmas, my family would put on a holiday dinner for all the regulars. People would show up during the day and evening and my mother would make raviolis with pasta sauce while other people would bring in a dish or two, something like meatballs or cannolis. Mrs. Mattos made the best cannolis, better tasting than even those from the bakery."

"One year things turned out a little differently. During the Christmas party, three men with guns and wearing masks came in and robbed the place. Dad was hit over the head trying to stop them, and they took all the money from the register and any money on the card tables. After the robbery, people didn't want to come back, too afraid that it might happen again. Papa decided not to keep the card room going after that."

Myrt said, "I can't blame him. I would be worried too."

About then, the theater lights went down and movie previews started. I don't like talking about me or my family very much, but talking with Myrt is so easy. Towards the end of the movie, we held hands, and I'm starting to feel close to her. I hope that she feels the same way about me.

***** ***** *****

I entered my first flat track race on a dirt track on the outskirts of Palo Alto. I got out on the track for practice laps with a goal of cutting down lap times and improving. The first thing is getting the hang of the hot shoe. The hot shoe is a steel plate that's on the bottom of your left foot, and it lightly slides along the dirt to provide balance as you let off of the throttle going into the left-turn corners, and the rear end of the bike gets pitched sideways. As you are coming out of the corner, the quicker you lift your hot shoe off the ground and put it back on the peg, the faster that weight is shifted to the rear tire which gives the bike more balance and traction.

When it is time to get lined up for my first real heat, I'm a little nervous as I made sure that my jacket is zipped up and that my hot shoe is strapped on tight. The stock Excelsior is not nearly as powerful or as light as the other racing bikes, so I'm at the rear of the pack. Although I didn't qualify for the main event, after getting in over an hour of practice and experiencing race conditions in the six-lap heat, I felt that good things are ahead.

Chapter 2 / The New Boss

I have been working for Mr. Merlow at the dealership for over a year and a half, but he recently decided that he didn't want to stay in the motorcycle business anymore. Mr. Merlow said that things were in the works and that the dealership is going to be taken over by Tom Sifton who is a subdealer under Dudley Perkins. Dud Perkins is well known in California; he opened one of the first Harley dealerships west of the Mississippi in San Francisco in 1914, and he was a hill climber before that.

They started having climbs at a 500 foot hill at San Juan Capistrano in 1916, and for the first couple of years no one made it to the top, so the winner each year was chosen based on how far up the hill they went. The first year's winner made it 327 feet out of the 500. In 1919, Dud Perkins showed up at San Juan Capistrano and topped the hill in 34 seconds. The second year he made it in 26 seconds and still no other rider had made it to the top of the hill.

I asked Mr. Merlow about Tom Sifton and I found out that Sifton wasn't a slouch either. In 1929 Sifton won the Pacific Coast Championship for flat tracks, the Pismo Beach Rally, and the West Coast Hill Climb Championship, all on bikes that he built and tuned. So Dud Perkins and Tom Sifton are true motorcycle guys and not just talking the part.

Sifton had been working for Perkins for a few years when the opportunity came up to take over the Merlow dealership, and Perkins gave Sifton his okay to take over as a subdealer. A subdealer essentially means that the person with the territory rights allowed someone else to open a dealership in their area and the dealer received 10% of the profits. As is usually the case, the guy running the dealership brings his own group of mechanics, and I figured that I wouldn't be needed anymore. So instead of showing up just to get fired, I got a job at the Continental Can Company working as a header soldering on can tops.

After working at the cannery for a couple weeks, I went by the old dealership to see how things are going. When I walked in through the shop door, Mr. Sifton is standing behind the counter, and when he saw me, he said, "Sam, where have you been?"

"I've been working."

"What? You don't want to work for me?"

"Sure I do, but I figured you already had your own mechanics."

"I still want you to work for me. You know everyone in the area, and I don't."

Then he said, "Where are you working?"

"Over at the Continental Can Company."

Then Mr. Sifton asked, "How much are they paying you?"

"$20 per week." Which isn't bad money for someone just out of high school.

"I'll give you $25 a week if you come to work for me."

I was sold until he said, "One other thing, all my mechanics ride new Harley Davidsons."

My hopes were quickly crashed. "Sorry, but I don't have the money for that."

Mr. Sifton said, "I'll tell you what, I'll take $5 out from your weekly check to pay for the bike. What do you say?"

I didn't hesitate as I stuck out my hand, "I say that you've got yourself a mechanic."

I can't believe it, instead of riding my 10-year old (1922, 61-cubic-inch) Indian, I will be driving a brand new Harley that costs $380. I'll make the same amount of money as over at the cannery even after deducting for the bike payment, so it's like I'm getting a new Harley for free. I also get to do what I love to do, working on and being around motorcycles. There and then, Mr. Sifton became like Jesus Christ to me, and he became my hero and mentor.

Meeting the Parents

I've been seeing Myrt a couple times a week, and although we had only known each other for a couple months, my parents have been asking me to invite her over for dinner. They knew that we were pretty serious, so they wanted to meet the girl that I'm spending all of my free time with. I had mentioned to Myrt that my Mama mainly speaks Italian, so the conversation might be a little one-sided. Even with those obstacles she is looking forward to meeting my parents Maria and Santo. My Mama can speak some English, she's learned enough to become a citizen, but she is embarrassed by her accent and doesn't speak it around many people. Papa is fine with English and can carry on a conversation, but he also prefers speaking Italian most of the time.

After picking up Myrt and bringing her back to our house, she got to meet my folks.

"Myrt, this is my Mama."

"Nice to meet you."

In rough English Mama replied, "Nice to meet you too."

"And this is my Papa."

Myrt stuck out her hand and Papa said, "Hello Myrt."

Myrt has met my brothers and sisters before, so they all said hi to her.

Soon after we sat down and enjoyed spaghetti and Mama's homemade sour dough bread that she makes in the stone oven in our backyard. I thought sitting around the table with all of my family might make Myrt nervous, especially since she is the center of attention, but she didn't seem to mind.

After dinner, we went into the family room where we could carry on our conversations. Mama whispered to me and I said, "Erwin and Eleanor."

Mama asked another question and I replied, "Muratore."

I turned to Myrt, "Mama wanted to know what kind of work your Father does, so I said a mason."

Papa said, "So your Father is working on the new Post Office on Santa Clara. It looks like it should be open before long."

Myrt replied, "They've been putting in a lot of hours to get it done."

Mama said something else to me and smiled. "Mama says that she hears you are good at roller skating?" That embarrassed Myrt, but she smiled while Mama smiled back. It was a very nice evening with my parents, and Myrt came through with flying colors. When it was time for me to take her home, Mama said as she held Myrt's hands and smiled, "bambolina."

She asked me, "What did your Mama say?"

"She said, pretty girl."

After I took her home, we sat outside on the steps talking about the evening.

"I love your Mother, and your Dad is nice. He's quieter than I expected."

I laughed, "He was on his best behavior tonight."

"I also think it's cute that your parents share the same plate for dinner."

As long as I remember, they share an oblong shaped plate which is maybe a foot and a half long and the width is about half that. Although they share a single plate, each person has their own side. "I'm sure it's something fairly common in Sicily. One good thing is that it's difficult to be mad for long with someone you're sharing the same plate with."

***** ***** *****

A few weeks later at the dealership, Tom wanted to show me something out back. When we got outside, I saw a shiny new Harley Davidson VL.

"Is that my bike?"

"That's the one."

It's a beautiful red and black combination, and with the new art deco eagle design on the gas tank, it's as pretty as can be. The hand-shifter has a chrome ball controlling the three-speed transmission bolted to the 74-cubic-inch twin-cylinder motor. I can't believe my good fortune.

Finnegan Spear's Bike

I've been racing at local tracks with the heavy Excelsior and I've been getting into the middle of the pack in most heats, but I can't match the guys on actual racing bikes, especially on the straights where they have the power to peel away.

One night Mr. Sifton was at the track watching the races, and he saw how I was struggling on the Excelsior. Later he came over to the infield and talked to me.

"Hey Sam, you were doing some good racing out there."

"Not too good, I didn't get into the money."

"So you really want to be a racer?"

"Sure I do" I replied.

"Maybe I can help. I have a bike in Los Angeles that you can use. Bill Crane (who is our shop manager) and I built a bike for Finnegan Spear, but things didn't work out, and he's not using it anymore. I'll get the short-tracker shipped up here and you can use it."

"That sounds great. I would kill to be able to use a real race bike."

He smiled and said, "Let's not do anything drastic."

***** ***** *****

Finnegan Spear's bike arrived two weeks later from Los Angeles. As Bill and I are taking the bike out of the crate, I notice that it's a much smaller motorcycle than I was expecting. The small dark green gas tank hanging on the black frame makes it look little, but the 500cc motor in the frame is a full-sized power plant. This bike is little more than an engine, two wheels, and a kill switch. Tom says that without brakes, the only way to scrub off speed is by hitting the kill switch in the corner. On top of being smaller, the bike weights over a 100 pounds less than the Excelsior I've been using, so the difference will be like night and day. Tom wanted to do some work on the motor before I could ride it, so I helped Bill remove the motor from the frame and we set it up on the work bench so he and Tom could get to work.

Tom is a highly intelligent engineer, brilliant at making things run faster. He's been reworking the Harley motors for years, especially the 45 inchers. Tom graduated from school as a machinist, so he understands design and loves working on a lathe. He mills lightweight valves and rods and reworks the heads, but his cam designs are the best around. He relishes the fact that his Harley's are usually faster than the factory bikes. I stayed with them through the evening, but by midnight Tom told me to go home and they'll see me tomorrow.

When I showed up the next morning, the guys were standing around drinking coffee and the bike is back together. Bill said to take the bike for a spin and I got excited. I fired it up and took it around the block and it's so light and easy to steer just by adjusting my body weight. It's also very responsive when I twisted the throttle to see what kind of power it had. The front tire felt like it wanted to come off the ground most of the time, that's not something the Excelsior ever thought of doing. But when I really gunned it, something didn't seem right to me.

When I came back to the shop I told them that I thought the clutch might be slipping. So they looked things over and things checked out. It took me a while to figure out that the problem is that the rear tire is braking free and spinning on the pavement. The bike has so much power, more than any bike

I've ever ridden, that it's too much for the rear tire to get traction. It's hard to believe that since I've started working for Tom over the past few months, I've gotten a new street motorcycle, and now I will be riding a true race bike. I am one lucky stiff.

***** ***** *****

My next event is a road race which is part of the Northern California Gypsy Tour being held at Lake Merced. You race the motorcycle that you ride up on; it can't be trailered to the event, so I'm using my new Harley with less than 500 miles to compete. I rode for nearly two and a half hours to get to the event and had a little time to relax before it started. When it came time, I topped off the gas tank, removed the headlight, and got ready to go up against 30 other riders.

One thing I've been doing before a race is to pop a couple sugar cubes in my mouth to calm my nerves and provide a little energy. Once I tightened my chin strap, and zipped up my jacket, I lined up with the others ready to start. We will be riding through the woods on trails that I'm guessing are narrow for most of the time, so if I don't get out in front from the get go, I will get stuck behind the slow pokes.

With all of the motorcycles at the starting line, their rumble vibrates my body as all of us are watching the start-man holding the green flag. As his arm went up, everyone is at attention, and when the flag dropped everyone took off. I got a good jump, but I am still behind maybe a dozen riders. The trail itself isn't in very good condition, so I must avoid any rough or muddy areas and not get pushed into those areas if I get bunched with other riders. I will need to pay attention to how the trail changes but still keep pushing forward.

By the halfway point, I'm pretty sure that I've passed all but two riders. As I started closing in on one of them, he did a quick look back and tried to make it difficult for me to pass. I started leaning down closer to the gas tank to cut wind resistance and as I moved to the inside for an upcoming left turn, he started edging over to cut me off. I tapped the brakes and veered to the outside and coming out of the corner my bike has more steam and by the time he saw me right beside him, it is too late to do anything.

I still have one other rider ahead of me, but the race is nearly over. It seems that I'm beginning to narrow the gap, but he still has the lead. My bike must have had a slight horsepower edge because I began edging past him and I slid out front in just enough time to get the win.

I got a first place trophy, but more importantly, nothing happened to my beautiful motorcycle. After the race I put the headlight back on and reattached the wires and started back to San Jose. As I was riding home, I thought to myself, I can get used to this.

Learning Experience

On nearly every weeknight during the summer, there's a flat track race within driving distance of San Jose in Northern California. I have been racing the Finnegan bike for about a month, and I've gotten really comfortable with it as I've been moving up the standings. Tonight I'm at the College of the Pacific in Stockton, and I've qualified during the heats, so I'm ready for the main event. I make sure that my hot shoe is strapped on secure and my chinstrap is tight, popped two sugar cubes in my mouth, and rode my bike over to the starting line. This is a four-lap scratch heat with four riders, and the same thing is on everyone's mind: get out to the front and be the first into the corner.

Everyone is anxious and watching as the start-man drops the green starting flag, and the whole group takes off down the straightaway. Three of us are clumped together, jockeying for position and trying to get onto the groove of the track. I pushed deep into the corner before backing off the throttle while trying to avoid getting locked in with the others. A little bumping occurs as we go into the first corner, but the group spreads out as we pull out of the second corner. As I lift my hot shoe off the dirt and put it back on the peg pulling out of the corner, the Finnegan bike takes me out to the front of the other riders as I fly down the straightaway.

As corner three approaches, I'm focused on getting deeper into the corner, and when it comes time to back off the gas, the throttle cable breaks. The way that the carburetor cable is set up, when it snapped, the throttle went wide open. Heading into the corner every rider lets up on the throttle, everyone except me. I don't have time to lay the bike down, besides the rider's behind me might have a tough time avoiding me, so I'll ride it through.

Once I got on top of the corner, I crank the handlebars to send the back end sideways from the momentum. The bike resembles a can opener as I take the corner with a pounding heart. To my amazement, I held on and made it through the turn as I rocket forward and the bike straightens out down the track. I'm trying to reach down and shut off the compression release to kill the motor, but I'm going too fast with one hand to be able to feel it.

My bike can't go any faster as the next corner approaches. If I can lightly touch my boot into the dirt and slide along, without ripping my leg off, then maybe it's possible to make another corner. The rest of the riders are far enough back, so if I crash they can avoid me, but laying it down in a corner is the only way to minimize damage to me and the bike. With things happening so quickly, I'll probably end up squashed like a bug against the outside fence, so what the hell. I jammed the handlebars sideways, the rear tire broke loose, and my left foot skimmed along the track surface like a seasoned pro. By some miracle, I survived another corner going all out and I'm far out in front from the rest of the pack.

Going past the grandstands I'm dragging my feet to slow down the bike, but it doesn't help much at this speed. For the next corner, instead of the back-end sliding as I broke it loose, the tire sticks and the bike jackknifes as I'm tossed like a cowboy off a bucking bronco. The last thing I remember seeing, is the bike twisting 10 feet in the air as I ended up face first in the dirt near the outer fence after rolling a few times. It took me a few seconds to regain my senses and make sure that I'm out of the way, but I think that I'm fine. After a couple deep breaths and making sure that nothing is broken, the other riders passed by under the caution flag.

Everybody is coming by to check on me after the race, many were amazed how airborne my bike went during the crash and that I walked away from it. One thing that I took away from this, besides the bruises and a sore body, is that I can go much deeper into the corners before letting off the throttle and still control the bike.

***** ***** *****

It's my 21st birthday (Oct. 30, 1933) tonight and I invited Myrt over to celebrate. After bringing her to our house, I took her into the kitchen where my Mama is. She saw Myrt and said, "Buonasera bambini," or good evening child. Mama makes the best bread in the stone oven in our backyard, and she just brought in two fresh loaves for dinner. I can be anywhere and think about Mama's bread, and I can practically smell the aroma. Besides bread, as usual, the scent of pasta sauce slightly bubbling on the stove fills the air. Nearly everything that we eat is grown out in our garden, we rarely eat meat because of the expense, but also Mama is a vegetarian.

We all grabbed a plate in the kitchen and piled on the pasta and sauce, and then found our seats in the dining room. Mama passes around a plate with grated parmesan cheese for everyone to sprinkle over their tomato sauce. Once everyone is finished with dinner, Mama brought out cake and ice cream. I blew out the candles while everyone sang Happy Birthday, then I opened the two birthday presents that my sister Sally handed to me. One is a new denim shirt and the other present is a black leather belt, which is good because my belt is nearly worn out. I felt like 21 is just another number, but Myrt joked that I am getting old.

Wall of Death

One afternoon, me and a couple guys went to a carnival at the fair grounds to see the "Wall of Death." The Wall of Death is a wooden barrel-shaped cylinder that's 25- to 35-foot in diameter with walls 15 feet tall. Besides being able to withstand the centrifugal force put on its inner wall by the motorcycle, the barrel structure can hold about 100 people standing at the top of the drum looking down at the rider making revolutions against the wall.

The rider is sitting on an Indian 101 Scout inside of the barrel as he starts at the bottom of the drum going around near the outside. As he rode around the initial ramped section he gained enough speed to move on the wall itself. Soon he is riding on the vertical wall 15 feet above the ground making countless circles as the crowd of people looked down from above. I was amazed as he took his hands off the handlebars for a couple revolutions before grabbing them again.

I talked to the rider afterwards about how difficult it must be to get up on the wall inside of the barrel. His named is Slim and the name fit him because he's skinny as a bean pole. We talked for a while and I told him that I was a racer and he said, "If you want to come by tomorrow, I'll let you take a spin inside the barrel before the carnival opens."

I didn't expect that invitation, but I figured what the hell. "Slim, I'll take you up on your offer." I'm not really sure what I'm getting myself in to, but I'm really improving as a racer, so at this point, nothing on two wheels fazes me.

I showed up the next day and found Slim over at the motorcycle trailer. Slim smiled,
"I didn't know if you would show up or not."

"I said that I would."

"Great. Are you ready to give it a spin?"

"Ready as I'll ever be."

He has two Indian 101 scouts that he uses in his act and if one bike isn't working he has a backup. I grabbed one of the Indians for him and pushed the bike over to the wooden barrel. Slim undid four latches on the outside of the barrel and laid down part of the wooden wall, then I pushed the bike up the ramp and into the inside. Slim followed me in and gave me some pointers. "You are going to have to shift your weight to compensate for gravity pushing you down as you try to go higher on the wall. The bike is fighting to track straight, so you'll have to work through it."

I started up the Indian and warmed it up for a minute and put on my helmet that I brought along.

Slim said, "Give me a minute to lock the outer wall into place." The sound echoed off the walls, and when I revved the bike, a bomb could go off 20 feet away and I wouldn't hear it.

Once the wall is back up, I started driving around the bottom in a continual U-turn, trying to figure out angles as I increased speed. I got to the initial angle along the bottom of the barrel, but when I tried to get just the front wheel on the vertical walls, I came back down. I tried to remember what Slim said, the higher up on the wall the motorcycle goes, the more weight I need to shift to increase my height along the sides. I forced myself to make a good attempt on the vertical wall, and I might have made it three feet up it before I came crashing down. Slim looked down at me and he's smiling as I got the bike back up.

I know that I have to lean up the wall to fight gravity, but although I tried to get it to work, after several attempts I gave up. It was nice of Slim to let me give it a whirl, but I better stick to dirt.

***** ***** *****

E.C. Smith is the Secretary of the American Motorcycle Association, so when I saw him at a hill climb we got a chance to talk. In our conversation E.C. said that #79 is available if I wanted it. When a number becomes available you can put in for it. I've had #103 since I started racing, but when Olin Moss quit racing his old #79 went unclaimed. Two digits are better than three, and it sounded like a good number to me, so on a handshake, I switched to #79.

In a handicap race, you have six guys racing for six laps. The best rider starts furthest back at the scratch line, which is 60 yards from the front, and the next best starts 10 yards ahead of him, then another row is 10 yards further up until the six racers are six rows deep, 60 yards separating front to back. There is a lot of ground to cover in the six lap heats if you start at the scratch line, plus you have to make it through the other riders within those six laps.

I've been racing four nights a week on the circuit starting in Fresno, then Sacramento, Emeryville, and finally San Francisco. I work 8 to 5, four days a week at Tom's shop, skipping the day after Fresno to make it to Sacramento. Since I've been riding Finnegan Spear's bike I've worked my way up the ranks. It took two seasons from the time I'd started racing the old Excelsior to becoming a scratch-man. Now I've became the one to beat.

Fresno Fairgrounds

This evening I'm racing at the Fresno fairgrounds and the bike has been running well. That's a plus because I'm gearing up for the big event being held at the Los Angeles Stadium in two weeks. So far tonight I've made it through the preliminary heats and the eight lap semifinal is about to begin.

I got a decent jump at the start, and two laps into the race I'm going gang busters behind Oliver Clow on his Indian Scout. As I move to take the inside track into the corner, Oliver lets off the throttle, and as he did, the Indian really slowed down from the backpressure. In an instant, my front wheel hit his rear wheel, and soon as that happened, I knew things were about to turn ugly. Once I clipped his rear wheel, my bike crossed up, and I went to the dirt going about 60 mph.

Coming up fast behind me is Sprouts Elder who didn't have time to react and plowed into my back. The impact knocks the wind out of me, and sends Sprouts and his bike crashing to the ground. I rolled several times on the track and ended up near the outer fence unable to breathe. This is the first time that I've ever had the wind knocked out of me and I figured that this must be the end. I'm struggling to fill my lungs with air, but after what seemed like forever, my breathing is slowly coming back.

They stopped the race, and the ambulance came out on the track to pick up Sprouts and me. Being that Sprouts is a legend, the ambulance guys gave him the couch, and since I'm just a young buck, they gave me a chair to sit in. When Sprouts looked over at me and saw how bad of shape I was in, he said, "Sam, you better take the couch."

He got up and helped me to the couch to lie down. As I lay there, I can't ever remember being in this much pain. As I am trying to recover, I wondered how I'm going to get home tonight because there's no way I'm in shape to drive. Ott Wilson is the Fresno Harley dealer and he paid out of his own pocket for my ambulance ride back to San Jose. Ott doesn't really know me, he just knows I'm Tom's rider, so it is very kind of him to help me. I'll never forget Ott's gesture.

***** ***** *****

I'm still recovering from my injuries of two weeks ago, and my back is still bruised but not as bad as it was, and I'm in Los Angeles for one of the biggest races of the year. The event is in the stadium where the Olympics were held two years ago. This is where Babe Didrikson Zaharias won gold medals in hurdles and javelin, plus a silver medal in the high jump.

As I'm looking around, I can't believe all of the big names that are here. I've seen Lammy Lamoreaux, Cordy and Jack Milne, Cliff Self, Byrd McKinney, even Sprouts Elder is here and back in action. We caught up with each other before the race, and while he showed no sign of problems from our crash two weeks earlier, the same couldn't be said of me.

"Hey Sprouts."

"Hi Sam, how are you feeling?"

"My back's still a little sore, but at least most of the bruising is gone now."

Sprouts said, "You going to be ready for today?"

I said, "I can't wait." But I'm not as sure as I'm trying to sound.

Today would be tough against this level of racers even if I was 100%, so things don't look too promising. The Olympic Stadium itself is very impressive, and although they say the event drew a crowd of 30,000 people, the stadium can hold over 100,000, so it's a little deceiving how empty it looks with so many unfilled seats.

Once the race began, it had a lot of lead changes throughout, but when the checkered flag fell, Cordy Milne is the ultimate winner with Lammy in second and Byrd coming in third. I didn't do that well, but even though I probably should have skipped the race, I'm still glad that I went.

San Jose Motorcycle Club

San Jose has a motorcycle club that was started a couple years ago, but it hasn't been winning over many new recruits. One of their problems is that the club is being run by guys who don't even own motorcycles, and it's hard to take marching orders from someone that doesn't ride. Tom and I figured that we can do better, so we started our own motorcycle club. We put together a short list of rules that the club must follow, number one being that you must own and ride a motorcycle, and we started having meetings at the Sifton dealership.

It didn't take long before we had 20-30 members crowding into the shop for weekly meetings. At the end of the year we will vote on a club president to serve as Road Captain who will be in charge of running the meetings and organizing club events, but this year we unanimously voted in Tom as our first ever Road Captain.

On the weekends when there isn't a race or hill climb, we try to organize a club ride. One Sunday about 20 of us are on a ride north of Oakland close to Martinez, and I'm out front setting the pace when a cop pulls the whole group over. The cop wants to write everyone tickets, but I said to him that I was the person setting the pace and it's my fault that we were speeding, so I should be the only one to get a ticket. The officer went along with it, and I was the only one sited. So with the ticket in my jacket, we continued with the ride. Although this isn't the first time I've had a speeding ticket, I usually outrun the police unless I'm in San Jose. I can't do that in my hometown because the cops know me by sight.

A few weeks' later I answered a knock at the door only to find two cops standing there to arrest me for the unpaid speeding ticket. I had forgotten all about the ticket I had received on our club ride. The cops put me in the back of their cruiser, and we drove up to the main courthouse in Oakland.

When I got up in front of the judge, he said that the fine is $15, and I have the option of paying the fine or serving a two-day jail sentence. For me, $15 is nearly half a month's wages, so I went with doing the time. For the next two days in the Pinole Jail, I spent most of my time sweeping floors.

When I got out of the Pinole Jail, I didn't feel like calling anyone for a ride, so I took streetcars as far south as I could and started walking from Hayward to Mission San Jose. As I'm walking on El Camino Real, a guy driving an Studebaker saw me wearing my San Jose Motorcycle Club sweater and gave me a ride the rest of the way home.

Chapter 3 / Florida Racing

During the summer of 1935, me and a few buddies went on a two-month race circuit through southern Florida. Most of the races are going to be centered in the Miami area where our contact is Mr. Pitts who owns the Miami Harley Davidson dealership. The other guys coming on the trip are Al "Snooky" Owens, Eddie Spadofore (his brother Mike owns the Excelsior dealership), and Cecil "Jug" Atkinson, who is along as our mechanic. He will get paid a cut of the winnings, so the better we do, the better he's going to do.

It is going to be tough being away from Myrt for that long, we've become very close and I'm going to miss her. She understands that I'm a motorcycle racer and that's what I do, but it doesn't make it any easier on either of us. The night before we are set to leave, she and I rode over to the "5 Spot" malt shop on First and Sutter so we could spend some final time together before I left on the trip.

We ordered our drinks and Myrt said, "I'll sure miss you. I want you to promise that you will write me every day while you are gone."

"That's a little much, how about I'll send you a postcard at least once a week."

"Alright" she said, "Just write as often as you can."

I can't believe that after tonight I won't see her for two months.

The following day the four of us loaded our belongings in Jug's 4-cylinder 1923 Dodge Touring Car, with our three motorcycles and parts being towed behind on a flatbed trailer, and left for Florida. I'm bringing Bill Crane's speedway bike, while Snooky and Eddie are bringing along their JAPs.

JAP is the nickname given to James A. Prestwich-built motorcycles that came over from England. Prestwich started out building engines, but he soon branched out into building complete motorcycles from the ground up. His flagship bike is a 190 lb., 500-cubic-inch alcohol-burning motor that produces 40 horsepower. These powerful and light bikes perform great on short tracks and are the bike of choice for many riders. Harley hadn't been building anything that size until the 1934 short tracker came out, but production is limited, and they are fairly expensive, so racers turned to JAPs.

The beginning of the drive was uneventful, although crossing Arizona in summer is close to unbearable during the day, but not long after the Dodge's muffler fell off. We found out that the exhaust pipe broke off right by the manifold, and only a muffler shop can do the repair. We can't afford to take it some place to get it fixed, so we just kept driving. With the engine noise coming straight out of the motor, the sound is deafening. Even when we stopped and shut off the motor, the ringing in our ears is so loud that we still couldn't hear.

We drove on through New Mexico and into Texas and made it into Florida without any additional problems. When we were about 200 miles outside Miami and as it's getting dark, we noticed that the headlights were getting dimmer, which meant that the generator is going out. We turned off the headlights and drove on as best we could in the dark, and just whenever another car came in our direction, we turned on our headlights until they went by and then turned them off again. It's close to midnight when we stopped on the outskirts of Miami to get some shut eye.

The following day as we drove around Miami, the area looks like paradise with the acres of orange trees and the blue ocean in the distance. We got to the Miami Harley Davidson dealership and found other out-of-state racers there. Mr. Pitts is the dealership owner and one of the local organizers for the summer race circuit and point man for the out-of-towners. He gave us a rundown of the upcoming races and what to expect. He also let us know where we could stay cheaply while we are in town.

Later that afternoon we drove out to the local fairgrounds and looked at a horse track where we will be doing some of our racing over the next several weeks. It is one of the nicer places that I've seen, and it has a large grandstand overlooking the track. All of us have raced on horse tracks back in Northern California which are typically quarter- and half-mile tracks, this is a 3/8-mile track which is right between the two, but it won't be much of a difference to us.

Mr. Pitts says that most of the races will be on Saturdays and only a few are planned on Sunday afternoons. With no weekday races, if you don't make money on the weekend, you have to wait a whole week before getting another shot. Mr. Pitts tells us of a race near Daytona, which they say isn't very far up the road, so we'll go look it over once we get some free time.

The first Saturday race turned out well enough, and I earned a little pocket money. The following weekend, I had engine problems that kept me out of the money, but the third Saturday, I came in first overall in the main event. Although I made money in the races, Snooky and Eddie didn't do well. What ended up happening is that Snooky, Jug, and Eddie boxed oranges for two bits an hour on the weekdays to earn money to get by. The area is choke-full of orange groves, so you can find work picking oranges. But when it came right down to it, whoever did well racing ended up buying food for the other guys, so nobody is going to starve to death on this trip.

Another way to pass the time between race days is to go fishing. You can sometimes catch a ride on a boat out of the marina to do some deep sea fishing, or some of the guys go fishing in the sloughs to catch eels. It's not like they would eat them, but the local Chinese men pay two bits each for them, so our guys would sell them the eels and use the money to buy a square meal. If things got a little more desperate, guys would resort to catching ducks in city parks and take them back to the garage and cook up a duck dinner.

Smokin' Joe Petrali

One afternoon I saw the great racer Smokin' Joe Petrali at the racetrack. Petrali is a legend, and even though he's still in his early 30s, it seems like I've been hearing about his racing skill forever. Joe won back-to-back Grand National Championships and back-to-back National Hill Climb Championships in 1932 and 1933. Not just one or the other, but both championships in consecutive years, which is unheard of. When Smokin' Joe is racing, the only question is who's coming in second. When I saw him at the race track, he was cooking spaghetti in a five-gallon drum in a small garage, while about thirty guys were standing around waiting to eat. When you are a racer, especially one far away from home, knowing where your next meal is coming from is always a big concern.

Smokin' Joe is here in Miami because the organizers are paying him to be an honorary referee at some of the races. Joe is a good Italian with much of the same background as me, so once we met each other, we got along fine. Joe was born in San Francisco and moved to Sacramento when he was a kid and started racing as a teenager.

Joe's had his share of excitement over his years of racing, so he has lots of entertaining stories, but one of the main stories that come to mind is how he got his mangled upper lip. Most of us have heard about the crash that caused it, but it's always better hearing it straight from the horse's mouth. As we were sitting around one afternoon shooting the breeze, someone asked Joe if he wouldn't mind telling us what happened that day.

"I was in Springfield on a half-mile track when Eddie Brinck laid his bike down right in front of a group of us, which caused a chain reaction of wipeouts. It happened too quickly for me to react, so I crashed into a pile of bodies and bikes and got thrown maybe 15 to 20 feet into the air. The aftermath was pretty ugly: Eddie died in the hospital that night, and the doctors didn't think I would survive because I had some serious head problems and was unconscious. Since the doctors didn't think I would make it, and I was missing a big chunk out of my lip, they allowed an intern to practice his stitching on me. They had actually found part of my lip that was torn off an hour or so later at the track and brought it over to the hospital. Well, the intern didn't do a very good job, but I survived and was back to racing again less than a year later. So I'm still around, but I have this to show for it," he said pointing to his lip.

***** ***** *****

I heard from some of the riders about an upcoming race called the Florida 200 Mile Road Race National. The race is several hours north of Miami, close to Jacksonville, at a place called Neptune Beach. The race is run on both beach and road surfaces, which sounds interesting, and I'm up for any kind of challenge. But before I could enter, I needed a motorcycle that could handle that type of race. My short tracker is a lightweight bike that holds only about a quart of gas, so I need something more durable.

I talked to Mr. Pitts to see if he had a bike that I could use and he took me to see an old Harley 45 out back of his dealership that they had been using for parts. Most of the dark green bike is there, it needs a carburetor, chain, and a back tire and rim, but it sure beat nothing. Before long, Mr. Pitts and I had started taking off the heads, sanding down the carbon and polishing everything smooth. We found a used carburetor in good shape and replaced the gaskets. One obvious thing is that the bike needs more power if I'm going to have any chance of competing.

Later that day Smokin' Joe dropped by Mr. Pitt's dealership and the conversation turned to the Neptune race. When I mentioned that we were putting together a bike, but we needed more ponies, Joe said that he would look into getting us a set of high performance cams. Sure enough, the next morning Joe came by with a new set of cams and now we were in business.

After Mr. Pitts and I put the bike together, I took it out to see how well it ran. As I'm riding out on the Miami streets, the throttle response isn't feeling right, so I stopped to make some adjustments to the carburetor.

The motor seems to be having a little trouble breathing, so I turned out the screw to add more air to the fuel mixture. About that time an old Ford roadster pulled up beside me and an old guy is inside saying something, but I could barely hear over the bike. I finally heard him say, "Let me see your license." I wondered, who is this guy? He's not driving a cop car, he must be crazy. It's not like he could catch me in that old junker, so I hit the gas and left him sitting there. As I sped off, I looked back and noticed that the roadster had two red lights in the grille. That can't be good.

I stayed out of sight for about an hour and figured that things had blown over by then. As I got closer to the dealership I made sure that I didn't see any cop cars and the coast is clear. But as I pulled around by the back of the shop and got off my bike, the roadster pulled up with the lights flashing. There is nothing that I can do at this point, so I told a couple of the guys standing around, "Tell Mr. Pitts they're taking me to the pokey."

Miami Hospitality

They put me in a cell with a bunch of rednecks that looked like they came right out of the swamp, so I'm going to have to watch my back in here. I've been sitting in the cell for maybe two hours when they came and got me to take in front of the judge. As I stood in front of the bench, the judge said, "You're guilty of entering the jail without the inmate's permission, how do you plead."

I was kind of dumbstruck. "What?" I asked.

The judge said, "Answer the question." I didn't have any options, so I had to plead guilty.

"Your fine is set at $450."

What the hell is he talking about? It might be a $25 or even $50 dollar fine, but not $450. I can buy a new motorcycle for $400 dollars. I guess the judge must want to do some work on his house and he wants me to pay for it. The thing is that I do have close to $500 dollars on me, but half of that is going back to Bill Crane for using his motorcycle, so even if I wanted to pay, I didn't have enough of my own money to do it.

When I said, "I don't have that kind of money." I could tell that he didn't like my answer at all.

Then things went from bad to worse when the judge said, "If you are not going to pay the fine, the punishment is 50 lashes."

They are actually threatening to whip me over out running a cop? What kind of backwater place is this? Maybe the threat of 50 lashes would make other people buckle under and pay, but I sure as hell ain't going along with it. The judge looked at me and said, "Last time, pay the fine or get the 50 lashes. What's it going to be?"

"I don't have the money."

"Your choice" the judge replied. "Take him away."

I'm hoping that this is a bluff, but I'm just a nobody from California, so I'm at their mercy.

They took me out of the courtroom and down a long hall into one of their back rooms and told me to take off my shirt. Then I saw someone bring in a leather whip and I knew that I was in deep shit. I'm not going to do this willingly, so when two deputies came over to grab a hold of me, I kicked the closest guy square between the legs and he dropped like a stone. At that point all hell broke loose as a half-dozen deputy's bum-rushed me and they weren't being gentle.

They got a hold of my arms and legs and held me spread eagle. Being whipped isn't something that you can prepare yourself for, so the first connection of leather to bare skin is a shock and stung like hell. After about 10 lashes, they all started to blend together, but I never forgot that another one is coming as they counted. The guy with the whip took a break at 25 and asked me if I was ready to pay the fine. In between my heavy breathing I told them, "Hell no!" They resumed the whipping and after 40 whips they asked me again if I was going to pay. I knew that I only had 10 more to go, or at least I hoped that they would stop at 50, so I said "Kiss my butt."

When they finished the 50, they half-dragged, half-carried me back into the holding cell. At this point I'm not in too good of shape and I can feel trickles running down my back that is either blood or sweat or a combination of both.

As I'm sitting there, one of the guys came over to talk. He said that an inmate heard me talking earlier about how I had a couple hundred bucks on me, and that started the chain of events. I'd been talking to a guy earlier from a Miami motorcycle club, and I had mentioned that I had a couple hundred bucks on me but half of it wasn't mine. I guess the punk that overheard us talking wanted to butter up the judge, so he told a guard that passed the word back to the judge.

Because of my big mouth the judge started seeing dollar signs, and from that point I was screwed. Then he told me about the officer I kicked in the family jewels. It's a funny story, depending on how you look at it, but a few weeks earlier the man had been shot in the groin, so that's why when I kicked him he dropped hard. At least that is one thing I can laugh about, but if I ever find the guy who ratted on me, I'll be in jail a lot longer after I'm done beating his ass.

About an hour after they finished with me, Mr. Pitts bailed me out. Mr. Pitts said that he had been waiting outside for a couple hours, but they didn't seem to be in any rush to let me out. Once we got outside of the jail to Mr. Pitts car, I gingerly sat down in the front seat and when he saw how I was moving he asked, "What happened to you, they rough you up?"

"You could say that."

When I filled him in on what happened he couldn't believe it. But for me, I can't sit back in the seat as Mr. Pitts is driving. I had to lean forward the whole time so nothing touched my back.

Once we got back to the dealership and inside his office, I pulled up my shirt to show him my back which by this time is covered with large welts.

"That's horrible! They can't do that."

Mr. Pitts started making phone calls and got a hold of the district attorney and the conversation got pretty heated. Soon after we were in the DAs office showing him the whip marks on my back and telling him what happened while I was in custody.

"This type of action is not condoned. I can assure you that we will put a stop to that."

He sounded like he is going to do something, but I don't have a lot of faith.

On the drive back from the district attorney's office, Mr. Pitts stopped by a pharmacy to get some pain pills and ointment for my back, and then he took me to my motel. He put ointment on my lacerations the best he could, then he left me so that I could get some rest. I'm dealing with a lot of pain just sitting here breathing, but I'll take a few pills and pray that I can sleep a long time and wake up feeling better.

The next day I dropped by the dealership and I'm doing slightly better, but I'm still hurting. Mr. Pitts said that the district attorney had called earlier to say that they dropped the charges against me for assaulting a police officer. How nice of them! I should be the person filing charges against them. I knew then that nothing was going to happen to the judge and his thugs.

Florida 200 Miler

After a couple days of recovery, I tried to put everything behind me and focus on the upcoming race. Jacksonville sounds like it's nearly at the other end of the state, so we're leaving early on the day before the race to make sure we arrive with enough time to look things over. With all of the mechanics around the track, we managed to repair the muffler and fix the generator on the Dodge, so it's now safe to drive.

This race is going to be quite different from any of the races I've been in before, and we don't even get practice laps. The course is on a combination of brick roads and sandy beach and I've raced on both, but not in the same race. The brick surface still has windblown sand covering most of it, so it will probably be a little slick in spots, especially the wide turn before getting back on the beach. I talked to some of the guys that have raced on this type of course, and they say to ride closer to the water's edge where the sand is more packed, and just avoid the incoming waves. One interesting thing is that since this is a beach race, the start time is based on the tide and when it's going out.

It's a warm sunny day, and other than still being a little sore from the whipping, I'm feeling pretty good. The Harley that Mr. Pitts and I put together in less than a week before the race is running strong. It's about 20 minutes before the race is set to start and Snooky and Jug are with me. I'm wearing my normal race clothes, leather jacket, leather pants, and my trusty football helmet. I wore a football helmet because that's what my idols wore, but Snooky has other ideas.

"Sam, why don't you use my helmet and look like a racer, not like some guy from the sticks."

Snooky has a real motorcycle helmet, and it looks better than mine, so I decided to wear his.

When the race is ready to begin, 60 to 70 of us are lined up across the wide beach for the standing start. All eyes are on the start-man, and once the flag dropped, the roars of the motors shatter the air. I got a good jump and stayed near the middle of the track for the first two corners to make sure I didn't get taken out by other riders. The first rule in racing is you can't win if you don't finish. Not long after the start, it became apparent to me that Snooky's helmet is too big for me, and even though the chin strap is tight, it's still bouncing on my head. I don't know what size head Snooky has, but if it's filled with brains, he must be a genius.

Racing down the beach, I can see a series of flags about a quarter of a mile away indicating the first corner. As I'm coming out of the second corner, the surface changed to brick as I went back into the other direction. The brick section is where you hit your highest speed because sand is a much slower surface and it knocks at least 5 mph off your top speed. There's a height difference from the sand to the road, and the first time I hit the road section, the jolt is so great that I barely keep ahold of the handle bar as I got airborne.

By the time I got past lap 20, the bike is running well and I'm going gangbusters, but all of the bouncing from the helmet just caused me to lose my goggles, so now I'm racing without any eye protection. I'm over three-quarters of the way through the race and things are going in my favor when the track officials gave me the flag to come into the pits. The pit crew is standing around as I pull in. I yelled over the noise, "What is it?"

"You need gas."

"Well, fill it up!" For some reason they are standing around like there's no rush. I knew that I'm making good time because I've been passing guys and so far no one has gotten past me. Then I got the word that I have over a five minute lead.

I need to get back out on the track, but there's a problem. Before the race the gas cap had been tightened with a pipe wrench to prevent it from loosening, but so many spectators are mulling around that they can't get to a toolbox to find a pipe wrench. They've been gone for a couple minutes and by this time I'm ready to kill someone. They finally got ahold of a wrench and filled the tank, but by the time I made it back on the track I no longer had the lead.

With the Keystone Cops filling in as a pit crew, my chance at winning a National Championship in an endurance run went up in smoke. Rody Rodenberg won the race while I finished a disappointing fifth. I figured out later that nearly seven minutes had elapsed while I waited for them to find a wrench and fill up my tank.

On top of that frustration, I had lost my goggles early in the race and continued without any eye protection, and now I'm having serious eye problems. The sand that blew along the course and got whipped up by the motorcycles is essentially ground coral, and it pelted my eyes throughout the race. By the time I crossed the finish line, I couldn't close my eyelids because they are stuck in place.

Luckily someone found an eye doctor in the stands, and using a bottle of solution, he flushed the debris from my eyes, and my vision slowly improved. The doctor said that without having the solution to clean the sand out of my eyes, I might have been permanently blinded. So far, this Florida trip has been much more trouble than it's been worth.

Florida Girl

One thing that I did notice in Florida is that there are nice-looking women around the track, which is odd because it's usually just guys that show up. After one afternoon race, I was thumbing through the Speed News when I heard a voice. "Nice racing out there."

I looked up to see a smiling tall and thin brunette which kind of took me by surprise. She has a pearly white smile and long straight brown hair down past her shoulders. She can't be here alone, not with as nice as she looks, so I wondered whose wife or girlfriend she is.

"Thanks, I appreciate it. You a racing fan?"

"Sure, it's fun watching you guys out on the track. It must be exciting out there."

"It is exciting, especially if you're winning."

"Not so much if you're crashing," she replied with a laugh.

"Yep, not so much. My name is Sam, nice to meet you."

"I'm Nessa. Nice to meet you too."

I glanced her over. She is wearing a light blue sundress with large white buttons going up in the front where the material overlaps.

"Are you with one of the racers?" I said as I looked around.

She smiled and said, "Not me. My girlfriend was set to come, but she couldn't make it, so I just showed up anyway."

I can't imagine what a pretty girl like this is doing alone here at the track. She ought to carry a club to keep the hounds off of her. I'm trying not to look her up and down, at least not more than twice, but it's hard to resist.

I asked, "Do you and your friends come here often?"

"Every week or so during race season we come out to the track and watch the races."

A buddy of mine called out, "Hey Sam, Petrali is looking for you."

"Okay, thanks. Well, I've got run. Maybe I'll see you around."

She smiled and replied, "Sure, talk to you later."

The following weekend at the track I heard a familiar voice. "Hello tall, dark, and handsome."

I looked around and saw Nessa walking up to me. I can't believe that she looks even nicer than she did the first time I saw her.

"Hi Nessa."

"What are you up to Sam?"

"Just making a few adjustments to the bike."

"I'm heading over to the soda machine, do you want to go grab a soda with me?"

"Sure, I could use a break."

We walked over to the machine and both of us got a grape Nehi.

She asked, "So where are you from?"

"San Jose, California."

"You're a long way from home. You came all that way just to race here?"

"That's it," I replied.

"What have you been doing since you've been in town?"

"Not much besides racing and spending time around the track."

"Some afternoon you ought to drive along Ocean Drive and look around. The ocean is beautiful, and there are a couple great new hotels that have gone up recently."

"I don't know if I would be interested."

"I tell you what, let me know when you're not doing anything and I'll show you around. You ought to see some of Miami while you're here, maybe buy a postcard or two."

"Sure, maybe we can do that sometime if things work out."

I don't know if she is just being friendly, but Myrt and I are an item, so I'm not going to do anything stupid.

One slow Tuesday it had been raining off and on for most of the afternoon, and Nessa picked me up in her white Ford coupe and we drove over to Ocean Drive. After parking the car and walking along the beach front, we went into the new Edison

Hotel to cool off with a couple drinks in the hotel bar. I've got to agree with her, this really is some beautiful hotel.

The outside of the Edison Hotel is painted a light yellow, while inside the lobby floor is a checkerboard of pink and green marble. Not my color choices, but it seems to work. Nessa said it is built in the art deco style that's becoming all the rage. Inside the bar they have murals of palm trees and flamingos on the walls which supposed to be like the view out past the palm trees separating us from the ocean across the street.

As we sat down the bartender asked, "Good afternoon. What will it be?"

I looked over at Nessa, "Choose for us, you're in charge."

"I like that," she said flashing those pearly whites. "Two Cuba Libres."

We watched him make the drinks and he set them in front of us.

I took a sip and asked Nessa, "Isn't this just rum and cola with a slice of lime?"

"Pretty much, but Cuba Libre sounds better."

I nodded, "Now I understand."

I'm sipping on a cool drink and sitting by a pretty girl who looks like someone that just stepped out of the movies, not a bad Tuesday at all. Nessa is easy on the eyes, and what you might call a temptation, but I have to remember that I'm spoken for. During the conversation it came around to whether either of us had a steady. For Nessa, she just ended a two-year relationship a couple months ago.

I had to come clean, so I said, "I have a steady back in California."

"What's her name?

"Myrt, actually Myrtle but she hates that name."

"That's nice." We had an awkward moment of silence and then she said, "So how's the racing going this season?"

"Doing well, I've been getting into the money more times than not."

"Great. Are you going to make it this way next year?"

"I really haven't thought much about it."

We talked a little more over a second Cuba Libre, but it's getting time to wrap things up. We did a short walk on the beach and then we got into her car and she drove me back to the track.

I said, "I had a good time. Thanks for getting me out."

"I'm glad that you went."

She smiled, but it isn't the same as before. I felt that I should say something.

"I hope that I didn't lead you on."

"About what?"

"Well, maybe I gave you the impression that I was single, and I feel bad if I did."

"No. I just thought that it would be fun to show you around town."

I could tell by her expression that she was a little let down. If it wasn't for Myrt, it's hard to say if something might have developed, but I'm a loyal guy. I saw Nessa one other time around the Miami track before the season ended and we talked for a while, but things were more stand-offish than before.

***** ***** *****

It wasn't long after I returned from the Florida trip when I received a letter at the shop from Putt Mossman. Putt is inviting me to join his group, the "American Motorcycle Rodeo Circus and Speedway Aces" for a six month tour. Putt and his group travel abroad setting up races against local riders, and on this tour they're going to New Zealand, Australia, and England.

He wrote that the tour will be a month apiece in New Zealand and Australia, then a short break back in the states, before sailing to England. There we would be racing at speedway tracks around London for three months, maybe a few weeks longer depending on how things go. The trip sounds like a lot of traveling, I figured out that just the time at sea would be nearly a month, but it sounds exciting just the same.

Chapter 4 / Overseas Racing

Motorcycle racing is drawing ever larger crowds, and there are a few motorcycle shows touring the world. So just like Buffalo Bill did years ago, Putt is taking his motorcycle rodeo overseas. From what I gather, racing is wildly popular in London, and it's a great market for the "American Motorcycle Rodeo Circus and Speedway Aces."

Putt Mossman was born in England, but he's been living in Pasadena for years. Putt is a natural showman and a great all-around athlete. Some of his accomplishments include winning back-to-back World Horseshoe Championships and pitching one spring for the Boston Braves baseball team. Now Putt performs stunts on motorcycles, everything from shooting balloons while riding, to going over jumps blind folded. He's even known to ride through a wall of wood that's on fire. In addition to organizing the tour, Putt is providing the entertainment during intermissions for the paying customers.

In Emeryville, a couple years back, I remember watching Putt ride his Indian Scout across a foot wide wooden platform nearly 40 feet in the air as a crowd of people were looking up from below. As he was riding along, his bike slipped off the narrow plank, and they both came crashing to the ground which messed up Putt pretty good. In addition to breaking his wrist, Putt got a major slash from his forehead all the way to the back of his neck. The cut was so deep that skin hung down on one side of his skull. I saw Putt a couple days later with his head bandaged up and a cast on his forearm while he was shooting pool. It's tough trying to slow Putt down.

Getting the chance to travel to New Zealand, Australia, and England sounded great to me. When else would an offer like this come along? Putt is supplying a JAP Speedway racer for each of the racers, so I'll have plenty of power on the tracks. These will be similar to the bikes Al Owens and Eddie Spadofore were using when we went on the Florida trip, but I don't think these bikes will be as worn out. On top of Putt providing motors, and the mechanics to keep them running, each of the riders get a $25 weekly check to cover expenses. So it's like

I'm being paid to travel, and any extra money that I make racing is just icing on the cake.

The only problem is that this tour is going to last a long time. I talked to Tom about getting the time off from work and he's okay with it. Myrt, on the other hand, will be more of a challenge to get an approval from. She didn't like my two month trip to Florida, and now I want to be gone for half a year. But that's the life of a racer, so I hope that she will understand that this is too big of an opportunity to pass up. Outside of the trip, I've been thinking about asking Myrt to marry me. My original plan was for us to get engaged first and then settle on a wedding date later, but now I think that we should get engaged before I leave.

That evening I picked up Myrt at her house and we went out for burgers at the 5 Spot. After we ordered our meals, I jumped right into it.

"I have a little bit of news, I got an offer from Putt Mossman to go racing with his tour group in New Zealand, Australia, and England after the first of the year."

She didn't say anything at first, she just looked at me. "That sounds exciting, but how long of a trip are you talking about?"

"That's the problem, Putt is saying about six months."

"Huh? That's too long."

"I know it's a long time, but it's a great offer. Going to London and Australia would be neat and I can't see that I'd get this chance again."

As our sodas were dropped off, Myrt didn't look too happy about things.

"So do you think that you're going to do it?"

"I want to. I talked to Tom and it's alright with him. I'm hoping that it will be okay with you too."

Myrt said, "When you went to Florida it felt too long for me, and this trip will be a lot longer."

We had a little bit of a silence, then I said, "We've been dating steady for a while now, so what do you think about us getting engaged before the trip?"

That took her off guard, and after a moment she said, "I think that would be great, if that's what you want."

"You're my girl, and there's no one else that I'd like to spend my life with."

I had bought a gold wedding band at Hart's department store two days ago, and as I pulled it from my pocket, I glanced at Myrt as I unwrapped the tissue that held the ring inside.

When I held the ring it in front of her, Myrt's chocolate brown eyes lit up.

"Myrt, will you marry me?"

She hesitated for a second. "Do I have to agree to your six month trip first?"

"No. But I hope that you say yes to both."

She looked at the ring and said, "It's beautiful. I'd love to marry you."

Then I slipped the ring on her finger and kissed her. As she looked at the ring with a smile on her face, I said, "Are we okay on the trip too?"

"Don't ruin the moment."

Myrt finally gave me her blessing to go on the tour with Putt, and I felt really lucky to have such a great girl. I will send Putt a telegram saying that I'm all in, just tell me when it's time to sail and I'll be there.

Sailing for Australia

In February of 1936, I sailed out of Los Angeles with the other members of the American Motorcycle Rodeo Circus and Speedway Aces. Along with Putt's business partner and fellow racer Pee Wee Cullum, Putt's wife Helen and his sister Dessie are with us. Helen and Dessie assist on some of Putt's stunts, while Dessie's husband Ray Grant is part of our group of riders. Ray won the 1933 National Speedway Championship, so he's a quality rider. Shortly after winning the championship though, he was in a bad crash and unconscious for nine days. He needed constant attention and several operations to drain fluid from around his brain, but he pulled through and began racing shortly after. Ray was also on Putt's first overseas tour last year, so he's someone good to have around.

The other riders include Bo Lisman, Byrd McKinney, and Manuel Trujillo who is bringing his wife Francis. I know Byrd from racing against him in Emeryville and Los Angeles, and I know Manuel from racing him in Tulare. Also along are mechanics Lou Brunache, John Norsigian, and Robert Diehl who will keep our JAPs running, so we look to have an even dozen in our troupe.

As we settled into life on board the ship, we don't have much to do for the 12-day trip except play cards, smoke cigarettes, and tell old racing stories. One day, as some of us are standing around talking, I said, "So Putt, what stunts do you have planned for the tour?" Putt is always trying out something new, so I figured that he would be creative on this tour.

"Well, I'll tell you Jimmy's: for one of them I'm going to ride down a long ramp, be propelled into the air, and land in a tank filled with water. And just to make it more exciting, Pee Wee is going to pour kerosene over the top of the water and set it on fire just before I do it. Then, as the bike lands, the splash will put out the flames and the crowd will roar." Putt is smiling as he finished.

Lou Brunache asked, "Don't you get worried about getting caught on fire?"

"Things can get sideways. A couple years back I was in front of about 100 people, ready to perform when I ran into a little hitch. I was to ride my scout off a ramp on the dock, while on fire, and launch into the middle of a lake. When it was time to start, I'm standing beside my Scout that was idling, and Pee Wee doused my clothes with petrol. As I swung my leg over the seat, the crowd was on edge as Pee Wee lit a match and set me on fire. Just when I sat down to take off, the motor stalled. Damn!"

Putt is telling his story as straight as can be, while we're glued to his every word.

"I'm trying like a madman to start the bike as my clothes are on fire and I'm getting burned alive. When the bike finally started, I raced up the ramp and into the lake looking like a human torch. I was hospitalized for two weeks with burns over most of my body for that."

The bunch of us listening roared with laughter.

"Sure, you bunch of toe rags," Putt said, "It *sounds* funny."

***** ***** *****

As we got closer to New Zealand, I watched from the deck of the ship as the island came into view. I didn't know about it until the trip, but New Zealand is two islands. We sailed to the Northern Island which looks really green for February, but its summer south of the equator, so the seasons are maybe six months off compared to the seasons back home.

One of the stories I heard on the trip was how my hero Sprouts Elder started racing in New Zealand and Australia nearly a decade ago. Sprouts even won the Australian Championship nearly 10 years ago against top riders from Australia, England, and the U.S. As the popularity of motorcycle racing increased down here in New Zealand and Australia, more British and American riders started spending their winter months here when it's their summer, so they could alternate between the two and race year around.

Once we pulled into port and got our stuff off of the ship, our group went to a speedway just outside of town in Auckland. They knew that we were coming, and we were able to break out the bikes and play around for a while. As far as the track itself, the surface has more gravel than I'm used to, even though I've been on some terrible tracks, but I'll be ready when the real races begin. Everyone's been feeling a little claustrophobic after 12 days on board ship, so we are all in a much better mood after getting out on the track.

It's always a question mark for the first time on a new track, but on the first evening of races when we got to compete, things went pretty smooth. We went up against three sets of New Zealand teams and our team raced well, but this is a home track for the New Zealanders. Still, I felt a little more comfortable about travelling half way around the world, and the locals seemed to enjoy the show.

For Putts performance, he did an act of balancing off his motorcycle while his right foot is on the left peg. As he's holding on to the handle bars by his right hand going 10 to 15 miles per hour, his free arm and left leg reaching out spread eagle. Once he completed that trick, he moved on to his second trick. This is where he performs his stunt of climbing a metal ladder attached to his motorcycle as it's moving down a track.

So, Putt is on his Indian Scout moving about 10 miles an hour as he locks the throttle, and keeping his balance, he moves to the ladder attached over the middle of the seat. Once on the backside of the motorcycle, he slowly climbs up the rungs until he's about 12 feet above the ground. If Putt makes a mistake now, he's got a ways to go before hitting ground. After climbing up one side and down the other, Putt gets back on his seat, turns the bike around, and waves to the crowd as he does a lap in front of the stands as the crowd is clapping.

We spend most of our time at the tracks, so we don't see much of the country, but the bikes are set up correctly, and we've gotten to know each other a little better on the track. After finishing our four evenings of racing in Auckland, we all helped load up everything and drove to the south end of the island, to the city of Wellington. After finding our way around town, our group checked into a nice little hotel called the Helen Rae, and I got the chance to mail Myrt a letter that I had written yesterday.

We're racing at Kilbirnie Speedway outside of Wellington and we have bigger crowds than in Auckland, but in both places the locals are really enthusiastic about the racing and Putt's entertainment. During this stretch, we started working better as a team and became more aware of helping teammates out on the track. These races are based on team scores, so we all need to do good to get into the money; just one guy doing well doesn't help the team. These local teams know how to work together and they often block out other racers or slow them down to protect a teammate's lead. The Harley Davidson racing team of the early 1920s, nicknamed The Wrecking Crew, used similar tactics to great success.

After our time in Wellington, we gathered our gear and took a small ship to the other island, some dozen miles away. The southern island is more mountainous than the northern island, and the mountains have snow-capped peaks. We sailed into a small harbor, and after loading into a few trucks, we made our way along the inland roads until we reached Christchurch.

Our time in Christchurch is going to be brief and we only have a few races. Once our races were complete, we are now sailing to Sydney overnight aboard the Maunganui. We arrived in Australia and disembarked, and then we needed help on getting directions to our lodgings. Shortly after, we got news that our team didn't have any races lined up. I guess the forward manager that Putt had employed to get races lined up hadn't done anything. By that evening Putt fired the bum and got busy trying to put things together himself.

Five days into our stay, Putt still isn't able to get us any races. It came down to Putt not having enough time to advertise locally or talk to the right people. The Australian portion looks like a bust and we won't be racing in England for nearly a month and a half. With me and Myrt already talking about getting married, I decided to move up the date. I talked to Putt first to make sure that I wasn't needed until the English portion of the tour, then once I figured how to put it into words, I sent Myrt a telegram asking her to marry me once I get back to home in a few weeks.

I've already checked on ships heading to the United States, and I can secure passage on a ship leaving next week. So if Myrt agrees to marry me, I'll buy my ticket and sail to Los Angeles, then we'll get married in San Jose in early May. After the ceremony, we'll have to drive cross-country to New York where we will catch our ship sailing for England. If all goes according to plan, we'll have just enough time to meet up with our group in London for the second leg of the tour at the beginning of June.

Four days later, I received Myrt's return telegram and then I took a deep breath before opening the telegram. "Yes I'll marry you. I will get things ready for when you arrive. XXXOOO, Myrt"

It took a moment for it to sink in, but there is no turning back now. I'll buy my ticket and send a cable to the folks letting them know of our plans, and then I'll get ready for the long boat ride back to the states.

Getting Married

Once I finally arrived in San Jose after the long trip, we had to get things done quickly. Myrt has already gotten most of the wedding organized, and the ceremony is set to take place at the home of Reverend Nell Vincent. Myrt's sister Eva had married Milton Vincent, and it's his mother who will be performing the marriage ceremony, while Eva and Milton are going to serve as witnesses.

We don't have the time to put together a church wedding, and Myrt's sister really wants her mother-in-law to do the ceremony, but it's not going over well with Mama. Although she loves Myrt, she's a devoted catholic and since our marriage isn't taking place in a church by a priest, she has told me that she's not coming to the ceremony. If I had the time, we could have a church wedding, but we don't, so our options are limited. I love Mama dearly and I hope she'll change her mind once the day comes. I tried talking with her, but so far she hasn't budged. If Mama isn't coming, I doubt that Papa will come either.

***** ***** *****

I've been nervous since I woke up this morning, and finally after all of the excitement, at four o'clock on May 7th, 1936, Myrt and I were married. Myrt's folks are here, as is Tom and his wife Stella and her sister Jessie, and some of Myrt's friends from the neighborhood showed up for the ceremony.

We had a small reception afterwards at the dealership, and guys from the shop, and some of my good friends like Snooky Owens, Jugg Atkinson, and Oliver Clow came by to wish us well. My parents even came to the reception to be with us, which made Myrt and me very happy. We both hoped they would have come to the ceremony, but sometimes that's how things turn out. On this happy day, we don't have much time to celebrate because we are leaving early tomorrow.

The following day Myrt and I loaded our suitcases and took off in my Plymouth for New York City where we will board our ship for England. On the second day of the drive as we are crossing Utah, we saw a dark cloud in the distance that kept getting closer, and we soon found out that it's a giant mass of locusts darkening the sky. The cloud is more than a block wide and looks to be several miles long and it's creating an image straight out of the Bible. I drove through the cloud as they splattered into the windshield and a few times the car actually hydroplaned across the bodies of the bugs, but we got past the locusts and continued on.

We finally reached New York and found out that our boat tickets that are supposed to be at the post office hadn't arrived yet. We got a hotel room and each morning I went to the post office to check for the tickets. With time to kill, Myrt and I took a boat tour out to see the Statue of Liberty and look at the New York City skyline. It made me think about my parents coming through Ellis Island thirty years ago and everything that has happened in their lives, and mine, since then.

After two days in New York we're preparing to turn around and head back to San Jose when the tickets finally arrived, and we were able to board the Aquitania. Both Myrt and I are amazed what a beautiful ship it is. They say that the Aquitania is a favorite of the movie stars and royalty, and now I can understand why.

The Aquitania is huge, nearly 100 feet wide and 900 feet long, with four majestic smokestacks rising high above the deck.

On our second evening on board, we went into the tourist class restaurant, and the steward brought over a bottle of champagne compliments of the captain. I guess that they heard that we had just been married. The steward popped the cork and Myrt and I drank to a long and happy life together.

During the evening as Myrt and I are talking about our families, the conversation switched to my Dad and some of his money making attempts. "About a dozen years ago Papa was involved in a business venture that wasn't exactly on the up and up. He and a buddy were making counterfeit coins, nickels actually. They say that the coins weren't very believable, no metal in them at all, but they tried to pass some of them off and got pinched. I was a young kid at the time and I didn't know where he had gone off to. When I asked Mama, she said that he was on a business trip, it just happened to last three years."

Our days onboard the Aquitania were enjoyable, but I'm getting antsy after so many idle days.

After seeing nothing but ocean for so many days, land finally came into sight. As we looked out at London as we came into port, it felt like a different world. Once we disembarked, Myrt insisted that we do a little sightseeing before finding the rest of the tour group. Myrt thought that if we waited, we wouldn't get a chance to see anything, and she's probably right. Once I get focused on racing, it's like I have blinders on, so we had our trunks sent ahead to the Carlton Hotel in Southampton where we would be staying.

We took a horse-drawn carriage around the city and saw Buckingham Palace, the Tower of London, and Big Ben. We also went to Madame Tussaud's Wax Museum, which has been around since the 1890s, and the wax figures really look life-like. I especially thought that the James Cagney image is impressive. Madame Tussaud's even has the original guillotine that beheaded Marie Antoinette, and with her wax image standing next to it, it is just a little too creepy for Myrt. We soon finished our sightseeing and went to locate our tour group and make sure that the racing schedule is in place.

Racing in England

Speedway racing is extremely popular in England, and the London area alone has eight major tracks ranging from a tenth to a third of a mile. They say that at some of the big stadiums, twenty-thousand fans can be in the stands watching. In the London area, we found plenty of racing at speedway tracks such as Leeds, Oxford, Hackney Wick, Harringay, New Cross, and Wimbledon. With so many local and foreign race teams competing, each team wore a thin vest over their jacket with either their countries flag, a crest of something like a lion or a dragon, or just team colors on the front so that spectators can tell who to root for.

Riders often team with a partner to watch out for one another and help protect your partner if they are in the lead, so I'm teamed up with Pete Colman. After New Zealand and Australia, Byrd McKinney went back to the states and Pete arrived for the England leg and brought his wife and their little girl. Pete's a really good rider out of Southern California, I've raced against him back home, and we've got a good feel for each other out on the track.

The biggest difference of racing in England is that instead of dirt, their tracks consist of cinder, which is basically coal dust. Since it always seems to rain in England, using dirt would create mud puddles, but water drains off of coal dust. On days when it isn't wet or raining, the track crew floods the whole racetrack an hour or two before the start making it look like a lake, but by race time, the water has drained off. Another thing is that they use short metal starting gates that drop flat to signal the start of a race instead of using a flag-man like we do in the states.

When we lined up for our first heat and the gate dropped, we took off like bats out of hell. Then we quickly found out an essential difference between cinder and dirt. Heading into the first corner, the two English racers shut off their throttles before us. Pete and I kind of glanced at each other thinking, this should be easy. That was just before we slid right off the track.

Besides finding out that cinder is much slicker than dirt, we also discovered that cinder is strangely like wet paint. Everyone starts the race with goggles on, but after the first corner the leading racer is taking off his goggles so that he can see better, while the rest of us took ours off because we can't see at all.

For the first two weeks we stayed at the Carlton Hotel in Southampton, and then we moved into the Ragland Hotel in London along with the other married couples in our group. It didn't take long to settle into a routine in London. The Ragland House is close to Wembley stadium, which is one of our main tracks, so the women can stay at home while we go nearby to work. We are in a shared furnished apartment with Manuel and his wife Francis, and our housekeeper Mrs. Hiley looks after us while we are staying here.

We've gotten really close with Manuel and Francis along with Putt and his wife Helen. Pete and Clara are a great couple too, and they have their little girl Sally Anne with them, so everyone kind of treats her like a kid sister. All three of the couples: Manuel and Francis, Putt and Helen, and Pete and Clara live in Pasadena, or close to it, and they are trying to talk us into moving down there to live. Myrt and I have our families in San Jose, so it would be hard to leave, but that doesn't keep them from working on us.

***** ***** *****

Compared to the previous leg of the tour where our racing was limited, in England we are racing as many as five or six nights a week which is a grueling schedule, but we're getting better as a team. We just finished a good meeting at Rye House in Hertfordshire and the score was 26 – 40 in our favor. During one of those nights in a six-lap heat, I got into a good battle with a British racer. We were neck and neck from the third turn and stayed that way for the remainder of the race. Going into the second to last two corner, his front wheel bumped my leg and it came down to the wire, but I edged him to win by about half of a wheel at the finish. Afterwards I saw him in the pits and went over to say what a tough battle it was.

"That was a good race out there."

"So you're the yank on the other motor. My name is Ezra," he said as we shook hands.

"I'm Sam." I looked at his bike. "You're riding a JAP too, no wonder things were so even."

We talked a little about the upcoming races and how I'm with Putt Mossman's tour group.

"So what have you been doing since you've been in England?"

"Not much besides racing."

"Spending all of your free time with a bunch of blokes?"

I laughed about him calling us blokes. "Actually, I brought my wife along for the English tour."

He shook his head and said, "Poor bastard. A cousin of mine owns a pub not far away, I'm heading there to get a bite to eat if you are interested."

"That sounds good to me."

An hour later, we walked into a little pub called the Black Eagle. It's not too different from back home, it's still guys standing around a long wooden bar drinking beer with a blue haze hanging in the air from all of the smokers.

Ezra asked, "What would you like to drink?"

"How do I know what you guys drink over here? I just have whatever you're drinking."

Ezra walked over to the bar and I heard him talk to the bartender.

"Pauly, two pints of Guinness."

Once Ezra brought over our drinks, he put a nearly black beer in front of me, I Ezra a little worried. I had never heard of Guinness, and it was the darkest beer I'd ever seen, but thankfully it didn't taste as heavy as it looked. We both ordered the fish and chips to eat, which I figure should be good here in London, and my beer went well with the meal.

Ezra said, "I'd like to try my hand at racing in New Zealand and Australia like you did."

Then I couldn't resist, "At least they have dirt on the tracks and not cinders."

"Bloody hell, you yanks always complain about that," Ezra said as he kept a straight face. We were only at the pub for an hour or so, but Ezra and I got along like old friends, even though his accent makes it tough to understand what he's saying about half the time. As we are getting ready to leave, I said, "Ezra if you ever get to San Jose, you need to look me up. Just find the Harley dealership and they'll know where I am."

"I hope that I can make it there someday, my gal Vera has always wanted to visit California."

We shook hands and parted as I walked back to Ragland House in the early London evening.

After races at Hackney Wick in the east London, we went to see Putt's show in action which is always entertaining. When we arrived just before intermission, the water tank that Putt is using for his jump has only a few feet of water. He needs a decent amount of water to create a big enough splash to put out the flames on top, but I don't think it's nearly enough to do the stunt.

Putt is a professional and people paid to see him, so he will do it no matter what. When it came time to perform, Putt is on his bike at the top of the ramp which leads down and up to the lip of the tank. Then Pee Wee poured petrol over the top of the water, and striking a match and holding it up for everyone to see, he set it on fire.

We watched as Putt rode down the ramp and got airborne before landing in the tank and putting out the fire. One problem though, without enough water to absorb the impact of the motorcycle touching down, the landing is much harder and Putt smashed his nose on the steering damper on impact. Putt climbed out of the tank of water, jumped on his waiting second motorcycle, and did a victory lap waving to the audience as he is bleeding all over the front of himself.

With just a few more days of racing until the tour winds down, our group is having one last get together at a London restaurant before everyone makes their way back to the States. Putt, on the other hand, is thinking about taking a future tour to Africa, so when the tour is over, he's going to Africa to see if it is workable. When the racing season wrapped up and they were recognizing riders, I made the official team of Hackney Wick, which is a big honorary title.

On our trip back from England, we are sailing on the Queen Mary, which is on the return trip of her maiden voyage. The Queen Mary is bigger than the Aquitania, so much so that it has an indoor swimming pool and an outdoor tennis court. Each day Myrt and I have been spending time in the observation bar which is an art deco-styled lounge with wide ocean views that we look out upon. There is not much time left on our extended honeymoon, so we are enjoying every day of it that we have together. We are anxious to get back home, but not so ready to get back into the daily schedule.

After retrieving my Plymouth from the New York harbor's parking lot, we started on our drive back to California. I try and put in 12 hours of driving each day, and we're making good time. We stop for a motel every few days, but we usually just find a place not far from a gas station where we can pull off the road to catch some shut eye. After we wake up in the morning, we go to the closest gas station and get cleaned up.

One of the things we did on the drive, even though it's out of the way, is to stop by the Grand Canyon. As we drove, I wasn't 100% sure we were heading in the right direction, but we were soon right by it. As we stood at the edge, Myrt said it took her breath away. It is impressive at first, but after about 15 minutes, it looked like just a big hole to me. The worst part is that we're out in the middle of nowhere and it's about 110 degrees in the shade.

Back on the road Myrt and I have been talking about how we need to find a place to rent as soon as we get back to San Jose. After making it back home and spending time with our families catching up, we went looking for an apartment. We found a nice furnished place at 9th and Santa Clara above Hall's Coffee Shop and as a bonus it's only two blocks away from her parent's house. The rent is $18 a month and our groceries for the month cost around $4. I'm making $28 a month at the dealership, so we have money left over to put into savings.

San Jose MC

Our motorcycle club is gaining in popularity and with so many members, the shop is no longer big enough, so we had to find a house where we can hold our meetings. One of the members located a place to rent on Virginia Street off of Third Street that's owned by Jim Malatto. Jimmy owns and runs Malatto's bar which is right across the street at Virginia and Vine, so a lot of the guys are happy with that being so close.

We've been talking about how our San Jose motorcycle club needs a mascot. After working over a few ideas, we've decided to officially name our club the San Jose Dons Motorcycle Club. Dons is Spanish for gentlemen, and with all of the quality guys we have, the name fits. We've also selected club colors of green and gold, so our long sleeve wool sweaters will have gold sleeves and the main body will be green. On the back of our sweaters we'll have an outline image of a Spanish Gentleman wearing a hat, and in red letters "San Jose" is scrolled across the top, and in larger green letters underneath is the word "Dons" with Motorcycle Club written in smaller red letters below. I already have a green helmet and I'm going to paint one gold stripe (yellow might have to work) going from front to back and another gold stripe going from side to side to match our club colors.

Our club has a one dollar initiation fee to join and the monthly dues are 50 cents which goes to the house costs, but that's not enough to cover the monthly rent. So we'll serve beer and whiskey shots for two bits apiece at meetings and get-togethers on the weekends. We are using an old door on sawhorses for a makeshift bar in the family room, but one of the Dons is a talented carpenter who is going to build a 12-foot bar complete with matching bar stools for the clubhouse. Another one of our guys has a pool table that he's going to donate, so after we throw in a few old sofas, we will be set.

For our weekly meetings, we go over the minutes from the last meeting, any costs associated with the clubhouse, and any announcements on upcoming events like hill climbs, poker runs, or pool tournaments. We always end the meeting with a "for the good of the club" open floor which is when anyone can bring up ideas for the club, and it's also when to nominate someone for the "Bone" prize. This is when someone stands up to tell a story about a club member that did something stupid or embarrassing, and whichever story gets the most laughs, the guy that embarrassed himself receives the bone prize. The prize is a cow leg-bone about a foot and a half long, and it has two clamps on the back that are used to attach to a motorcycle's front forks. The "Bone" is the highlight of our weekly meetings, and there's never a shortage of funny stories to go around.

Watsonville Dealership

Tom has been keeping me in the loop since he started the process of buying the Harley Davidson dealership in Watsonville. The current owner, Lyle Muth, is a smart guy, but not really a motorcycle guy. He ran the dealership for a couple years, but he's tired of the business, so Tom stepped in.

Tom will stay at the San Jose dealership, and I'll be the guy running the Watsonville dealership for him. The Watsonville area is wide open because outside the Harley dealership, everyone has to go to San Jose for parts. One thing about the area is that it's rather sleepy, so the dealership will be a one-man operation. I'll either be helping customers at the counter or doing repairs in the shop out back. Then Myrt hit me with some other news, she is pregnant with our first child. We're excited, but we've decided to wait until after she has given birth before moving, so I'll be riding to work each day from San Jose.

***** ***** *****

I've been running the Watsonville dealership for about five months now when Myrt called one day to say that she's going into labor. I raced home, breaking a few speed limits in the process, and grabbed Myrt and her prepacked suitcase and got to the hospital. Within a couple hours, on October 29th, 1937, Myrt gave birth to a baby boy that we're naming Sammy. If the kid could have waited one day, he would have been born on my birthday.

Two weeks after Sammy's birth, our family moved to a small rental house on Lincoln Street in Watsonville, and if things go well at the dealership, maybe I can afford a nicer place before long. I didn't know if I would be able to get Myrt to move out of San Jose, but the saving grace is that her sister Eva lives down the street, so they'll be able to spend time together, and Myrt won't feel homesick. Eva's husband Hubbie drives a delivery truck for Kraft. He and Eva recently moved from Chico when he was transferred to Watsonville a few months ago.

Louie Margarettich and I are starting to promote the Apple City Motorcycle Club around the local riders. The club has been around before I showed up, but I want to organize some club events which can also help business at the dealership. The colors for the club's long sleeve knit sweaters are yellow for the main body and red for the sleeves. On the back of the sweater is a big red apple patch with the name Apple City Motorcycle Club stitched across the top.

Oakland Speedway

The biggest race in the bay area is the Oakland 200, and it's only been around since 1935 in its current version. It's not a typical mile flat track. With the high-banked corners, it's more of a speedway track, so top speeds hitting 100 mph are likely. It's already being called the fastest one mile dirt track in the nation.

A mile long speedway tracks is a different style of racing than shorter flat track races. The steep angles of the track help push the bike down for traction, and the wide corners allow you to push the bike's speed without having to take your feet off the pegs. The dirt on the Oakland track is lightly oiled to keep the dust down, but it also makes the track a little slicker, and as the race progresses, the groove gets even slicker yet from tire rubber and any leaking motor oil. The main groove also gets bumpy throughout the race, and with the fences only a couple feet outside the groove, there's little room for error.

During the 1937 season, Gus Hunter joined the team as another rider for Tom. Gus is from the area, and after Tom saw him in a couple local races, he offered Gus a ride. Tom spent a few days making improvements to his bike and now Gus is ready to roll. When I got a look at Gus's bike, mine looks kind of sad. Gus has a nice-looking paint job with black on the top half of the gas tank and gold on the bottom half, while mine is painted basic gray.

During the season, Gus and I have been running partners on some of the half-mile tracks, and this will be the first mile track we've done together. The day before the race, both of us went to Oakland to do some laps and get a feel for the track. It's good to get in some practice if you can, but you didn't want to risk harming your newly rebuilt motor prior to the race.

Gus and I did a few laps at three-quarter speed to warm up the bikes, and then we pushed them up to racing speed. We figure to do 20 laps, take a breather, and then do another 20 and then we should be ready for tomorrow's race. About fourteen or fifteen laps into it, Gus is running full out and somehow lost control of his motorcycle and slammed into the outer wooden barrier. By the time I can get slowed down and came back around to him, Gus is already dead. His bike is 50 yards away, crumpled and smoking. I'm in shock trying to figure out what happened and what, if anything, I can do.

The safety crew should be here soon, but as I waited, I knelt down beside his body and said a few words. Gus has a wife and young child that are going to be hurting after this, so I prayed that they would be taken care of. When I finished, I tossed a small handful of dirt upon his body, sort of a baptism for a flat track racer. As other riders came up, most of them didn't say much - we all knew that the same thing could happen to us at any time.

That evening I reluctantly told Myrt about Gus' death. She is devastated and sick with worry that it could happen to me too. I tried to put it out of my mind, but I had a hard time sleeping that night. The mood of the riders is somber in Oakland the next day. I still raced, but I didn't do very well. In the back of my mind, I was probably still thinking about what happened to Gus.

This is the last race of the season, and besides an upcoming hill climb, it's time to wind down for the winter. To tide us over until next racing season, we'll go through the back roads on weekend rides and race each other along the trails and firebreaks up in the hills. I also plan to set up a poker run for the Apple City motorcycle club one of these Sundays, and everyone can bring along their ladies to join in on the fun.

Daytona 200

After the ongoing success of the Florida 200 Mile Road Race in Jacksonville, the organizers of the event needed a bigger venue, so they moved down the road to Daytona. The Daytona 200 is the first national championship of the season, and now it's one of the year's biggest events. For the inaugural race in 1937, Ed Kretz won with an average speed of just over 73 mph, so he's the favorite for this year's race. Kretz is a long time mechanic at Floyd Clymer's Los Angeles Indian dealership, and he's a good friend of mine, but he's a tough S.O.B. in the dirt.

I haven't been to Florida since the 1935 Neptune Beach race, and Tom must think that I need a bodyguard after my troubles last time, so both of us are going to Florida this year. Tom and I left San Jose for the cross-country drive to Daytona Beach in late February with the trailer loaded with my bike and all of our parts and tools, and the trailer is hooked to a sturdy GMC pickup and not a broken-down Dodge.

Tom is always coming up with ideas to get an edge, and for this race, it's no different. Tom put together a spring mechanism attached to my bike's shift lever, and when the clutch is pushed, the tight spring pulls back making the bike downshift. He set up a stop on the spring so that it will only downshift one gear at a time when you pushed the clutch, but for increasing speed, you have to shift like normal. Tom designed the spring-loaded shifter expressly for the long straights of Daytona, and by not having to take your hand off the handle bars to downshift going into the corner after a long straightaway, it will be a big time-saver over the 200-mile course if everything works out.

The course is a combination of road and beach over 63 laps with one and a half miles in both directions on the straights and quarter mile turns on banked sand. A sandy surface is somewhat of a challenge, for one sand is more resistance on tires than pavement, which in turn, requires more effort over the long haul. Motorcycle racing works your body all over, and racing for 200 miles will flat wear you out. You also need to decide what part of the beach to race on. The sand is more compact near the water, but waves come into play, and closer to the shore the sand is deeper and therefore slower, so you are looking for a happy medium. Besides watching out for the incoming waves, and the changing track surfaces, you also have to keep an eye out for spectators running across the track to the infield.

With over 100 riders, using our regular numbers causes too much overlap, so everyone is assigned random numbers and I have #28. Also, with so many riders, the officials have switched from a standing start to a staggered lineup. We'll be in rows of 10 with positions based on lap times taken earlier in solo runs.

The first row is lined up across the wide beach, and as the start flag drops, the sand is spraying backwards as they take off. Ten seconds later the second row heads out while I'm waiting in the third row. The two sugar lumps have dissolved in my mouth and as my row gets the flag, I twist the throttle and take off. The goal is always to get into the first turn before the rest of the riders, anything to create space over the next guy, and then I'll contend with the rows of riders that left earlier. Once I got three quarters through the first wide corner, I got a little airborne going from the sand to brick, but the brick surface is where my bike excels, and I began passing riders.

I'm starting to feel a little wore down by three-fourths of the way through the race, but I'm in the top half-dozen riders, and things are going well with Tom's spring shift setup. I'm roaring down the beach going well over a 100 mph just ahead of Ben Campanale somewhere near the 50th lap, and corner one is approaching. I wait to the last second to push in the clutch and make the bike to downshift, but the spring mechanism hangs up, which forces my bike into neutral. It's too late to try and downshift again, and too late to slow down when I'm going this fast. Even worse, a group of spectators are on the outside turn of the track, and I'm not sure that I can avoid going straight into them at this point. As I laid the bike down in the sand, it corkscrews and propels me airborne about 20 feet as I land on a couple people.

The people helped me up, and somehow I'm not hurt, and it doesn't seem any of them are either. Compared to some of my previous crashes, landing on people is rather soft. I looked out on the track to see my bike on its side and, thankfully, it didn't hit someone. I ran over to get the bike up on two wheels to look it over, and I see that the air filter is torn off, so the carburetor probably sucked in a bucket of sand before the motor died. Even if I can get the bike started, it won't last long before the sand destroys the cylinder walls and explodes the motor. For me this race is over. Ben Campanale took over the lead and went on to win the race.

***** ***** *****

Once we made our way back home in mid-March, the buzz is all about Seabiscuit's return to Bay Meadows. Last year it was mayhem as tens of thousands of people showed up to watch Seabiscuit beat Exhibit by one and a quarter lengths. This year Seabiscuit will race against Gosum, and the race is expected to draw 50,000 people. The seats in the grandstand can only hold a fraction of that number so, for most people, it will be standing room only. But for all of the excitement in the days leading up to the showdown, and all of the people coming to town by train and car, the actual race lasts less than two minutes.

I'm not going to fight the crowds to see it firsthand, so I'll be listening to it on the shop radio with the guys on Saturday afternoon. When the race is about to begin, we huddled around the radio to listen to the race announcer. From the start of the race until the end, it took one minute and 49 seconds, and Seabiscuit won by three lengths over Gosum.

A minute and 49 seconds is quick, but it's a lunch break compared to a hill climb run. The following day I went to a hill climb near Visalia which is being put on by the Visalia motorcycle club. This is the first climb at this location and as I looked up the hill, I knew it will be rough going. I'm guessing that near the top it's about a 60 degree incline. The hill is somewhat torn up, but it's not like you can do anything about it. I always have the attitude that I'm going to win or break the bike in half trying, so why worry about what you can't control.

I only brought a 45-cubic-inch today, but it feels like it could pull a plow across a field. On my first attempt, the path got so bumpy towards the top that, without warning, the front of the bike came off the ground and I flipped ass over elbows about 30 feet shy of the finish line, and the bike damn near fell on top of me. My handle bars look like a deformed pretzel from the crash, but I'll find someone with a bar bender and get the bike ready for my next pass.

A couple hours later, it's my turn again and, this go-around, I'm planning out a different route. I lined my hill climber in front of the catcher wall and got great traction at the start and I practically flew up the hill. That run worked out well enough, I had the day's fastest time in the 45-cubic-inch division and came home with a gold trophy.

Nevada Speed Race

Tom always said he would beef-up my motorcycle, and in early 1938, he asked to use my Harley for an upcoming speed race. Tom is going to build up the motor to use for the speed race, and afterwards I'd get the bike back with most of the modifications still in place, so I handed over my key. The event is about a hundred miles north of Reno on a dry lake bed in Black Rock Desert, so it's similar to the speed races they have at Bonneville. Tom is having Sally Gotto pilot the bike and Sally weighs only about a hundred pounds, which does wonders for the horsepower-to-weight ratio.

Tom spent a week preparing the motor and transmission for my bike, while I rode a trade-in that I borrowed from the shop. After Tom finished with his upgrades, we took the bike out to Balsa Road near Hollister for a speed test. The bike has dropped down handlebars to cut down on wind resistance and thin tires for less contact with the ground. We had hooked up a high-mph speedometer to get an idea on overall speed and, although it's a slow starter, I took it past 110 mph and slowed it back down. Balsa road is nice and flat with very little traffic, but hitting a pot hole or even a ground squirrel going 110 could be curtains.

Tom and I met at the shop at 3:00 in the morning and headed for Reno, while Sally is going to meet us there. Once we made it out to the dry lake bed, it looks like well over 200 other riders are here, but there are several categories to compete in today. With this being a speed race, the bike is built with a very tall gear, so it won't be moving fast at the start, but as speed builds up and Tom's improvements really kick in, things are going to happen.

At 11:00, they called for the 14 riders in our category to line up. I pushed the idling bike over to the starting line, and Sally got on. The officials lined up the riders along the painted white stripe and spaced them about 10 feet apart. After the starting flag dropped and the riders took off, Sally is near the back of the group, but that was expected. We watched the riders getting smaller as they zoomed down the two-mile course towards the finish line. When the race was completed, they announced over the loudspeakers that Sally had won with a time of two tenths of a second under 132 mph.

When Sally came back, he filled us in on what happened. "I started slow at the beginning, but by the middle of the dry lake bed, the bike is gaining ground. I came rocketing through the middle of the pack and crossed the finish line first by nearly 100 yards." I always find it amazing how Tom can always put together a contender no matter what type of race it is.

That week at work, I switched out the gears and rear sprocket to make my bike more street friendly. It's noticeably quicker putting around town, but I hope to take it out on Balsa Road in the next few days to see how much speed the bike still has.

Chapter 5 / Oakland Victory

In a few weeks from now, the Oakland 200 will be here and I've been looking forward to the race. The WLDR is running strong and I've been clicking on the tracks lately. It's also the last race of the season, so I want to go out with a bang. Last year's race was traumatic and something I'd just as soon forget. Hopefully, this year will be injury free for all the riders. Several of the big names will be in Oakland: Jim Kelly, Cliff Self, and Jack Cottrell, all of them trying to be among the 36 riders qualifying for the main event.

The biggest problem with Harley Davidsons and racing motors in general is keeping the motor lubricated enough. Tom has been working on the oil system to produce a thicker and more consistent layer of oil on the cylinder walls to keep the heat and friction down. If things work out as planned, I should be able to keep it running wide open and not have to worry about blowing up the motor. Before the race Tom said that if I let off the throttle very much, I'd foul the plugs with the motor running so wet, which means that I need to keep the RPMs as high as possible. With the high banks and wide corners of the track, it shouldn't be a problem.

I had no problem qualifying, and after doing a final check on the bike, I got ready for the start. At the beginning of the race, I got into a groove early and didn't let off the throttle for well over 120 laps. When I got the sign to come in for the mandatory fuel stop my mechanic Sam Stevens quickly started filling up the tank, but while I was off the track, Jack Cottrell took over the lead. The good thing is that he hasn't refilled yet, so he won't hold the lead for long. Not more than 10 laps later, when Cottrell came in for fuel, I got out front again and increased my lead over the remaining laps. By the time the 200 lap race was over, I shattered the old track record by 19 minutes and 20 seconds and averaged nearly 10 mph faster than the previous record.

It's mayhem after the race, as photographers are taking pictures of me holding the trophy while the reporters are asking Tom questions about the bike and our big win. Tom and I are thrilled by the victory and how well the bike performed, and for me, this is my biggest win so far.

Tuesday morning Tom got a call from Bill Davidson congratulating him on the big win. Then the talk soon turned to them wanting the technical information on all of his modifications. Besides being a tuner and engineer, Tom is a businessman, so he wants to get fairly paid for his work. When Bill Davidson low-balled him, Tom had no option but to turn him down, which didn't go over well in Milwaukee.

Tom put the motor from the Oakland 200 victory in the front window of the dealership with a placard stating "Sifton Engines." He had reason to be proud, but within a week, the factory jumped in and accused Tom of promoting himself with "Sifton" engines, although it's still a Harley-based motor. Everyone knew what this is about, if Tom would have played nice before, nothing would have been said. Tom left the motor in the window for a few more weeks, just to annoy the powers that be, then pulled it out. Now it's time to hunker down for the slow winter months and come up with improvements to make our motorcycles better for next year.

Back to Daytona

Tom and I are going to Daytona like we did last year. Tom has put together a strong motor for the race, so we feel good about our chances to compete, although I can't say we've had much luck here so far. Along the way I heard about some of Tom's old races like the Pismo Beach Rally. While nearly all of the riders had 74-cubic-inch (1200cc) motors, Tom raced a 45-cubic-inch Harley motor that he modified and, with it, he smoked the competition. Tom was using double cam springs and high-strength aluminum before anyone else, so he's been at the forefront of racing engineers for some time.

A few weeks after the Pismo Beach Rally, Tom won the Pacific Coast Hill Climb Championship and then retired from competition. Tom was already working for Dud Perkins as a builder, so that's one reason he stopped competing, but the main reason is that he tore up his knee on a hill climb. Tom slipped off his bike when the front end lifted, and when he put his foot down, it got caught in a gopher hole and as the bike spun, it wrenched his knee. His knee still bothers him, especially when the weather gets cold.

We arrived in Daytona to a swarm of motorcycles and people. The city is jumping, and it's amazing to see how the race's popularity has really grown since my first time here.

When race day came, it's time to put up or shut up. I got into position with the other riders, and after the start, I'm making good progress and passing riders in every lap. As far as I can tell by the half-way point, I should be leading or really close to it. Then, out of the blue, I start hearing one of the pistons hitting the top of the cylinder head, and my heart sunk. That's a sure sign that the motor isn't going to make it for long, certainly not to the end of the race, but I'll keep pressing ahead and hope for the best. I'm riding the bike wide open down the beach portion when the motor explodes, the flywheel locks up, and I came skidding to a stop with part of my motor missing and oil trickling onto the sand.

Ben Campanale goes on to win his second Daytona in a row, which is pretty remarkable considering that only one out of every four or five riders complete the race at all. Engine failure is always the number one problem in racing, but beach races are especially hard on motors. The blowing sand gets into everything and acts like sandpaper on moving metal parts, which often don't have a lot of durability to start with.

***** ***** *****

When we made it back to San Jose, Myrt is happy to see me, and I can't believe how much Sammy has grown since Tom and I left on the trip. I spent my first Sunday back from Florida with the family, but next Sunday I'm going to a flat track race near Merced to try and pick up a little cash.

The following weekend, I had a great start at Merced winning my heat by two bike lengths, and the bike still has more power to give. After the heats and the semi are over, we lined up for the main. This will be a staggered line-up with three rows of two, and the rider with the day's fastest lap time gets put on the outside of the back row, so that's where I'm sitting.

When the flag drops, I spun out too much and didn't get a good jump. As the riders funnel into the first corner, I saw a little bumping take place, so I'm okay with bidding my time behind the pack. Once I hit the straightaway, I knew I'd be passing most of them anyway. Going into the second corner, a rider went down not 15 feet ahead and I'm heading straight for him, I veered outside and clipped someone's handlebars, which got my bike squirrely. As I head for the outside fence, I laid the bike down, but I'm still moving too fast and prepared to collide with the fence. I had my foot out to brace for the impact, but that only twisted my ankle as I slammed into the fence. I'm limping as I try to set my bike up and restart it, but I see a couple broken spokes on the front rim, so my day is done.

Relaxing in the pits afterward, I can barely walk, but I'll take a few aspirins once I get home and my ankle should be fine in a day or two. Unless your bike can't be ridden after a crash, it doesn't mean that you are done for the day. Last year during a heat that knocked down three riders, my buddy Harry Bertram got back up and stayed in the race with a broken nose. Harry is quiet off the track, but fierce on it. He just stuffed a small piece of a rag in the one leaky nostril causing him problems, and kept racing. We look forward to racing all week long, and it takes a lot to keep us from getting out in the dirt.

1939 Oakland 200

The Oakland 200 race is this weekend, and after last year's record breaking win, I'm favored to repeat. These high-profile events always bring in the top riders, and I know Ben Campanale, Paul Albrecht, Armando Magri, and Ed Kretz are showing up, so I'll have tough competition again this year. The way that the high-banked track is laid out, you can ride through the corners at nearly straight-away speed. Compared to a normal mile track, on a speedway track you can cut a couple seconds off a normal lap time, so I should get it down to maybe 38-39 seconds.

Our starting positions are based on qualifying times, and I'm in the second of five rows with five riders per row. Once the race began, a few laps in, I made my way to the front and set up a quick pace. The bike is running strong, and I've got the lead, but I have to keep it for nearly two hours. At the half-way point I've lapped several riders by double digits, and I'm still comfortably in the lead. At least up to lap 108, that's when the explosion occurred that blew the front cylinder off my motor, and just like that, my chance to repeat is over.

Jack Cottrell is one of Dud Perkin's riders and he went on to take the checkered flag, but the race isn't without controversy. Coming in second was Armando Magri who is the Harley Davidson dealer in Sacramento, and it sounds like one of the lap checkers didn't credit Armando with one of his completed laps, which would have made him the winner. It doesn't help that they have similar numbers, Jack has #21 and Armando has #2, plus their bikes and helmets are identical, so it's possible that someone could have made a mistake. But once the officials declared Jack Cottrell the winner, it will be hard to reverse. Looking at Jack's overall time, it's more than three minutes slower than my winning time from last year.

***** ***** *****

The Watsonville dealership generates enough income to cover the monthly nut, but not much of a profit. Tom and I hoped that the dealership would do better, but this is a farm community without much daily traffic. The weekends can get busy during the summer, but the weekdays are quiet, so after two years of me running the dealership for Tom, he decided to close it down.

Since returning to work at the San Jose dealership, Myrt found a nice rental on South 22nd Street for us to move into. Then Myrt sprung some big news on me, we have another baby on the way. A second child is going to make life even busier, but we're both excited about it.

Endurance Run

The club has been trying to organize a local endurance run for some time, and after promising the police department that we would not break any laws and clean up afterwards, we finally received the green light from the city to hold the event. One of the Dons has an old WW1 helmet that we decided to use for the race's trophy. After we drilled a hole in the top of the helmet, and bolted on an old eagle radiator cap hood ornament from a 1930s Chevy, we had the whole thing chromed. With the helmet trophy setting the tone, we are calling the event the Tin Hat Derby.

This event will have a distance of over 180 miles along the trails, but it covers so much ground that we must use city streets in a few places to get to other sections of the course. The goal of an endurance run is to average 24 mph over the complete course, and for this distance, it's going to take up most of the short winter's day. It should take about seven and a half hours to cover the course, in addition to a 30 minute break at the half-way point in Boulder Creek. The weekend before, we will set out markers along the trail to make sure everyone goes in the right direction, and about two hours after the last rider takes off, we'll have a couple guys riding the trail to make sure that no one gets left behind.

The run will start and end at the Don's clubhouse with each rider leaving one minute after the previous rider. From the clubhouse, you ride over to Almaden, then turn right on Coleman and keep going until you get into woods of Almaden Valley, and then it's on through the mountains. The Saratoga summit usually has snow on the ground if it isn't falling during the race, and it often rains at the lower elevations this time of year, so mud is practically guaranteed throughout most of the ride.

We'll have 14 checkpoints set up at unknown locations every 20 to 30 miles along the trail, and at each checkpoint, the rider gets a receipt of the current time, while the checkpoint person keeps a duplicate copy. They'll have coffee at the checkpoints, but most of the riders will probably just want to get their receipt and keep going at the speed they've set for themselves.

At Boulder Creek, everyone is given a 30-minute food and bathroom break before continuing up the coast to Pescadero and then south to Whitehouse Canyon road. After coming back through the Santa Cruz Mountains, you finally come through Los Gatos on the final stretch back to the clubhouse and the final checkpoint on the course.

It's been raining off and on for the past several days, but bad weather isn't going to hold off the run. The temperature will be in the 40s, so we don't have to worry about snow, but it will certainly be muddy. The one big concern is that the further back you start in the crowd, the muddier the trail will get as dozens of riders pass through it. I can imagine that it's possible to sink up to the foot pegs in mud if you don't watch it.

We have numbers on pieces of paper in a bucket and as each person pulled out one they wrote down their number by their name on a clip board. Once I took off from the clubhouse in the number nine slot, I quickly set my pace and focused on being consistent as possible. As I got higher into the mountains a couple hours into the run, the muddier the trails became, but since I'm one of the first riders, the trails aren't as bad as they will be for those coming through later. I made it to the half-way point a little less than four hours into the run, and got a much needed stretch. As I'm eating a sandwich I had packed, I looked over my checkpoint receipts and seem to be doing well according to my times, but there's still four hours left of riding.

When I hit the pavement in Los Gatos on the last stretch of the run, I feel half frozen and I can't wait to warm up my cold bones and get something hot to drink back at the clubhouse.

When I made it to the last checkpoint, my forearms are worn out and I'm saddle sore. At the clubhouse, some of the Dons are already adding up times to figure out who is the closest to averaging 24 mph for the day. When it came to add up my checkpoint times, I thought I did okay, but I wasn't even in the top five. It's been a really long day, and I've seen a dozen guys stuck in mud and one rider slide off the side of a trail and disappear into the brush at 24 plus miles per hour, but for a first-time event, things went pretty well.

Lake Port Crash

Last season I went undefeated in every half-mile heat and main event that I've been in from Stockton and Galt, to Tulare and Bolado Park, and after four races into the new season, I'm still unbeaten. I've been planning for some time to make the flat track race at Lakeport near Clear Lake, but it's really close to Myrt's due date. When I thought about it, the chance of her going into labor on Sunday is pretty small, and I'll be back in the evening, so it shouldn't be a problem if I go ahead and make the race.

At Lakeport, the competition is pretty solid, but my bike has been running strong lately and I'm feeling good today. We have an hour or so before qualifying, and I got out on the track with about 10 other riders to do some warm-ups. About a half dozen laps into going all out, a rider took a spill in front of me and I'm heading right for him. I turned into the infield, but it's as rough as a freshly plowed field as I'm holding on. It's a tank-slapper as my handlebars crossed and I went crashing to the ground. Pain shot through my arm, and I didn't need a doctor to tell me that it's broken. A couple guys pushed my bike to the infield for me, and the medics wrapped my arm in a tight cloth to keep the bones in place until a doctor can put my arm in a cast.

I left before the races began to get back to San Jose, and on the way, I'm thinking that I'll quickly go by the hospital on my arm, but something just didn't seem right. I decided to go home first to check on Myrt, then I'll get my arm tended to. When I got to our house, there is a note from Myrt saying that she's left for the hospital. My day has gone from bad to worse in a hurry. I made it to the hospital in less than 10 minutes, but they informed me that the baby hadn't arrived yet, so they sent me off to the waiting room. Since my arm is throbbing and causing me a decent amount of pain, I went to find a doctor to set my arm while I'm waiting.

A few hours later, the doctor came out to say that I'm the father of a beautiful baby daughter. Later I went over to see Myrt, and she's holding our little girl on the other side of the glass windows that separates the nervous Dads from the newborns. As I'm standing there looking at them, Myrt smiles at me, and then she sees my arm in a cast and shakes her head. I'm sure that Myrt jinxed me for going to a race, and that's why I have a broken arm, but it's still a good day. Our daughter weights a healthy eight pounds and three ounces; thankfully she isn't a 10 pounder like Myrt was at birth. Myrt has already settled on a name, Judith Ann Arena.

I wish that I could hold her without my arm being in a cast, but that's the breaks. What really bugs me is that the Oakland 200 is less than a month away and now I'm screwed. It's also the last race, so this isn't how I wanted to wrap up the season, but I'll be back in shape for our winter rides and the Tin Hat Derby. I've already decided that I'm skipping Daytona this year. At this point, it's doubtful that I'll ever race in Florida again.

***** ***** *****

Last season I was undefeated, so my goal is to go undefeated again this season. One thing that is for sure, this year again I am the guy that everyone's trying to beat. One race night a buddy of mine is talking with a couple other racers when he saw me working on my bike.

"Sam you're racing tonight?"

"That's why I'm here."

"Crap! I wonder how much the purse is for second place."

I laughed to myself, but I did end up winning the main event that evening.

At today's afternoon race in Modesto, I spanked everyone in my heat and had the fastest lap time. When it came time for the main event, I decided to have a little fun. When the start flag waved, I didn't move I just lowered my helmet so I wouldn't get pelted by dirt as everyone peeled away. I counted to three Mississippi and then took off. Playing catch up is good practice anyway, you never know when a mechanical problem might delay your start. By the back stretch of the second lap, I made it out to the front of the pack on my way to another win.

Myrt and I are looking into buying our first house, and I talked to my friend Don Gaglardi (the second "g" is silent) who's a home builder, to get his opinion. He says that we can borrow $4000 from the bank, buy a house lot for $400, and use the rest of the money to build the house. With him doing all of the work, it would save us money, the payments would only be $25 a month, and we will be getting a better house. So Myrt and I got a loan from the bank, and Don found a building lot for us on Minnesota Avenue in Willow Glen, just outside the San Jose city limits.

Over the span of a couple months we watched our house being built from the foundation to the framing, and then to the roof and walls. It's looking really nice, and we are very excited about having our own place. But when Don finished everything, the monthly payment came in at $26 per month, not $25 like he said it would be. I'm close to telling him to kiss my butt, but after talking with Myrt, we decided to move in anyway. I'm making $32 a week at the shop, and being that I double my monthly income during race season, I can live with the payments.

Last Oakland Race

The final race of the season is the Oakland 200, and it's become the Bay Area event to attend each year. While you see many of the same guys at local races, for high-profile events they come up from Los Angeles and San Diego and come down from San Francisco, Oakland, and Sacramento. For the 1941 race, some of the top riders coming to town include Ben Campanale and Ed Kretz.

On race day, the atmosphere is charged and the number of spectators tops 6,000 easy. The event gets bigger each year, and the checks are getting bigger too. This year's first place winner gets a $500 check. From an entry of 66 riders, they cut it down to 25 for the main race. Once they got our bikes lined up, it's a short wait until the flag fell, then the sound of horsepower erupted and the dash began. While a certain amount of jostling took place going into the first corner, everyone worked on getting into their rhythm coming down the back stretch and settled in for the long haul.

About a half hour in to the race, probably less than 50 laps, a couple of riders went down in front of me as I came out of a corner. Ben Campanale is off to the side of me and he's trying to avoid the bikes and bodies lying in the middle of track and hit the outer fence. I laid down the bike and somehow slid between the wreckage, while out of the corner of my eye I was shocked to see Tommy Hayes spin out over the fence.

As I'm sliding, something smashed into my arm with such force that I figured I must have broken something. I got up and went over to stand against the outer fence, my arm is throbbing, but everything seems to be working, so no broken bones. I ran over to my bike that is some 30 feet behind me, and it somehow managed to shift into neutral and is still running, but the back wheel is bent from the crash. All of us are rattled by the wipeout as the ambulance came onto the track to attend to the racers.

I got the bike back up and rode it into the pits under the warning flag and my pit man Sam Stevens quickly replaced the rear wheel. Ed Kretz was in front for most of the time before the warning flag, and after the long delay and restart, Kretz took the lead again. On lap 148, Kretz's motor died and Ernie Holbrook took over the lead and carried it for the win on an Indian, although his overall time was 18 minutes off the record.

After the race, we heard that both Tommy Hayes and June McCall had been killed, while Jimmy Kelley and Ben Campanale were in serious condition at the hospital. As the riders and mechanics were talking afterwards, everyone said the same thing, it is the worst crash that they had ever seen.

Racing is a dangerous sport and, as riders, we know the risks, but the oiled dirt track and the high-banked corners added up to a lethal combination. The Oakland 200 track has claimed several lives over its short existence, and in the aftermath of the 1941 crash, the organizers decided that the dangers far outweighed the benefits, and motorcycle racing at the Oakland 200 came to an end.

World War 2

On the morning of December 7th the newspaper headlines read that Pearl Harbor was attacked by the Japanese. Shortly after, the United States declared war against Japan. Many of my racing friends are enlisting in different services, many of them hoping to fly planes. I went down to the recruiting station to fill out my paperwork, and they sent me home afterwards saying that they would be contacting me.

I kept waiting for my notice and someone told me that I am performing one of the highest civilian duties, which is keeping the police and military motorcycles running, so I just kept working at the dealership and figured that they would contact me if things changed. One day when I came into work Tom said, "Hey Sam, guess what?"

"What?"

"I've been drafted."

"Are you kidding?"

"Wish I was. You're going to have to run the dealership while I'm gone."

"Sure, I can do that. I guess that it's a good thing the military didn't want me," I chuckled. I thought that it's odd that they are taking Tom and leaving me, but Tom has specialized skills that make him a valuable asset. Soon they informed Tom that his new job is working as a machinist at Hendee Iron Works over at Moffett Field Naval base in Sunnyvale.

I took over running the day-to-day operations at the San Jose dealership when Tom began working at Moffett Field. Bob Chaves has been one of Tom's friends since childhood, and he started helping at the shop working part time, but when he went into the service as a paratrooper, running the dealership became a one-man operation. All motorcycle production is strictly being used by the military, so we won't be able to sell new motorcycles, only used ones. We'll have to keep the dealership afloat mainly from parts and service.

One morning, a couple of Army trucks brought in over 40 Harley's to be worked on, which is about three months of normal business for the dealership. It will be a time-consuming job, and take up a lot of parts, but it will bring in some good money for the shop. They provided a rough list of repairs and once I looked them over and picked a couple easy ones to repair, I got to work. As I made my way through the motorcycles, I found out that two of the motorcycles were too far gone, so they were cannibalized for parts. I finished repairing the last motorcycle 24 days later and called the phone number that they left to report that the bikes were ready.

Soldiers showed up two days later to pick up the motorcycles. I'm waiting for payment when the guy in charge handed me a piece of paper.

I asked, "What's this?"

"That is a receipt for all of the work on the motorcycles. Send it to the address listed on the back, and the government will reimburse you for the costs of the repairs."

I don't like IOU's so I asked, "Are you sure about this?"

"This is how the military runs things. Don't worry, you'll get paid."

They loaded the bikes on the flat-bed army trucks parked out back and drove off. Once they left I went inside to get envelopes and I did just as instructed: I mailed in the paperwork and copies for all the receipts to the address listed. I hope that it won't take long to get reimbursed because I used a big chunk of the parts we had at the shop, and I need to replace what I can.

A month later I still haven't been paid on all of the repairs when different soldiers brought in more motorcycles to be serviced. I want to do my part to help with the war effort, but these expenditures are all coming out of Tom's pocket, and I'm not going to fall for this twice. I'm standing at the shop counter when a soldier came inside and said, "We were told to bring our motorcycles here to be repaired."

I replied, "We tried this before, but I never got paid for the last batch of motorcycles that our shop repaired. You'll have to pay up front before I can start working on them."

That isn't the response he was expecting. He went back outside and had a short conversation with another soldier sitting in one of the trucks. As they are talking, I can see that neither of them is too happy. After a few minutes, the first soldier came back inside the shop and said, "We'll get back with you." Then they left with their motorcycles and still haven't come back.

***** ***** *****

I paid Tom a visit to see how things are going for him over at Moffett Field. Even from miles away it's easy to spot the naval base, just locate the biggest buildings on the horizon that tower over everything else in the area. This is where they house massive airships, or blimps, and the buildings they need to park them in have to be huge. I rode over to the front gate of the naval base on my motorcycle and said to the guards that Tom Sifton is expecting me. One of them made a phone call from the guard booth and came back to tell me to wait.

About 10 minutes later, Tom drove up in his car and, after signing the visitor log, we drove over by the giant airship hangar so I could take a look. Tom said, "The first hangar was built for the USS Macon about 10 years ago, while the other two hangars have just been built over the past couple years. The USS Macon was 785 feet long and had 100 crew members, and the amazing thing is that it had five Sparrowhawk planes on board that could be released from harnesses. But after only two years of service, the USS Macon went down near the Big Sur coast."

When we looked into the main hangar I couldn't believe the size.

"This building is gigantic!"

"It can fit 10 football fields inside and it's close to 200 feet tall. Sometimes clouds appear inside because of it is so massive."

I told Tom, "I notice how busy the base is with all of the planes flying in and out."

"Most of those are anti-submarine planes that are patrolling along the coastline."

We went to large building, but not as large as the others, where Tom works, and we climbed a ladder to get to his work platform some twenty feet up. I watched as a lathe, nearly the size of a small car, peeled thin sheets of steel off of a huge revolving wheel like they were strips of tin foil.

"These will become gears for the steam-powered engines that propel Liberty ships. A block-long shaft will run through the center of this gear to the far end of the shaft which will have a four-blade propeller. The Queen Mary has four propellers this size."

It's been interesting to see what he's been doing, but I've been gone from the shop long enough. Tom took me back to the front gate where we said our goodbyes, and I hit the road so I could get back to work. It's not just people that get called up to serve, the Dons had to give up our clubhouse because it's needed by the military for a warehouse.

With so many club members off to war and losing the clubhouse temporarily, we suspended the Dons. In its place I started the Roamers Motorcycle Club from the leftovers of different local motorcycle clubs. Most of the Dons are Harley faithful, but during the war, we set aside those differences, and any motorcycle rider is welcome. With no other options, Myrt said that she's okay with us having the club meetings at our house in Willow Glen. Myrt and I have a big den with two pin ball machines and two slot machines to pass the time. I have a neighbor that fixes slot machines for Vegas casinos, so he loaned two of them to me. We also have a pool table and two couches in the den, so it's a comfortable place for the Roamers to meet once a week.

***** ***** *****

Sammy is six years old and has been riding a bicycle for a while, so I thought he should start riding something with a motor. The bicycle he has right now is a good fit, so I will use his bicycle frame as the basis for my project and work from there.

I found a small gas-powered pull-start Briggs and Stratton motor taken off a washing machine that would fit the bill for the power. I built motor mounts and welded them to the frame and bolted in the motor. For the rear wheel I made a brake hub for the rear balloon tire and switched to heavier spokes so that the rim can handle the extra power. Next I fabricated a chain drive going from the motor to the back sprocket in the center of the rear wheel. I also added a rocker clutch, so that the bike will have a neutral position, and by rolling the clutch backward, the bike went into gear and started moving forward.

On his current handle bars, I replaced the right grip with a throttle, and next to the left grip I placed a brake lever to control the brakes pads that I fashioned on each side of the front wheel. I also set up a foot pedal to control the rear brake. I built working mini-springer front forks to match the set on my hill climber, and to get them working right took a fair amount of work. The small gas tank is actually a fake. I have a pint can hanging along the frame to hold the gas.

After a couple weeks to get everything right, it's time for a test run. I brought the bike out into the front yard, pull-started the motor, and Sammy got on the seat. He pushed down the clutch and put it in gear like I said, then he gave it a little gas and once he rolled the clutch back, the bike started moving. After a few minutes in the front yard he is riding like a pro. Myrt has been watching, and although she doesn't care much that I motorized his bike, she knows that Sammy wants to ride a motorcycle like the rest of the guys he's around all the time. It's in his blood, and it's only a matter of time before he will start racing himself.

The war has been terrible, and we've known several riders that lost their lives, but in May 1945, we got the news that Germany surrendered, and Hitler shot himself in the head. Then three months later, the United States dropped two atomic bombs on Japan, and they soon surrendered too. Now the war is over.

As everyone began returning home, Tom came back to the dealership, and I went back to being shop foreman. With local riders also coming back, the Roamers disbanded, and the Dons started back up.

Racing Resumes

They don't have a racing schedule put into place yet, but I'm getting excited about getting back out on the track. I've missed four years of my prime during the war, but I still have some good years left and I'm in to win.

In central California we have numerous places to race, but there are eight main tracks: Stockton, Hollister, Antioch, Brisbane, Tulare, Lodi, Watsonville, and San Rafael. Many of these are half-mile horse tracks located at fairgrounds, although not all of them are horse tracks. The track at Lodi is just a quarter-mile track around a small football field, while the San Rafael track goes around the outside of a baseball diamond. Most of the short tracks have lights for running night races, but it's too hard to light up the longer tracks, so they are only for day races.

Tonight is the opening race of the 1945 season at the Dixon 5/8 Mile, and Tom has put together a great WLDR. After all of the years off I'm ready to roll again. I have about five minutes before my heat starts, so I double-check everything. I popped a couple sugar cubes in my mouth, made sure my jacket is zipped up and my helmet's chin-strap is on tight, double-checked that my steel shoe is strapped on firmly. Then I rode out of the infield to the start line and joined the other three riders.

The four of us have our motors revved, waiting for the flag to drop. As the start man flashes down the green flag, an explosion of horsepower erupts. There's no other feeling to compare to that split second when all of that brute power is unleashed, and then it's a mad dash to the first corner.

Approaching the corner is dictated by the groove of the track and once you pull out of the corner, you want to keep any sliding to a minimum and track it out of the corner. The quicker you lift your sliding foot and put it back on the peg, the faster the weight shifts to the rear tire giving the bike balance and more traction.

I won the qualifying heat and followed it up by winning the main event for the season opener. It felt good to knock off the rust after four idle years. After Dixon, I won the race at Brisbane two weeks later. It felt like I didn't miss a beat from the years off as I knocked down every main event through the last flat track race of the season at Hollister to go undefeated.

After our successful season, Tom and I are talking about going to some national championships outside of California next year, but we haven't made any definite plans. Racing for the #1 plate at Springfield would interest me most, but with two kids and all of the hours I put in at work, it would be difficult to pull off.

Chapter 6 / Friant Dam

Another project of Tom's is to build a "Class A" hill-climber from scratch, and over the winter, he started working on it. All of my hill-climbers have been Class C bikes, which are primarily stock with very few changes besides adding tire chains. When it comes to Class A bikes, you can make all the modifications you want. Tom started with building a very lightweight chrome-molly spaghetti frame with extremely thin down tubes, hence the spaghetti nickname.

The next step is putting together a highly modified 45-cubic-inch motor, and Tom is doing everything to maximize power and reduce weight, even the flywheel has been shaved down to get a quick-as-possible start. If the rear tire chains can handle the power, the bike should be a bull on the hills. There's a hill climb along the slopes of Friant Dam located northeast of Fresno on the San Joaquin River, and that's where we're taking the new hill-climber for its maiden run.

On the day of the event, we arrived at Friant Dam and received the day's line-up. We will wait until two riders are ahead of us before warming up the bike. Although the hill is shorter than most, it gets steep quickly before tapering off near the top. With the power of this bike, I need to be careful to keep the front end down, otherwise, it wants to lift off the ground and lose traction.

When it's our time, Tom and I pushed the idling bike to the starting area in front of the wooden backstop and I got onboard. As I tightened my chin strap, I look from the bottom of the hill to the top, double-checking the route I plan to use. It's a different kind of feeling when you are staring up a hill that looks damn near impossible to ride up. You can't walk up a hill like this without using your hands at some point, and you're sliding down even then. In addition, hundreds of people are on the flat lands and surrounding hills watching to see if you make it, but they love a good crash too. When they gave me the okay, I cranked the throttle and blasted to the top of the hill in 4.6 seconds. In my first time out on the new bike, I shattered the Friant Dam record.

This bike is on a whole different level from my other hill climbers, and Tom and I are looking forward to conquering other hills and breaking more records, but it isn't meant to be. Shortly after, we got word that the AMA is abolishing Class A and only continuing with the Class C division. So the bike that Tom spent hours building to top every mountain will never get a chance to go at it a second time.

Stockton Half Mile

After going undefeated the past two seasons in all of my main events, I'm focused on keeping that winning streak alive. The first race of the season is the Stockton half-mile, which is a couple hours east of San Jose, and it's a nice opening night with solid competition.

After the qualifying rounds, the fastest six riders were picked from the two ten-man heats. We are in position at the starting line waiting on the signal to begin. My Harley is in gear, my foot has the clutch pushed down, and I'm watching the flag man with the other riders. I'm ready to crank the throttle, let off the clutch at the same time, and take off like a bullet.

As the start-man waved the green flag, everyone took off, everyone except me. I looked back at the rear wheel thinking that the chain must have snapped, but it's still in one piece. I quickly figured out that the heavy vibration of the bike caused the transmission to slip into neutral. By the time I realized the problem and got going, I'm a half lap down. The crowd sees how far back I am, and things aren't looking good for me.

After I completed four laps, only the excellent rider Lammie Lamereaux is ahead of me on a JAP. I stuck on his tail for the next 15 laps, waiting for the right time and with just a half lap to go, I drafted him through the corner and got a slingshot move to cross the finish line first for the win. Lammie threw up his hands in disgust as we slowed down. He had been winning the race from the very beginning and couldn't believe that he lost at the very last moment. For my win I took home the trophy and a $75 dollar check.

Racers are a fairly small group, and you just never know who you'll run into. One Saturday night, I was at the San Jose Speedway watching jalopy racing when I saw my old friend Pete Colman. Pete and I traveled together with Putt Mossman and the Speedway Aces in England. I haven't seen Pete in a couple years, and I was interested in how he's doing.

"Pete, how the hell are you," I said as we shook hands.

"Sam, it's good to see you. What have you been up to?"

"Same crap, different flies. What brings you to San Jose?"

"I was over at Cancilla's dealership earlier, so I thought I'd drop by and see what's going on. You still with Sifton?"

"Yep, still with Tom. I was running a dealership for him in Watsonville for a few years, but we didn't get enough traffic to survive. How's Putt these days?"

"Good, the last I heard. He got married again."

"He divorced Helen? I didn't know that."

"Their falling out is kind of sad. You know how Putt would ride blindfolded across a thin ramp with Helen lying on her stomach under it."

I nodded.

"Seems that on one of the later tours, Putt thought Helen was messing around with one of the racers. I don't know if she was or not, probably not, but love is a fickle thing. During one of the shows, Putt accidentally missed the ramp and ran over Helen, breaking her pelvis."

"Ouch," I said.

"Tell me about it. Especially since the blindfold had slits in it, so Putt could see just fine."

I said, "Myrt might need to write Helen a letter and see how she's doing. I heard that after our tour, Putt got stuck for a while in Africa, but I didn't hear how he made it out."

"I got the story from Manuel. Putt was in Africa when the war broke out in Europe, and he couldn't find a way back to the United States. Ships weren't taking anyone that didn't have a ticket because they were worried about someone planting bombs, and Putt was getting desperate. He found a ship that just arrived from the U.S., but he needed a way to get on board. He decided that if he had some kind of injury, they wouldn't turn down an injured American. So Putt got a knife and cut open his leg and it looked really bad and blood was all over. Putt went to the dock beside the ship and screamed he needed an American doctor to help him, knowing that the ships always have a doctor on board. Once they made sure he wasn't carrying a bomb they brought him on."

"What did he say happened?"

"He probably said he was mugged. So that's how Putt made his way back to the U.S. from Africa."

It was good talking to Pete, and it made me smile thinking about those days back in England.

Tin Hat Derby

This will be the first Tin Hat Derby since before the war, and it will be the biggest group of riders ever. When the Tin Hat Derby started in 1938, we only had one class of riders, but now, with so many riders, we split it into 80- and 45-cubic-inch divisions. There will be a winner for each division, and an overall point's winner who gets the Tin Hat trophy.

Everyone starts with 1000 points, and at the end of the race, the times are tallied, deducting one point for each minute a rider is late, and two points for each minute that a rider is early. Besides having watches, most everyone has a schedule taped to their gas tank to calculate their time and miles to help keep consistent over the course. The Tin Hat Derby covers the Santa Clara valley along the Hamilton Mountain range and over Mt. Umunhum to the Santa Cruz Mountains and, since we've added some additional trails to make the course 200 miles long, it's known as the longest one-day endurance run in the United States.

From the start at the clubhouse until returning afterwards, its nine hours of riding from dawn to dusk. We have a fair amount of snow this year in the higher elevations, and everyone is cold and miserable by the time they arrived back at the clubhouse, but it's warm inside, and there's a big pot of navy beans and French bread waiting for the riders. We have a map of the complete course laid out over two tables and, after adding the checkpoint locations and calculating the distance between them, we can figure out everyone's points. It's close to midnight by the time we were finished tallying the times, and I beat out nearly 200 riders to win the overall event with 980 points out of a possible 1000.

***** ***** *****

After last year's season, the powers that be let me know that I'm the face of Harley motorcycles in the Bay Area, and they wanted me to spruce up my bike to projects a better image. The bike that I've been riding isn't much to look at; it's covered with gray primer, but it's a winner, and that's what matters to me. A paint job isn't going to make it go any faster, but I found a chrome rim to put on the front, and I even washed the bike.

I'm at Tulare just south of Fresno, and it's the main half-mile race of the season. Tulare has two races each year; today's is the early race in May for the Pacific Coast Championship, while a second non-championship race is held in September. Riders from Northern and Southern California come together in Tulare to fight for the title and bragging rights. Since the war ended, Triumph motorcycles have become very popular, and riders like Lammie Lamereaux and Ed Kretz are bringing Triumphs to the race in hopes that they now have an edge on me.

We were about ready to get out on the track when I saw my good friend Larry "Sleepy" Headrick. Sleepy is a great guy, and he's just getting started in flat track racing.

"How's things Sleepy?"

"Good, Sammy. I'm getting better with each race, but I need to get deeper into the corners before backing off the throttle. Do you have any tips?"

"Watch me and when I let up going into the corner, do the same about 20 feet back."

"That sounds good, thanks Sam."

When I got on the track, it happens to be pristine, and I rode the complete track with the throttle wide open. The track conditions didn't change much for the remainder of the heats, and I took the checkered flag in the 20-lap main event. On top of that, I crushed the old track record and left those Triumph riders empty-handed to become the Pacific Coast Champion of 1946.

After the race, I saw Sleepy leaning on a guardrail, his foot is all bandaged, and it looks about the size of a watermelon.

"What the hell happened to you?"

Sleepy looked me right in the eye and said, "You son of a bitch, you told me to turn it off 20 feet behind you, but you never let off the throttle, so I never did!"

I felt bad about his foot, but I couldn't help but laugh.

***** ***** *****

Besides success on the tracks, such as winning the Pacific Coast Championship, and at Dixon winning the time trials, my heat, the trophy dash, and the main event, and winning the Tin Hat Derby, I'm also doing fine in hill climbs by winning at Visalia, Modesto, and South San Francisco. So far, 1946 is turning out to be my biggest year.

With the success we've been having, Tom started putting together a plan for us to go east in August to compete in the Springfield Mile. Although I don't like being away from the family, if I'm ever going to race back east, the time is now. Tom sent in the paperwork for the race, and we got our travel plans organized. A few short weeks later, we received news from the Springfield officials stating that our entry was denied.

They're saying that the reason our entry was denied is because it arrived too late, but we sent ours a month ago, and since they take probably 100 entries to deny us didn't make any sense. People from the Midwest don't like West Coast racers to start with, but maybe since I've been undefeated for so long, it's got them worried. I went through the 40 and 41 seasons undefeated, and since after the war, I've won every quarter- and half-mile main event that I have been in, so maybe they're scared of a West Coast rider winning it.

We did get some good news from AMA though; they gave Tom the okay to host a national hill climb championship locally. Tom had contacted people about having an AMA-sanctioned national in the south bay area, and after nearly two years, they approved the request.

Before the war, nearly all of the hill-climb nationals were held back east, but after the war, the hill climbs slowly started coming out to the West Coast. Now we need to find a location that can handle a championship sized event. Besides the obvious of having a steep and tall hill, we'll need room for the rows of cars and several hundred spectators. The Santa Clara valley is ringed by foothills, so Tom and I feel good about locating a worthy hill. We're going to focus on the eastern part of the valley because it has more options.

A couple weeks into the search, we located a steep hill near Milpitas off Calaveras Road that we thought should work. The hill is fairly steep and looks to be about 400 feet tall, and the side hills form a natural amphitheater. Nearby it has plenty of flat areas for parking, but now for the tough part, convincing the owner into letting us hold the event on their property. Tom and I went to the house close to the property and knocked on the front door. The property owner came out and introduced himself as Mr. Covo. We introduced ourselves, and Tom started in on his pitch.

"Mr. Covo, we are looking for a place to put on a national hill climb, and we saw a great hill off the road that we think will work. We wanted to see if you would consider letting us have our climb there. The AMA is sponsoring the event, so you'll be paid for having it on your property."

Mr. Covo thought for a moment, "Lot of people?"

"Probably a few hundred, but the fans are usually well behaved."

"If I let you use my land, it has to be returned in good shape. I don't want my property torn up."

"We will only use the one hill and we'll make sure that everything is cleaned up afterwards."

He waited and said, "I will have to think about it, but I'll let you know either way."

We left the shop phone number, now all we can do is wait for his call.

Much to our relief, Mr. Covo called Tom at the shop two days later and said that as long as he gets paid, he's fine with having the hill climb on his land. Tom said that he'll notify the AMA, and they'll contact him to work out a written agreement. We have five months to get things ready, but the hill is in fairly good shape, and the parking area is good as is. So we'll start getting ready after the rains end.

***** ***** *****

It hasn't rained much over the winter, so the Tin Hat this year shouldn't be too muddy along the trails, and it will be easier to keep a consistent speed. This will be our second post war Tin Hat Derby and, with the nicer weather, there's less chance of messing up your bike, which is especially important, since the motorcycle most of the guys are using is also their daily rider.

When the points were tallied this year, I won the 45 division, but I wasn't the overall winner, that went to Herman Liebenberg who works at the dealership. The key to the day-long event is steadiness to average 24 mph over 200 miles of trails, and Herman is consistent as a watch. He won the Tin Hat Derby in 1939 and 1940 too. Starting with the first Tin Hat Derby in 1938, the winner's name and points have been engraved onto the chrome helmet, now Herman's name will be engraved a third time.

Herman is a great mechanic and an ingenious guy. A couple years ago he invented a clock and speedometer combination to use for endurance runs. When the needle of the speedometer and the needle of the clock are pointing to each other, you were on the money at 24 mph. Herman loaned his setup to a buddy for an endurance run in the Sierras, but the judges wouldn't let him use it, and Herman's invention was banned not long after.

Tuesday morning at the shop, after his Tin Hat Derby win, I saw Herman. "Herman, it looks like I'm going to have to put sugar in your tank next year."

"Come on Sam, don't do that," he said with a chuckle.

"Three times is enough, so you can retire now."

Covo Hill Climb

Two months after the Tin Hat Derby, we got to work at Covo Ranch. Typically most of the effort is in clearing plants and rocks along the path, so the hill is just dirt and grass. The San Jose Dons pitched in to help one afternoon, and it didn't take long before we completed the heavy work. The hill is going to be fairly easy to make it up as is, so to make things more interesting, we're going to add two big berms across the hill, one a third of the way up and the other about two-thirds of the way up the hill. Berms can toss riders, which are exciting for the fans, and they also slow down speeds, especially the higher up berm.

We worked with the AMA on advertising the "1947 National Hill Climb Championship of Milpitas California," although most of us just call it Covo Ranch after the property owner. Tom got a call from a buddy that offered his 74-cubic-inch knucklehead for the open division. So far, I only have a 45 for the climb, and his buddy knew it, so Tom took him up on the offer. Out of the two divisions, one is for the 45s, and the other is the 80-cubic-inch division. The big 80-cubic-inch flathead motors that came out in the mid-1930s are still a favorite for guys to hill-climb with, but most of the motorcycles coming out today are 74-cubic-inch. Once we get a hold of the bike, we'll go through the motor, beef it up, and drop in Tom's cams, but, we don't have a lot of time.

In the days leading up to the climb, the Dons helped set out the side boundaries for the pathway and spaced out wooden markers 10 feet apart, going up the left side of the hill. We also added a 100 foot rope on the side of the hill for the hill crew to hold on to during the event. At the bottom, we set up the wooden backstop that we built to block the dirt from shooting backwards at the start. We have other volunteers to help with parking and concessions, and it looks like we have everything ready for the big day.

The morning of the championship, Tom and I trailered the bikes over to Covo Ranch to put the final touches on the hill. Five feet out from the starting point, we put down a chalk line and then we set up the electric eye. The electric eye puts out a light beam across the starting point and, when the beam is crossed by the rider, the counting begins in fractions of seconds on the timer.

We have an electric cable going up the hill connected to the timer at the top. We are using a string trip wire at the finish line and when it is pulled by the passing bike, the clock started by the electric eye stops. We've tried using an electric eye at the top to stop the clock, but sometimes heavy dust can trip the sensor, so we're sticking with the old fashioned string method to make sure things work correctly. We have flagmen at the top and bottom of the hill, the flagman at the bottom lets the rider know when he's clear to go, and the flagman at the top waves the flag once the rider crosses the finish line so that the crowd can tell if he made it.

At check-in, the stewards did a quick safety inspection on everyone's motorcycles, and then they gather all of the riders for a quick meeting to go over rules and racing order. The riders competing in national hill climbs are based on a points system with only the top 12 hill climbers invited. Most of the national climbs are held late in the season, but our climb is early in the year, so the invitees are based on last year's standings. The point's leader has the option to be the first rider up the hill, but some decline because they don't want to be the guinea pig for everyone else as they show how to take the hill.

The novice riders got ready for the 45-cubic-inch division while the others watched and waited. It's been a very dry spring, so the clouds of dust following each rider make it nearly impossible to see how far up the hill they made it, unless the dust cloud goes all the way to the top, and the flagman is seen through the dust cloud.

After the novice group finished, the expert riders got ready. With two riders before me, I pushed the bike to the waiting area and got ready. When the previous rider finished his run, I rode the 45 over and lined up in front of the wooden backstop. I've already decided on my path and, after checking my helmet, I'm ready to roll.

When the flag-man gave me the nod, I twisted the throttle and took off. Things were choppier than I hoped, so I lost too much traction and didn't get a good time. An hour later, when it came time for my second run on the 45, it was more of the same, and I didn't have a prayer of winning. When the runs for the 45s were finished, my buddy Snooky Owens had the best time.

The berms have worked out well and, although the lower berm didn't affect the riders much, the top berm flipped a few and caused others to spin out. In case any bikes really get banged up, there's a cable on the right side of the pathway connected to a tow truck winch at the top to pull up damaged bikes if needed.

After the novice riders completed their open division, it came time for the experts. When I lined up, the 74-cubic-inch loaner did well. I dominated the division and I have the best time by about a half second over the next best. On my second pass, I turned out a pinch better time. Nobody could top my second run, so I was pretty happy to take home my first National Championship trophy. For the event itself, things went really well, and our club even made a little money.

On the drive home, Myrt said, "We had a little excitement earlier. I was helping set out concessions and Judy got about half way up the hill before I saw where she was. One of junior's kids went to go get her and, when Judy saw him coming, she started running down the hill. It didn't take much before she started tumbling and got scrapped up pretty good."

"Judy, did you get hurt?"

"A little," she replied.

"Those hills are too steep for you to play on."

Myrt told me later that Judy really got rolling ass over elbows down the hill, so I don't think she'll be doing that again anytime soon.

Shortly after, the AMA contacted Tom and approved a national for next year at Covo, which was a surprise because they usually don't give their okay for a second year at the same site. So they are happy with the turn out, and we're happy to have a West Coast hill climb championship so close by.

Hollister Invasion

The Gypsy Tour and rally takes place over the three-day long Fourth of July weekend in Hollister. The rally brings together the Northern California motorcycle clubs for some fun and an AMA-sponsored flat track race. The race is held just outside of town at the Memorial Park track, and we also have events such as precision riding, motorcycle decorating, and a motorcycle parade on Saturday. On Saturday evening, a band will be playing at the American Legion Hall so everyone can come and dance, enjoy a few beers, and then go home the next day to get ready for work after the long weekend.

The Gypsy Tour is put on by the Salinas Ramblers Motorcycle Club, but I also got involved in organizing and promoting this year's event. The Gypsy Tour has been in Hollister since the mid-1930s and it's well known, but this is going to be the first rally held after the war, so we're expecting a big turnout. Most of the Dons know about the rally from being around the dealership, but once we started adding event information to the flyers that we post for upcoming events such as hill climbs and endurance runs, it created a lot of buzz.

In Hollister, the main drag of San Benito Street will be blocked off for the weekend to contain the crowd, and Hollister's seven police officers will be joined by 30 or so Highway Patrol officers to help out. The city of Hollister looks forward to the yearly event because it brings in good money into the local economy from the hotels and restaurants, to people renting out rooms, and to the kids setting up lemonade stands, so everyone is ready for the crowd.

Friday night after I closed the shop, Myrt and I hopped on my new 1947 Harley WL with a two-tone red and silver paint job and white wall tires and drove to Hollister. Myrt's folks are watching Sammy and Judy, and we have hotel reservations for Friday and Saturday night, so it will be a fun weekend for us. Because everyone we know will be at the Gypsy tour, it didn't make much sense to open the dealership on Saturday, so we'll be in Hollister all weekend. By the time we arrived near dusk, the streets are lined with motorcycles and folks are having a good time.

Besides the San Jose Dons and the Salina's Ramblers, members from other clubs like the Peninsula Motorcycle Club, Capital City MC, my old Apple City club, and even guys from the Rose City MC out of Portland showed up. For most motorcycle events the crowd is mostly guys, but on this holiday weekend, there are plenty of girls in tight sweaters sporting the colors of their guy's motorcycle club. Our friends Stan and Annie Schmidt are here along with my youngest sister Sally and her husband Don. Although we went into a couple bars for a drink or two, we took it easy because Saturday is going to be a busy day.

After breakfast, Myrt and I rode out to Memorial Park for the preliminary racing and the 20-lap main event. I've raced on the half-mile track at Hollister over a dozen times and know it well, but I'm not competing today. It was a good day of racing, although one crash sent a pair of riders to the local hospital, but nothing serious. When we made it back into town later that afternoon, the main drag is packed with parked motorcycles and the sidewalks are crowded with both riders and locals watching the excitement.

While most of the riders are from the Bay Area, this year some clubs from Southern California had heard about the good times and came north. One of the rowdier motorcycle clubs from the Los Angeles area that showed up are the Boozefighters. They wore green and white sweaters with a beer bottle patch on the front and a patch with their name across the back. Their club members rode the big 74- and 80-cubic-inch Harleys and were pretty good on those heavy bikes. With their feet on the floorboards, they would crank the handlebars and do power circles in the middle of the street as smoke rolled off the tires.

We also heard about guys who were riding their bikes on the sidewalks earlier, and a few detoured into a bar or two, Hollister has nearly 20, but they weren't causing trouble so much as just having fun, and the bar owners didn't seem to mind. Myrt and I walked into one bar that had a bike in the middle of the room, and people just walked around it like it was a piece of furniture.

For the motorcycle parade on Saturday evening, everyone got a chance to show off their decorated bikes, then after the parade, everyone went over to the American Legion for the dance. I haven't danced in ages and I could have easily skipped it, but Myrt loves to dance and she looks forward to it each year. I was having such a great time with our friends that I went a little overboard on drinking beer. I might have a beer on a hot day, or a glass of wine here and there, but that's about it. After the dance, we walked back to the hotel sometime after midnight, and I was out like a light.

As the sun came up Sunday morning, parts of the streets are littered with hundreds of broken beer bottles, which isn't the smartest thing because it's causing motorcycle flats. As the morning went on, the riders are streaming out of town and, within a few hours, Hollister returned to its normal sleepy self.

Then I saw the morning newspaper's headlines, one had "Hollister in Chaos" and another's was "Motorcyclists Take Over Town." The reporters just exaggerated the goings on to sell more newspapers. Considering that over 4,000 riders showed up in Hollister and doubled the population, the incidents that weekend were fairly limited. I talked to locals who said that the cowboys from the Salinas Rodeo caused more trouble than we did, but the newspapers worked it up. They failed to mention that over 30 police officers were watching everything and arresting people when needed, mainly for drinking in public or reckless driving.

Once I got back home, I called the different newspapers in San Jose and San Francisco, as did several members of the Dons and the Ramblers, demanding a retraction to the made-up stories. A few days later, near the back page of the newspaper, the editor added a couple of lines stating that the Gypsy Tour wasn't accurately depicted, although their retraction was so small that it was even hard to read.

With all of the negative publicity, the AMA and the local organizers decided against having a Gypsy Tour until things cooled down. Hollister is still planning to have their annual hill climb in a couple months that is sponsored by the Salinas Ramblers, so it must not have been that traumatic for the locals. We'll also be here in two months for the Hollister half-mile, just as usual.

Retiring from Flat Tracks

The Gypsy Tour was over a month ago, and today I'm at Bayshore Stadium in Brisbane waiting for the start of the race. I've been thinking about retiring from flat track racing for a while, and with just two races left in the season, I decided that after the last race of the season at Hollister, I'm hanging up the hot shoe.

Myrt doesn't really enjoy watching me race, but she still comes to all of the events. She's tried staying home on race days, but she's a nervous wreck the whole day and not just during my races. Friends have told me that her hands are literally shaking when I'm out on the track. She has also started getting stomach problems, which she blames on the stress of my racing. Myrt knew that I'm a motorcycle racer from when we started dating, but I understand how she doesn't want me getting hurt. When I told Myrt about my plans to hang it up after the season is over, she's really happy about it.

I've been racing on the flat tracks for so long that I'm not sure what I'll do once I'm retired, but I'll need to find something to occupy my time. As we were getting ready to head over to the starting area, I joked with the other riders, "You guys fight over who's coming in second." For the past three years since racing restarted after the war, I feel like no one can beat me, and today turned out to be no exception.

Today at the Hollister half-mile, I'm a little torn about this being my last flat track race. I've raced here dozens of times before, but all good things come to an end. I popped two sugar cubes and got everything tightened for the heats. After the preliminary heats were out of the way, I lined up for the main event. Once the flag dropped, I led the 20-lap race from start to finish and took the checkered flag.

I rode around to the winner's circle to receive the trophy and take part in the season closing ceremony. The announcer came down from his booth to the winners circle to interview me, and our voices will be broadcast through the grandstand speakers. As he held the microphone, I thought that the wire on the microphone must be two blocks long for it to reach this far.

"Here he is, ladies and gentleman, the Great Sam Arena in his last flat track race. Why don't you say a few words Sam."

He handed the microphone to me. "Thanks everyone. I've had a lot of fun over the years, but it's time for me to step aside and retire."

When they handed a trophy to me, the photographers started clicking.

A friend of mine joked, "Get a picture of the Great Arena while you still can."

While I sat on my bike with the trophy, Myrt appeared out of the crowd and came up to give me a kiss on the cheek as I put my arm around her.

"Can you guys get a picture of me with Myrt?"

This picture will be a nice memory of my final flat track race.

Although I feel I can still compete, I'm 35-years old while most of the other riders are still teenagers or in their early 20s, and those 20 and 25-lap mains take a lot out of you. I'll still continue to compete in hill climbs, but I'm going to leave the flat track racing to the youngsters.

On the Back Deck

Sam stopped talking about retiring from the tracks and said, "I'm a little dried out" as he sipped on his glass of wine.

I replied, "Not a problem, it's time for a break anyway."

As we sat relaxing, Myrt brought out some cooked kielbasa that she sliced up for us. "Is that for us?" I asked.

"Yep, for my two favorites."

"Thanks Myrt." Then I said, "I've got a question for you: how was your honeymoon in London?"

"It was a lot of fun and we had a great time, but Sam can't go back."

"Why is that?" I asked.

"After we returned from the trip, Sam got a letter saying that he owed back taxes."

I looked at Sam and he had a little grin on his face.

"Sam figured that we weren't ever going back, so he threw the letter away."

Then Myrt added, "The Queen sent him a letter recently though."

"Really?" I said doubtfully.

Myrt went inside to retrieve something and brought back a postcard with a picture of the Queen on one side and on the other it read, "Come back Sam, all is forgiven."

Myrt smiled and said, "John sent this to Sam when he was in England." Then Myrt went back inside to her television show, while we sampled some kielbasa.

I feel lucky to hear these old racing stories, but once Sam passes away, they will be gone forever. Hopefully that's many years down the line, but he's not a pup anymore. That reminds me of the poster that I mentioned earlier. My absolute favorite poster in Sam's garage, the one that I've looked at dozens of times over the years, is of his huge win at the 1938 Oakland 200.

It states, "Six thousand speed-loving fans shouted themselves hoarse as Sam Arena piloted his 45-cubic-inch WLDR Harley Davidson over the slick, treacherous 200 mile speedway to win in 2 hours, 22 minutes, and 38.4 seconds, smashing the old record by 19 minutes, 20.6 seconds."

I've always been amazed by how much he won that race by.

"Hey Sam, I think we need a little more wine," I say as I reached into my grocery bag. "I picked up some good Chianti from Trader Joe's on the way over."

Sam and Myrt Arena

Sam Arena – mid-1930s

Myrt Arena – mid-1930s

Emeryville, CA – 1935

Miami Florida – July 1935

Sam Arena – England 1936

Dagenham Speedway – England 1936 (Sam in the center)

123

Putt Mossman – 1936 England

Sam Arena – 1936 England

Aquitania – 1936 Postcard

Queen Mary – 1936 Postcard

Sprouts Elder – Approx. 1927

Joe Petrali – Approx. 1932

Sam Arena at the 1938 Oakland 200

Sam Arena at the 1939 Daytona 200

Sam Arena with Armando Magri – 1939 Oakland 200

Racers at the 1939 Oakland 200

Sam Arena on a Harley Davidson WR – 1946 Lodi

Sam Arena – Tin Hat Derby (approx. 1947)

Snooky Owens and Sam Arena – 1947 National Championship

Sam and Myrt – 1947 Dixon (Tom Sifton at far right)

ARENA

BOOK 2

TYLER A. TAVRIEN

Table of Contents

"The San Jose Bunch" 3
Saturday Afternoon 3
Chapter 1 / West Coast National 6
    Road Captains Run 7
    San Jose Riders 11
    Match Race 14
    Larry Headricks 15
    Vogel Ranch 17
    Learning about Trabia 25
Chapter 2 / Bay Meadows Mile 28
    Opening Night 37
    New Facility 39
    Pacific Coast Championship 40
    Stockton Mile 42
    Street Crash 44
    New KR Model 48
    Local Racers 51
Chapter 3 / Drag Race 55
    Return to San Jose 59
    Cams Are King 60
    Gypsy Tour 62
    Poker Run 67
    KR Frame 71
    BSA Sweeps 72

Chapter 4 / Springfield Mile 76
    Grand National Champion 79
    Last Tin Hat..80
    Upcoming Season 81
    Sleepy's Return 86
    Tommy the Greek 88
    Stolen Cams...90
    Factory Racers..92
    Dealers Banquet 94
Chapter 5 / San Jose Mile..96
    Sprouts Elder 98
    Daytona 200 101
    BSA Project 102
    San Jose Mile II 103
    Joe's Knee Problems...105
    Modesto National 107
Back to the Present 109

"The San Jose Bunch"

Saturday Afternoon

It's another beautiful Saturday afternoon at Sam and Myrt's house. The weather is perfect out on the deck and his apple and peach trees are shading us against the late afternoon sun. The white buildings of Lick Observatory on top of Mount Hamilton are perched along the golden brown hills and are easy to spot because the air is so clear today.

Earlier, when I went inside their house to get a glass of water and say hello to Myrt, I looked out into the garage to see the progress on the hill climber. Since the last time I came over, Sam had the heads ported and polished with new pistons and rings put into the 45-cubic-inch motor. He also had everything on the motor either chromed or polished, so it looks really nice in the white frame as it sits upon a wooden box. Sam's been busy hunting down parts, he found a big rear sprocket from a place in Oakland, while former Sifton mechanic Lee McReynolds made the rear rim, and another friend made a set of hill climbing chains for the project.

The most noticeable part on the original frame was the springer front forks that Harley used before tube forks came out in the early 1950s, and Sam is trying to copy those too. During his racing years Sam always used forks from the 1926-1929 Harleys because they were half the size and lighter than the newer versions. He found some of springer front-ends from the 1940s, but with those going for a thousand dollars a pop; Sam isn't going to break the bank for a set.

For plan B, he opted to use the front forks off of a 125 Honda Enduro that was donated to the cause. It provided a reasonable replacement, light and fairly strong, and since this bike is for show and will probably never even see a hill, it will work just fine. Sam will be able to use the fork and rim setup off the Honda after tweaking the steering head on the old frame, so it completed a few things on his checklist. For a personal touch, Sam bent the new handlebars to resemble the "Arena" style that he used on all of his former bikes.

One problem Sam faced was trying to put together a small gas tank for the bike. He worked with Tap Plastics to fabricate a tank of the correct size and shape, but trying to seal it correctly was becoming a problem. It took a couple tries, but the cast sealed up well and the beads are smooth. After shooting several coats of candy apple red over it with a small air tank out in the garage, the gas tank looks good. He has yet to build a seat and create headers for the exhaust, but the bike is coming together nicely.

After I was back outside opening a bottle of red wine, I said, "I like how the gas tank turned out, you did a good job on it."

"Myrt was the one who picked out the color."

"She picked out a good one; it looks sweet against the chromed motor."

Since I got here at 4:00 before any of the neighbors showed up, the other metal chair is mine for the afternoon. This chair is across the table from Sam and has awesome views of the valley, plus it's next to the table with all of the food on it, so you can't go wrong. For those coming later, they will have to pull up one of the plastic chairs to get close to the food and wine, and while their view consists of fruit trees and the waterwheel revolving on Sam's goldfish pond, it's not as impressive as the view of the Santa Clara valley. We can see the Boulder Ridge golf course on the south hills above Almaden Lake, although you need binoculars to see any movement on the course besides golf carts.

Sam's neighbor John never makes it over at 4 o'clock. It's typically sometime after 5 before he makes an appearance. He lives next door, so you think it would be easier for him to make it over on time, but he's usually working in his backyard garden on most Saturday afternoons. I heard him talking to someone earlier in his yard, so I know he's in town. John travels so much that Sam tells him that he needs to just live in a condo close to the airport, that way he can save time driving because he's always going or coming from the airport anyway.

John is a family friend originally from Kansas, and it was my grandfather who called John and talked to him about me considering a move to San Jose, so I'm grateful that my grandfather made the call. Later when I contacted John, he invited me out for a visit, and shortly after, I took a week off from work and flew out to look things over. After I arrived, John picked me up late in the evening from the San Jose airport, and we got into his blue Porsche 911 with the targa tops off and headed for his house. After about 20 minutes we turned onto his street and went up a big hill that veered left and about half way back down the hill we pulled into his driveway.

We walked inside his house and I met his lovely wife Donna, who, I found out later, shares the same birthday as myself, no wonder we get along so well. After introductions she asked if I wanted a drink, and since I'm not big on flying, she mixed up a rum and coke for me. Then because I didn't get any food on the plane, she put together a plate of chicken shish kabobs. We went out on the back deck to sit down, and that's when I got to see their spectacular view of the valley. The Santa Clara valley at night is something to see with a million twinkling lights and it looks as big as the ocean. I'm relaxing on their deck with a drink and a plate of food while looking out over this incredible view and I think to myself: this is the place to be.

The next day was a Saturday, and that afternoon John took me next door to meet his neighbors Sam and Myrt. John knows everyone and he often brings people over to the Arenas, so I'm sure they thought that I was just another stranger, who they'll never see again, coming by for a drink. I remember drinking wine that afternoon with Sam and hearing some of his stories, and I must have really enjoyed my visit, because six months later, I made my move to San Jose.

That's been a few years back, and on this fine Saturday, Sam and I are out on the deck with plenty of wine and cheese. It's a beautiful day, so life is good. It was just the two of us and I wanted to hear more of the old stories, so to ease into a conversation I said,

"The last time we talked you had just won a National Hill Climb Championship in Milpitas and retired from flat track racing, what was up next for you?"

Chapter 1 / West Coast National

"The following year, the second Milpitas National Hill Climb was being held again at Covo Ranch, and since I won the 80 division the year before, I was looking forward to it. We did all of the heavy work on clearing the hill the first year, so getting things ready for the 1948 national championship event was going to be fairly easy."

When the big day came around Tom and I loaded my hill climbers onto the trailer, one for each division, and made the short trip up the highway to Milpitas. As far as I'm concerned, Windy is the guy that I need to top. Clifford "Windy" Lindstrom is my main rival on the hills, and he has been for the past couple of years. Windy and his business partner Cliff Self, who is another great rider that I faced many times on the flat tracks, own the Lindstrom and Self Harley Davidson Dealership in Oakland. Once Tom and I arrived at the hill, it didn't take long before I ran into Windy.

"Hey Windy. Ready for today?"

"I was born ready!"

I replied, "I'll see you at the top."

This year it isn't as dry and dusty as last, so you can actually see the riders making their way up the hill. My first run on the 45 went really well and I topped the hill in 14:56 seconds, which is the best time so far. Since I had the group's fastest time, I didn't need to make a second run but I decided to go ahead anyway and things turned out differently. I got a great start and jumped the first berm, but on the second berm cutting across the hill I got a little airborne and the rear tire spun without any resistance, but once it made contact with the earth, the chains dug in and the spokes couldn't take the power and snapped like tooth picks. My rear wheel is jammed at an angle inside the frame and didn't budge, so the bike had to be dragged off the hill. At least my first run is still the fastest time out of everybody.

After my two runs in the 45 group were over, I started working out on the hill crew. They need guys to help out because the hills are so steep that once a rider's forward progress stops, it's tough to hold the bike from going backwards, so guys rush out and grab it before anything can happen. There are different ways to come to a stop: some guys put their feet down and lock the brakes once they can't make it any further, others pop a wheelie or spin out. One guy fell off his bike but held on to the throttle long enough that the bike shot across the hill, and everyone scattered before the kill switch cut the power and the bike slowed down and fell over.

I'm about three quarters of the way up the hill, close to the big oak tree off to the left of the main path. The tree is a favorite with the kids because it's big enough for them to climb and play in, and the bikes racing up the hill are just twenty feet away. I've been helping maybe 20 minutes, and as I'm watching a rider come up the hill, he lost control and got bucked off as his bike darted to the right. The kill switch isn't working, and the bike is heading towards the tree where Judy is playing on a low branch. I'm close enough to grab her and get out of the way as the bike bounced off the tree. And here I'm thinking that being on a motorcycle is the dangerous part.

In the second half of the day I did fairly well in the 80-cubic-inch division, but Windy ended up winning it with his time of 12:34 seconds. In a display of his talent, Windy also took runner-up in the 45-inch class. For my time of 14:56 seconds in the 45-cubic-inch division, I earned a second AMA championship trophy.

Road Captains Run

The Dons have an annual winter ride called the Road Captain's Run, and each year a different member comes up with a route for a Sunday ride, while the rest of the club members are kept in the dark on where we are going. Last year we took a ride from a trail near Mt. Umunum all the way to the ocean. It was a great ride with only a few bad parts along the forest trails, and the weather at the beach was great once we emerged from the trees. Our rides are typically off-road since most of the Dons are dirt riders, and this year, 14 other Dons and myself left the clubhouse in the morning towards the hills of Almaden valley.

After a few hours of riding, we are miles away from civilization when the clouds started getting darker, and before long, the rain started coming down. Fritzee is the leader this year, but this route must be new to him and, without much visibility, he soon got us lost. We are out in the boonies, and while we have a general idea of where we are, no one is familiar enough to know which logging road might get us back in the right direction.

The trail isn't that bad when we started, but it's turning into mud, and soon guys are getting their bikes bogged down, and it's only going to get worse if the rain keeps up. The sun has long since dropped over the horizon, so any daylight we had is gone, and that's making things more difficult. After a couple hours of no progress, we decided to find a spot to leave our bikes that we felt we could find later and started walking. We did consider riding in different directions to find a way out, but we thought that we should stick together as a group so that no one would get left behind.

We are cold, wet, and miserable and after walking in the pouring rain for at least an hour we spotted a light from a cabin in the distance. Good thing that the light is on or we could have easily walked by. I don't think that strangers get this way too often, especially at night, so I hope that when we knock on the door, someone doesn't start shooting.

An old farmer opened the door, and after we explained that we were lost, he invited us inside his small cabin, which is pretty nice considered we're 15 wet strangers. As we talked, I got the impression that he thought that we are flyers out of Moffett Field and our plane must have went down nearby. It's true that we are out in the middle of nowhere, some of the guys had leather-covered helmets and many of us wore one-piece jumpsuits, so in a way it made sense. We really appreciated his hospitality, so we didn't say anything to indicate otherwise.

The farmer told us how to get to the main road, and after 15 or 20 minutes of everyone warming up, we headed back out into the rain and darkness. We made it home well after midnight, but at least we made it home, which was our main concern. We'll meet at the clubhouse tomorrow morning before going out to get our motorcycles, but we're going to set up some guidelines to prevent something like this from ever happening again.

***** ***** *****

I've been working for Tom over a dozen years and while I still enjoy it, I have a growing family to take care of, and I'd like to have my own dealership or at least be a part-owner of one. With Tom having the territory rights to Harley Davidson dealerships in the Santa Clara County, I will have to get his blessing to get my own Harley dealership locally.

One day it is just the two of us by the counter, so I thought that I should bring it up.

"Tom, I'd like to ask you something. I want to get into the ownership side of things, and I'm wondering if I can become a partner with you in the dealership."

Tom thought for a second. "Sam I'm a loner, and if I were to have a partner, there's no one in the world I would rather have than you. But if I make a wrong decision, it only affects me and I pay for it out of my pocket. I'll tell you what I can do: I plan to retire in a couple years and when that day comes, I'll sell the dealership to you."

I'm pretty happy about him saying that. Then he added, "I've been thinking that Palo Alto would be a good market for a dealership. If you can find a small place to open this spring, you can run it as a sub-dealer under me until the time I retire."

"That would be great. I really appreciate that you would help me out like this."

"Sam, I've always liked you, and I think you would do just fine as an owner."

Tom is the general around here and what he says carries a lot of weight, and that extends to the people that hang around the dealership. If Tom doesn't care for you, the welcome mat isn't out and you got the hint before long. If you were a stand-up guy and didn't make excuses, Tom wouldn't have a problem with you. Some might say that Tom isn't very likeable, but he tells it like it is and he's always done alright by me.

***** ***** *****

It's easy to tell that this year's Tin Hat Derby is going to be one giant mud pit. It's been raining for at least 10 of the last 14 days, and so the big obstacle will be avoiding riders stuck in mud and hopefully avoid getting stuck myself.

During the 200-mile race I got bogged down a couple times in mud deep enough to cover my boots, and it took some effort to get out of one of them, so I bumped my speed heading to the next checkpoint. The next stop is in Scotts Valley, and Myrt is working at that checkpoint filling out time slips as I pulled up.

"Hey Hon."

She smiled, "Having fun?"

"More than I can stand." Myrt's wearing a heavy coat with a hat and gloves. "Are you cold?"

"What do you think?" She said smiling. "Want some coffee?"

"Just a half cup and then I've got to go. How are the times so far?"

"Most guys are running behind, at least for this checkpoint."

"Yep, that's what I figured."

By the time I made the final checkpoint near the clubhouse, my bike probably weights an extra 50 pounds from all of the mud caked on it and I'm splattered from head to toe. Besides that, my forearms are worn out from holding the handlebars straight through the trails of mud. With points being deducted for being too early or too late, it didn't take long to figure out that most riders were out of the running.

But simply finishing is an accomplishment because many riders fail to complete the event. Today, several guys went as far as the halfway point before saying that they had enough and headed home. After we tallied everyone's times at the clubhouse, I managed to take second place in the 45 division, but who counts second. Herman's younger brother Ray got the win this year. Ray is somewhat of a character. Last winter when some of the guys went to his place up in the Santa Cruz Mountains, they said that he had at least 20 boxes sitting on the floor and on counter tops with several rattle snakes hibernating in each.

San Jose Riders

I might joke around and say that guys are following in my footsteps, but San Jose is becoming a hot bed of talented racers, and the Sifton dealership is ground zero. With me no longer flat track racing, Tom has put together a team of local riders including Al Rudy and Bob Chaves.

Rudy is a great guy and I've known him for many years. He was briefly in the Roamers Motorcycle Club during the war, and I know that he's a good rider from riding together in the Santa Cruz Mountain's on weekends. The guys in the Dons are among the best riders in the state, so when you are out racing wide open in the hills trying to keep up with the leader, usually me, that's where you find out who the good riders really are.

When Rudy got out of the service, he started working as a delivery man for a drug company and raced on his own, then he started racing for Bill Haugh because he had a better bike available. Rudy was doing well in local races, but Bill knew that Rudy would be doing even better on something Tom built. One day Bill is at the dealership talking with Tom and said,

"Tom, you should hire Rudy to race on your team. He's one hell of a rider"

"I have a bike sitting here for him to ride; he just needs to come by and ask."

The following weekend Rudy started racing for Tom with half of the season left to go. I became a sort of mentor for Rudy and gave him advice on how to ride different tracks. We would walk the course before a race to check the surface and how problem spots might come into play as the track changed from wear during the race. One of the great things about Rudy is that he has a passion for the sport of racing which accounts for a lot. Rudy likes to kid around and say that he is my biggest fan, but when it comes to racing, he's serious and has the talent to back it up.

Tom's other pilot is Bob Chaves and he's best buddies with Rudy. As a teenager Chaves used to hang around the San Jose dealership and even worked for me during the war until he got called up. Chaves is one of Tom's mechanics and, while he's a good rider, he's not as serious about racing as Rudy is. Chaves is a couple years older than Rudy, and he used to beat Rudy out on the track when they were younger, but now it's Rudy that's topping Chaves on a regular basis.

The Pacific Coast Championship at Tulare (May 1948) is here and this is a big event that draws the Southern California riders north. During qualifying, Rudy turned some of the fastest lap times, and he's one of the four riders making it into the trophy dash. Rudy is up against top pro riders, Floyd Emde, Burt Brundage, and Tex Luce, but when the green flag dropped, Rudy beat all of them in the four-lap dash to take the trophy. Rudy is still a novice, so he can't be in the expert main event, but in the novice group Rudy crushed the rest of the lineup to become the Novice Pacific Coast Champion.

***** ***** *****

The winter months are spent working on bikes to get ready for the upcoming race season. Our guys, Rudy and Chaves, are preparing for a cross-country trip to Florida for the 1949 Daytona 200. Tom is building two nearly identical motors for Rudy and Chaves. The guys painted Rudy's bike robin's egg blue which is a factory color, just not for the WR model, while the WR that Chaves will be riding is in basic black.

A week before Daytona, the guys have the trailer loaded and hooked up behind their car ready to go. The coupe they are taking has the back seat removed and, in its place, a mattress is slid back into the trunk. Now they can take turns sleeping in comfort, or driving on the way to Daytona. Al Fernandez is going along as the pit man. He is a quality guy and a great mechanic at the shop. Tom is going to Florida also, but he's taking the easy way by flying out later in the week to meet them there.

They have two races at Daytona: a 100-mile amateur race on Saturday which Rudy and Chaves will be in and the 200-mile race on Sunday for the experts. While at Daytona, all of the riders get time on Friday to take some practice laps on the half-beach and half-pavement course. Tom compared Rudy and Chaves lap times with everyone else's during the day and saw that their bikes are running 12 mph faster than any of the experts.

With so many guys entering the event, the riders will be in rows of 15 taking off ten seconds apart with Rudy in the third row and Chaves in the sixth. As the first two rows took off, Rudy is just waiting for the green flag and, when it waved, he took off and disappeared down the beach. Even with starting three rows back, Rudy is the first rider to complete a lap on the 4.1 mile track, and he's out in the lead.

Rudy kept the lead for the first 50 miles of the 100 mile race, but he got a flat tire heading down the backstretch. He should have limped into the pits with the flat, but since Tom told him earlier how hard the tires are to replace, Rudy didn't want to ruin the tire, so he got off and started pushing the bike down the track. He pushed the bike for nearly 10 minutes and when he was close to the pit area a couple guys saw him and ran down the track to take over pushing. While Al is switching tires, he's giving Rudy hell for not riding back to the pits - he was leading for Christ's sake. Al quickly replaced the tire, and Rudy got back out on the track.

Chaves is making good time, and he and Don Evans got into a battle on about midway, and it was back and forth for over a dozen laps, then Chaves's bike started leaking gas from a defective tank seam. Chaves kept riding, but he had to make two pit stops to refill his tank so he wouldn't run out of gas. You can complete a 100-mile race on a single tank of gas, so any extra stops really hurt your overall time, but Chaves still managed to come in third even with having to stop for gas twice. Rudy finished the race (in 44th place), but who knows how he would have done if he had ridden the bike into the pits with the flat instead of pushing it. Don Evans ended up winning the 100-lap amateur championship race.

In Sunday's expert race, Dick Klamfoth won in his first time there, with Billy Mathews coming in second and Tex Luce in third. The big news was that Norton motorcycles swept the top three spots, even Don Evans won the amateur race on a Norton. Nortons aren't known as the fastest bikes around, but they are reliable, and on a tough course like Daytona, that's exactly what you need.

Match Race

I haven't been out on a flat track in two years, but when Rudy went to the Belmont track to put in some practice ahead of the race that night, besides bringing his blue WR, I also brought along my old WLDR. After watching Rudy turn practice laps, I got a chance to get out in the dirt and warm up my bike a little. I took two easy laps and then let it rip for six more. My bike might be old and not a thing of beauty, but it's still one hell of a bike, and when everyone's lap times came out later, I had the fastest lap time of the afternoon.

Cliff Self is a good friend and former rival. We had a match race at Belmont before the war that didn't turn out as I hoped. I was winning by a comfortable margin, but on the last corner I tried to make it look good for the crowd by shooting out a rooster tail. The problem was that I got too sideways and the bike slid out on me, creating the opening for Cliff to get the win and the trophy. Ever since that happened, whenever we bump into each other, I always ask him about my trophy and he gets a kick out of it. Belmont doesn't have a match race every Friday night, but when they do, it's always a crowd favorite. Cliff and I had a conversation a while back, and we're going to have our rematch tonight.

Cliff showed up with two speedway bikes from the late 1930s that he had recently restored, and he brought along the trophy from our last match race which will go to tonight's winner. Harley hasn't produced short trackers like these since before the war, and they are special motorcycles. Instead of a Class C bike, which is basically a stock street model; these bikes run on fuel instead of regular gas and have smaller frames than normal bikes.

Since they are built specifically for short tracks at a place like Belmont, they really shine. Belmont has a smaller inside track that's cushioned with a couple inches of loose soil, and we'll be racing on that track tonight because the usual track's surface is too hard for these bikes. In any case, it should be a fun race. With speedway bikes, you might let off on the throttle slightly before the corner, but you steer through the corner with horsepower as the bike is sliding.

A few hours later, when it came time for our match race, Cliff and I got out on the track to do a few laps to warm up the motors. It's going to be a flying start, so as we approached the start-man with the flag raised, we eased off our speed and, as the flag fell, we lit out. By the time the four laps were over, the race wasn't even close, and I blew Cliff off the track and got my trophy.

Larry Headricks

My buddy Larry "Sleepy" Headrick is back in town after two years away. Larry and his wife were living in Tennessee, and while he had a good job, his wife was homesick for San Jose, so they moved back. Before going to Tennessee, Larry wasn't really that good of a racer, so when we started seeing his name listed in American Motorcyclist magazine for winning a bunch of races around Tennessee, we were wondering if there was another Larry Headrick out there. But his riding really improved since he left, and when he returned, everyone was surprised at how good of a rider he has become.

Tom hired Larry as a mechanic, and he began entering local races. In short time, Larry won his first main event at Belmont. Belmont's quarter-mile track has jalopy (basically stock cars without fenders) races each Wednesday and motorcycle races each Friday night under the lights from April to September. With Belmont being just up the road, it's like a home track for us, and it's a great training ground too.

Unlike most tracks, Belmont is progressive, so the 12 fastest riders from the heats make it into the main, no matter what class they are in. For the heats and the semifinal, they use an inverted start so the fastest rider is on the back outside, while in the main event, the riders are lined up in two rows of six for the 15-lap main. It's a quirky place to ride, and the track surface changes though out the evening. The reason is that the Belmont track is at sea level, and being so close to the San Francisco bay the track is affected by the tide and becomes slick as the evening rolls along and moisture comes up through the dirt.

***** ***** *****

I've been trying to find a decent place to open a dealership in Palo Alto and, after looking for three months, I still couldn't locate a place that would work. I've been getting so discouraged that I nearly gave up on the idea, but then I found a former tire shop on High Street right off of University Avenue. It has a small showroom that can hold five or six bikes lined up in a row, a small office to the side, and a service bay in the back about the size of a one-car garage. It's not very big, but the location is good.

In order to cover the rent and finance the new and used motorcycles that I'm going to need, Myrt and I put our house on Minnesota Avenue up for sale, and we'll use the equity to get the dealership up and running. Just to be safe, I've already talked to Dad about borrowing a thousand dollars so that we'll have enough cash on hand for the day-to-day expenses.

In a few weeks our house sold for $9500, and the first thing I did after depositing the check was order four new bikes from the factory. I'm also on the lookout for a couple nice used Harleys to purchase and put on the showroom floor. Myrt is going to start doing the books for the dealership, and it looks like we'll be ready to open in May.

The final piece of the puzzle is finding mechanics, so I asked Bobby Boyd and Al Fernandez to come with me to the new dealership. Bobby is in the Dons and we've known each other for years, so when I offered him a job, he accepted. Right now, Al is at the San Jose dealership, but he's coming to Palo Alto for a while to help me out. Tom didn't mind Al coming over to help with the new place, as long as he's still Rudy's pit man on race days no matter where it is. In a way, our two dealerships are connected, so it's not like I'm stealing a mechanic from a rival dealership. Now that I'm in Palo Alto, Herbie Bosch is taking over as Tom's foreman at the San Jose dealership.

Like most of our mechanics, both Bobby and Al have been in the military. Bobby was an ace fighter pilot in World War II that flew Spitfires for England before the United States got into the war. Al joined the Navy and probably lied about his age to get in. Although Al doesn't talk about it, he was aboard the USS Franklin

(March 1945) when it was attacked by the Japanese. Several hundred crew members were killed in the attack, and the Franklin was heavily damaged, but the ship managed to keep afloat and stayed in service.

Within a month of Larry winning the main at Belmont, he followed it up with a win at the Galt half-mile. Larry is just coming into his prime as a racer, but his wife wants him to quit. Of course Larry doesn't want to stop, especially after he just bought a new ruby red WR. Larry's wife Dot is a sweetheart, but sometimes spouses don't see eye to eye. After Larry left for work one day, Dot took a hatchet to his new bike and just destroyed it. I don't know what happened to set her off, but I would have liked to be a fly on the wall when Larry got home and saw his once beautiful bike.

Vogel Ranch

The San Jose Dons often put on Class C hill climbs sanctioned by the AMA to help promote our club and, hopefully, bring in a little money, and besides, it's a fun way to spend the day. We've been on a search for a new place to host a climb, and Myrt and I have been riding the back roads of south San Jose and Hollister to scout for locations when we found a spot in San Jose that we thought would work for us.

The owner of the property is Mr. Vogel, and he isn't too keen on our proposition because he doesn't want a bunch of hooligans on his property. After I told him that we'd have a policeman or two present and everything would be cleaned up afterwards, he warmed to the idea. I'm sure that having Myrt along helped; she has a way of making you go along with her.

The hill at Vogel's Ranch isn't very steep, but it's long and we'll have faster speeds than our usual hills. To make it more of a challenge for the riders, a bunch of the Dons helped out and dug a two foot ditch across the face of the hill. The rest of the hill is in good shape and not much else needs to be done, so we'll have everything ready when the big day comes along.

A couple times each year the Dons have raffles for local charities, or we sometimes have a benefit to help someone down on their luck. Most of us know the Fuller brothers, and when Glen got hurt in a motorcycle accident, he racked up some big medical bills.

Glen doesn't have much money. His only possession is his crashed motorcycle which he'll need to sell to pay down his medical bills.

The Dons want to help him, so the guys at the shop got ahold of Glens 74-inch Harley and started repairing and upgrading the bike to bring in more money for the raffle. Tom is providing replacement parts along with a new set of tires, he's even sending out pieces off the motor to be chromed to add a little flash. The Dons will start selling raffle tickets at a dollar a pop and the winner will be picked at our upcoming Vogel Hill climb.

Just about each Sunday from March to June, there's a hill climb somewhere within a short distance of the Bay Area that I can enter. Most of the climbs are held in the spring before it gets too dusty and the grass is still green, so it's not a fire hazard. We always bring Judy and Sammy along, as do most of the riders, so on Sundays, all of the kids are able to play together. One of the things that the kids like to do before the climb starts is ride cardboard boxes down the hill.

While the kids are off playing, Myrt helps in the concession stand selling cokes or beers if the event is sponsored by the Dons or the Yellow Jackets, otherwise she is usually sitting in our car with a program of the day's riders marking down their times as she's watching the riders. Most of the time, she's with her buddy Jessie, who is married to my good friend Snooky Owens. Sometimes, if it's hot, they'll be sitting in the car drinking beer, and Myrt is a little tipsy by the end of the day. Myrt is also close to Jessie's older sister Stella who is married to Tom, even though Stella is closer in age to Tom who is about 10 years older than me.

The weather is perfect today, and the turnout of riders and fans at Vogel Ranch is good. Being an informal event, the referee drew names out of a hat to decide the riding order, while the stewards do a quick inspection on the bikes lined up for battle. The hill isn't as bare as some others, but the ground is soft, and it will really get churned up with each passing rider.

Once the climbs started, most of the riders are making it up the hill, although with the faster speeds, the ditch has taken out a few riders and provided some exciting wipeouts.

After all 45 professional runs were finished, Windy edged me when he got the best time of 8.83.

During the break between the 45 and 80 divisions, they selected the winning raffle ticket, and the winner was George Sepulvada. George is one of the young guys that come around the Palo Alto dealership. The motorcycle will come in handy because he doesn't have any transportation right now, so he's walking a couple miles to work each day. George isn't here today, so Tom will have to get ahold of him later and tell him to pick up his bike at the shop.

By the time the hill climb wrapped up in the late afternoon, I got the win in the 80-cubic-inch division after cresting the top with a time of 8.64, but it wasn't much faster than Windy's time in the 45-cubic-inch group. Overall, the event has been a big success, and the San Jose Dons did a great job of putting it on.

***** ***** *****

Rudy is hitting his stride and unless the bike has problems, he wins nearly every race he's in. We just had the Santa Maria half-mile, which is a big event for the Southern California riders, and Rudy topped them all. Rudy is also the current point's leader at Belmont, so he's at the top of his game.

After one of Rudy's Friday night wins at Belmont, he and Stan Schmidt took off towards home on their bikes along Bayshore highway. Rudy and Stan have a longstanding rivalry about who has the fastest street bike, and they were soon racing each other and topping 100 mph. Both of them are laying flat on their gas tanks and keeping their heads down to cut through the wind as they followed the white lines on the road. At that speed things happen quickly, and just ahead of them is a slow moving sedan. Stan saw the car in time and went around, but Rudy didn't and collided into the back of the sedan. His left leg sustained the brunt of the damage when it smashed into the thick steel bumper crushing the bones in his lower leg.

For a flat track racer, you have to put your left foot down for balance through the corners as the metal skid slides along the ground, there's just no other way around it. If your left leg can't handle contact with the ground, you really can't race on flat tracks. Just a few hours before the accident, Rudy had a promising racing career ahead of him, now his racing days might be a thing of the past.

After they got Rudy to the hospital, they found out the extent of the damage to his leg, and it's not good. The bones of his left leg, both the tibia and fibula, are so beyond repair that the doctors had to remove about 5 to 6 inches below the knee. If his right leg would have been the one that got broken, he might have still been able to race, but as it is, those days are over.

Chaves, Tom, and I started talking about putting on a benefit for Rudy to help with his medical expenses. We knew it had to be something big for it to really help, so Tom reached out to Ted Smith. Ted is a great guy who owns the Belmont track, but he's also tight with a dollar. After some convincing, he offered all of a Friday night's ticket sales to go to Rudy's medical bills. A bunch of people started volunteering to help with the event that's set for three weekends away on August 12.

Soon, we began advertising in the Palo Alto and San Jose papers and on the flyers that we put out weekly on upcoming motorcycle events. The flyers have a picture of Rudy sitting on his #66 with a caption on the left side stating, "All proceeds to go to the Al Rudy Hospitalization Fund," and on the other side, "Races sponsored by the friends of Al Rudy." Along the bottom of the flyer it reads, "Featuring "OL 79" Sam Arena," so I'm coming out of retirement.

I switched my race bike over to a hill climber a few months ago, but it won't take long to change it out for the track. Tom and Al offered the use of Rudy's light blue WR in the match race, but I'll stick with my trusty WLDR. It's too bad that Rudy is still in the hospital and won't be there, but they are bringing Rudy's WR to the track and will have it out for folks to see.

On Friday of the benefit, I got out in the dirt during time trials and took the third fastest time. I'll match up with a rider having a similar time and Tom Turner's is nearly identical, so he and I will be racing each other in tonight's four-lap match race.

Tom Turner might weigh close to 200 pounds, but he's a good racer and often in the Belmont main with the rest of the fastest riders. Tom is an Oakland cop, and the police department used to have a rule against officers racing because they don't want them getting injured. One night at Belmont as they were announcing the line-up over the loud speakers for the main event, they had a guy called Ernie Ammons which no one had heard of before. When the new guy got on to the track, it didn't take long for the regulars to recognize that it was Tom Turner. He still wanted to race, so he skirted the rule by using with a new name and number and raced under an alias.

All the fans know Rudy from watching him race over the years, and they want to help out, so it's a huge turnout. When it was time for the match race to begin between Tom and me, we headed out on the track and did some warm-ups. I must not be too rusty, because even though it was close, I pulled out the win for the four-lap race. Shorty Thompkins won the main event, and the crowd enjoyed the night of racing. The benefit turned out really well and the money should help with the doctor bills.

***** ***** *****

It's been five months since I opened the Palo Alto dealership, and things are going well. During the first month of business, I made $60 over my base salary, and in the second month, I made $200, so I can breathe easier about using my own money to run the dealership. Motorcycle riders are a fairly small group, so to drum up business and get more involved with the local motorcycle community, I started the Palo Alto Yellow Jackets Motorcycle Club. Sammy is only 12, but he came up with the original drawing that we're using for the club's logo: a bumble bee grabbing handle bars.

After Rudy's accident, Larry came on as one of Tom's riders, but he'll continue to race his own WR on the short tracks where horsepower isn't a premium. This is also the bike that his wife Dot took the hatchet to, but now it's good as new. The seat and especially the gas tank got most of the damage, but those were easily replaced, and his wife hasn't tried a repeat performance. One other benefit to using his own bike he doesn't have to split his winnings, but when it comes to the mile tracks where power is a premium, Larry will ride Rudy's old blue bike and split things 50/50 with Tom.

***** ***** *****

I have been making plans for the National Hill Climb Championship in Dubuque on September 25th, but I have one small issue to work out. I need the family car to tow the trailer, and since we just have the one car, Myrt's main option for getting to work is by motorcycle. She's been on a motorcycle hundreds of times, but she's never driven one, so we'll see how this plays out.

One night at dinner, I brought up the topic. "Hon, I don't know if you've thought about it, but since I'm going to need our car when I go to Iowa, you're either going to have to take the bus or learn to ride a motorcycle."

She replied, "I've thought about it, and I'm not too happy."

So I began teaching Myrt to ride and, at first, it looked like it might not be possible to get her up and riding in time. Myrt kept dragging her feet because she thought that she'd have to put them on the ground if she started falling over, but her feet got bruised from bouncing off the ground and into the foot pegs. I had to yell, "Stop dragging your feet and put them on the pegs," for her to stop dragging them. It took her many tries, but she started getting the hang of it and, before long, she thought that she could handle the two-mile ride down El Camino Real past the Stanford stadium to the shop.

Pete Peterson is a member of the Yellow Jackets and he's going on the trip with me to Dubuque. Vince (Andres) and Bill (Curran) are some other guys from the Yellow Jackets and they are around socializing as I was talking about the trip to Iowa for the Dubuque National.

"Tom put together a new 74 incher, so I'm pretty excited about the climb. I don't know if you guys can make it, but it should be a lot of fun if either of you wants to go with Pete and me."

Bill asked, "How long of a trip are we talking about?"

"We would be gone from a Wednesday to Thursday the week after. I figure that it will take four days of 12 hours of driving. We might make it back on Wednesday if we make good time."

Bill said, "I don't think my wife would mind, she'd like a week away from me. Count me in."

Vince said, "Let me talk with the ball and chain and get back to you, but it sounds like fun."

Pete chimed in, "I'll have to pick up a couple more cases of beer if it's going to be four of us."

Later, I was amazed when both Vince and Bill took me up on the offer.

Shortly before the event, I started loading the trailer with both of my bikes, spare parts, and all the tools that I might need. Then on Wednesday morning, all four of us met at the dealership and loaded our gear into the trailer and the trunk of the Oldsmobile and started out for Iowa.

The national in Dubuque is a huge draw with a lot of talent gunning for a trophy and when we showed up the place is jumping. The hill conditions look great, the dirt's not too dry, and the hill is in good shape. Windy Lindstrom is my biggest rival, at least on the hills, and I ran into him before the climbs started.

"Hey Windy, I knew you'd be here," I said as we shook hands.

"Sam how goes it?"

"Good. Now take it easy out there, don't hog all of the trophies."

Windy laughed, "Well, that's what we're here for."

During the climbs for the 45-cubic-inch division, I felt good about my riding, but Windy topped the hill with the quickest time of 10.68 seconds. I came in second by a couple hundred's of a second slower at 10.75, which is quicker than a bumblebee's fart, but it's also the difference between a win and a loss.

After the break, we got ready for the 80-cubic-inch expert division. When it came time for my turn I lined up the new 74-cubic-inch in front of the catcher wall, and once I got the nod, I cranked the throttle. The bike is running strong, and I covered the 329 feet in 9.62 seconds, which is the quickest run of the day so far. Since I had the fastest time, I don't have to attempt a second unless my time gets beat.

As I waited through everyone's second pass, no one could top my first run's time, so I secured my third hill climb National Championship in three years.

When we arrived back at the Palo Alto dealership after eight days away, Myrt is in the shop's office, and she's happy to see me. I asked, "Hon, how are you?"

"I'm doing just fine."

"Good. How are the kids?"

She replied, "They've been fine too."

Now for the biggest question, "How did riding the motorcycle work out?"

"I didn't have any problems, although driving with a bag of groceries wasn't my favorite."

Myrt is being very nice about it, but unless it's an emergency, I'm pretty sure that she'll never ride by herself on a motorcycle again.

Myrt had other news too: we're moving again. We've only been in our rental for two months, but she says that the house is haunted. I guess that while I was gone, she's been hearing odd noises and something like the sound of footsteps. Myrt is very superstitious, and I can tell that she's convinced that the place really is haunted, so arguing won't do me any good. The house is a decrepit old place with a weird smell that never goes away, so it's no keeper, but I'm not looking forward to repacking and moving again. Myrt has already found a nice house not far down the El Camino on Olive Street, and she's talked to the owner about us renting it.

Learning about Trabia

Judy is working on a school project about our family history, and she needs grandpa's help. So we're going over to my parents' house for dinner and they will be able to talk. We had a nice dinner, and after we finished and cleared the dining room table, Judy grabbed her notebook and sat down at the table with Grandpa.

While they are going to talk, Sammy is over on the rocker and Mama, Myrt, and I are going to sit on the nearby sofa to hear what Papa has to say. Although Papa's English is a little broken, as they say, Judy has been around enough to understand what he means.

Judy said, "I'm writing a story for class about my ancestors, and I want you to tell me about where you and grandma came from in Italy and what it was like."

"So you want to know about the old country."

"Yes I do," Judy said with a smile on her face.

"Both your grandma and I were born in Trabia, which is a coastal town on the island of Sicily. It's about 60 miles away from Palermo, which is the largest city in Sicily. Trabia is a beautiful town with sun-washed houses that stand two and three stories tall, and the houses are built along the hills. Women go to the town square to wash clothes and hang them out to dry with the other Trabian ladies. The central square is where people gather to socialize, celebrate holidays, and have weddings near the fountain in the center of the square."

"From the shoreline, you look out to the blue waters of the Mediterranean Sea. The weather is much like here in San Jose, fairly mild, which is great for gardens, and everyone has a garden in Sicily."

Judy asked, "Can you tell me about our family?"

"Well, the Arena family was, still is, fairly well-off. We own acres of olive trees and have vineyards in the Trabian countryside. That part of the country has many orange and lemon groves too, so it's very beautiful."

"Our families have known each other since before either of us was born, so for grandma and me, being together was always meant to be. In 1903, I left Sicily to come to America, while your grandmother (Maria DiVittorio at the time), waited for me to get things started in America, then she would come over. We knew that we would be married one day, but after I was gone for two years, her Dad started getting impatient and wanted his daughter married, even if that meant marrying someone else. Maria wrote me a letter asking for me to return before her Dad gave her away," Papa looked over to Mama and smiled.

"So I sailed back to Trabia where we got married at our town's church, the Monastero Santa Chiara Termini Imerese, which is a beautiful church built in the late 1500s. A year later we welcomed the birth of your Uncle Danny, whose birth name is Gaetano."

I butted in to ask Judy, "Is he going too fast for you?"

"No I'm getting it" Judy replied as she scribbled furiously. Then she asked how to spell the church's name, as Papa answered, he gave her a little time to catch up.

After a while Judy asked, "How did you make it to San Jose from Italy?"

"Ah, good question."

"In 1906, your grandmother, Gaetano, and I sailed to America aboard the Konig Albert. At the time, it was a German ship, but it was later seized by the Italian government and renamed the Italia."

"For your Grandma, this was the first time she had ever been away from Sicily, so it was a new world for her. I remember standing on the ship with Grandma and Gaetano as we saw the Statue of Liberty, which was a wonderful sight. We settled in Syracuse, New York, where a large number of Italians were living, but in that first winter New York had a big snowstorm, and

Grandma didn't care for the cold weather, so after hearing about sunny California, we decided to head west. We lived in San Francisco for a couple years, but it was too cold for us, so we finally settled here in San Jose."

"Over the years in San Jose, Joe was born, and then Annie and Josephine came along, and then your Dad Santo was born (October 30, 1912). Mrs. Brassini is a midwife that helped with your Dad's delivery as she did with most of our children. After your Dad, Babe (Angelo) was next, and then Celeste (Sally) was born. And many years after that, your brother and you came along, and here you are sitting in our living room."

"You're funny papa," as she finished her writing. "That was a great story, thanks for telling it to me," then she got up to hug him.

"I enjoyed telling it to you."

Even though I had knew about most of those stories, it's still fun hearing them. On the drive home, the kids said that they enjoyed them too, so besides Judy finishing her book report, I'm glad we got to hear about my folks in the old days.

***** ***** *****

A lot of characters come around the Palo Alto dealership, some are a little off, but most of them are okay. One of the good kids that drop by is George "Bobo" Sepulveda, the guy who won the raffle for Glen Fuller's bike last year. Bobo rides a single cylinder Matchless and he's a member of the Tri-City Motorcycle Club. The Tri-City club is based out of Redwood City, and they have a small clubhouse over near the Belmont track.

Anytime Bobo stops by the shop on his Matchless, Bobby Boyd tells him, "That's not a Harley, park it down the street." Bobo is just a kid and doesn't know that Bobby is just razzing him, but Bobo moves his bike so that it's not in front of the dealership. Bobo also tags along with Rudy and Chaves and, if they head to the bars, he'll go along but since he isn't old enough to drink, he plays shuffleboard while they are bending their elbows.

Chapter 2 / Bay Meadows Mile

Outside of the championship race at Daytona that kicks off the AMA series, the big event close to home will be the inaugural 20-mile championship race coming to the Bay Meadows track in San Mateo (May 1950). We've waited a long time for a national, and it's going to draw a lot of top talent from the West Coast and beyond.

It's been less than a year since Rudy's crash and he's already riding street bikes with his prosthetic leg, so it's good to see that he can still ride. Even with what Rudy has been through, he still has the passion for the sport, and with Bay Meadows holding its first national in a few weeks, we encouraged him to get out on the track again. Larry is using the blue WR, and Rudy knows that Larry has the best chance of winning with it, so he has no desire to ride it anyway. Art Boos is the brother of Larry's wife Dot, and he told Rudy that if he needed a bike he could use his new WR.

A few weeks before Bay Meadows, Rudy, Tom, and I went to the Stockton Mile to see how Rudy would do on the borrowed bike. Rudy has never raced on a mile track before and he's just going to do some laps today, so he's under no pressure. When it came time to practice, Rudy got out on the track and did some warm-up laps without taking his feet off the pegs, but as he got upwards of 70 mph, the wind blew his prosthetic leg off the peg. After slowing down and getting his foot back up on the peg, he circled around and pulled into the infield. He'll be going much faster than 70 mph in a real race, so dealing with the increasing wind is something that needs to be figured out pretty quickly.

Bay Meadows is a mile track with wider corners than Stockton, and with Rudy's prosthetic leg, he's going to have to ride the track without putting his inside foot down. He might not be going as fast as the other riders in the corners, but he'll do okay on the straights, so hopefully he can still get a good overall time. After talking it over, we are going to add floor boards to the bike, and for the race, we'll find a way to strap his left foot down to it.

This is the first time that the East Coast riders have come this far west for a national, and many of them are dropping by the dealership to visit. Compared with its status in the racing community, the great Sifton dealership isn't what most would expect. They probably imagine a nice big clean place with the best tools and equipment, but this is an old dealership typical of a small prewar motorcycle business, and it hasn't changed much since the 1930s. The service area has tools and parts all over, and if you were to clean up and put all of the tools away, the guys in the shop probably wouldn't be able to find anything. The first dealership in Palo Alto that I opened was a lot like that too, just a small old shop with a couple employees, but at least our new building is more like what the East Coast racers are expecting.

On race day we drove up to the track to make sure that the bikes are dialed in. Later on as people started filing in, the atmosphere felt like something big was going on. The Bay Meadows grandstands can hold something like 16,000 fans, and it looks like the crowd will be spilling into the infield before long. They will have all three divisions of racing as usual, but only the expert race is for a national championship. In the amateur division today, Kenny Eggers, another one of Tom's riders, is competing. Kenny is a local guy that has been winning some Northern California races, and after pulling out a win in the main at Belmont, Tom hired him to join the team. Tom has Kenny on a great bike, so he should be in the thick of things.

After the novice heats and main race, the amateur heats are up next. Kenny is in the third heat, and he crossed the strip first to qualify for the main. The first three riders out of each of the four heats qualify, plus the four fastest riders from the semifinal race, putting sixteen riders into the final race.

When it came time for the amateur's final, Kenny rode over to get into position in the staggered four rows of four riders. As the green flag waved and the race began, Kenny got a good start and after a lead change or two he led for most of the 20 laps to take the checkered flag. So far so good! Now we'll see how Larry and Rudy do in the professional division.

Just before it's time for Rudy's heat, we put sheet metal screws up through the bottom of the floorboards and screwed them into Rudy's wooden foot to keep his left leg in place. When it came time to line up, we jump-started the bike and pushed him onto the track. As they lined up for the start of the heat, Rudy leaned the bike to the right side on his good leg. For most of us in the pits, and the fans in the stands that know him, our eyes are glued on Rudy from start to finish as he made the six laps without putting his foot down. Rudy might not be as fast as some of the others going into the corners, but coming out of them he's like a rocket, and he managed to come in fourth for his heat. With that placing he'll be in the semi and, hopefully, in the next top four riders and make it into the final 16.

Once the semi began, Rudy did well in the dirt, but didn't qualify for the main. It might be just as well because he's having second thoughts. After the semi when Rudy and I were talking, he said, "Maybe it's a good thing that I didn't make the cut." I didn't expect to hear that.

"It might not be the safest thing for the other riders if I'm on the track."

I said, "Al, you've got to do what you think is right. It's your call."

"I know, I just think that it's time for me to call it quits."

Everybody is still amazed on how well Rudy did out there, and all of us had nothing but admiration for the guy.

We still have Larry representing the Sifton team after he qualified for the main event in the professional group. Larry is on a great bike, but without any high-profile wins, he's more-or-less a nobody, at least compared to someone like Jimmy Chann who has won the Springfield Mile (and number #1 plate) three years in a row, and who's sitting a couple riders over.

When the flag dropped, Larry gunned it too much and spun out, so most of the other riders got a jump on him. He's near the back of the pack, but he's easily passing the slower riders down the straights. Within a few short laps, Larry made his way out near the front with only Dud Perkin's rider Paul Albrecht ahead of him. It's a back and forth between Larry and Albrecht for the lead as they went into the last lap. On the final turn Larry came perfectly out of the corner with the momentum he needs to cross the finish line over Albrecht by two bike lengths. This is Larry's first national win, and the season is still young.

A few weeks after his Bay Meadows win, Larry traveled up the coast with Tom to enter the Portland mile at Portland Meadows. Just like Bay Meadows, Portland Meadows is owned by Mr. William P. Kyne, and the two horse tracks and grand stands are near duplicates of each other.

With Larry's riding and Tom's tuning, he came out on top again to take the checkered flag. At this point, Tom made the decision to have Larry go east and compete for the national title in Springfield, Illinois. With Kenny winning the amateur event at Bay Meadows, Tom is having him go along with Larry and Al to compete in the amateur division at Springfield. While they will be driving, Tom is going to fly out later in the week and meet them there.

Springfield's championship race is the biggest race out there. In addition to earning a nice check, the winner also gets the #1 plate for the following season. If things go well in Springfield, Larry and Kenny will compete in the Milwaukee Mile the following weekend, and while they are in town, maybe they can stop by the Harley factory before the drive back.

After a couple days of driving, they arrived at the Springfield track, and Al changed into his white mechanics clothes to prepare the bike. Outside of the racers, the dress code in the pit areas is white pants and shirts. The main reason for the white is so that it's easier to see through dust and dirt-covered goggles as they pull into the pit area, and also when it gets dark the white is easier to see. Another reason is it helps keep out people that shouldn't be there to start with.

Kenny won his heat on the mile track, and once the amateur main event started, he beat out the other 15 riders to win the amateur division trophy. Once the pro heats began, Larry easily qualified for the main, and the bike isn't even breathing hard. As they are getting ready for the final, Larry is telling Tom how well the bike is running. "Hold back a little and pace yourself off the leaders, don't get out front. Once you get the signal from Al, pour it on."

"Sure Tom, I can do that."

Being in second has its benefits. If you are close enough, you can draft the leader to get pulled along and then use that momentum to make a move in the last corner. You also don't have to worry about protecting the lead and fending off the rest of the riders.

During the race, Larry is hovering around third place and staying right in there for the first 15 laps. When he got the sign from Al going into lap 18, Larry cranked up the power and, in a short time, he stunned everyone by getting out to the front and passing Bill Tuman to take the checkered flag. With that win, Larry became the first West Coast rider to ever win the Springfield Mile. When the news reached the San Jose and Palo Alto dealerships that Larry won and will have next year's number #1 plate, the places went crazy.

The following weekend is the Milwaukee Mile, which is about five hours to the north of Springfield, and it's the last of the three one-mile nationals. Larry isn't going to be able to sneak up on anyone this time around, but with how well he's riding, he'll be tough to beat no matter who he's up against. Less than 20 minutes after the race ended, we got the phone call from Al that Larry had come out on top again and won the Milwaukee Mile. In his first full season of riding for Tom, Larry only raced in three nationals, each of them on mile tracks, but he won all three of the high profile events. He went from being unknown to the top rider in one season, and he did it on a Harley Davidson painted robin's egg blue.

When Larry made it back to town from his trip back east, he came into the Palo Alto shop.

"Hey Sleepy, how did it go?"

"The trip went well. We had some fun."

"Have any problems?"

"Springfield was the only place that things got a little testy. About half-way through the race, I was trying to pass Paul Goldsmith when he went on the high groove to pelt me with dirt. The joke was on him, because not long after, his bike broke down. Then I got into a dogfight with Bobby Hill for the lead, and for a few laps we were neck-and-neck, but his Indian started fading and I took the lead and held on."

I told him, "Great job, Sleepy. But next time you tell the story, leave out the parts about their motorcycle problems and stick to winning by being the better rider." He got a kick out of that.

***** ***** *****

The San Jose police department rides Harley Davidsons, and the Sifton dealership has the contract for selling and servicing their motorcycles. The dealership is fortunate to have that contract because it provides over half of the dealership's business, and it's one of the reasons that the department needs five or six mechanics most of the time. In addition to selling the police department new motorcycles every two years, we take their old models in on trade to resell, and we service their current motorcycles.

Tom is building a new hill climber for Dick Austin, and he's going to use one of the police departments old FL Panheads with the new hydraulic front end. Dick runs the shops parts department, and Tom promised to build him something strong for the hills. The police trade-in looks like a good start. The shop guys started in to stripping off all the heavy street equipment while Tom started in on building a new cam for the 74-cubic-inch motor.

After a couple weeks of Tom tuning the motor and working his magic, the bike is really strong. To complete the makeover, the guys painted the gas tank and fenders a dark blue color, which does a good job of covering any of the old black and white paint. Right out of the gate, the bike performed like a stud as Dick put together a couple quick wins at Modesto and Visalia. With that strong start, the old police motor got the nickname "The Big Inch".

***** ***** *****

The hill-climb championship at Corvallis north of Eugene, Oregon, is coming up, and we are making the trip into a family vacation. The day ahead of the climb we piled into the Oldsmobile and left San Jose before the sun came up. We made it to Corvallis with time for the kids to get into the swimming pool and still go out for dinner.

The next day at the hill climb, it's a huge turnout. The place is packed with thousands of fans and dozens of riders. Oregon has some quality hill climbers, and this is like a hometown event for them, but I'm here to win, so they can pull my finger. On my first run in the 45 division, I nearly flew up the hill and had the best time out of all the riders so far. Although I have the quickest time so far in the 45 group, I decided to go ahead with my second run. The second pass worked out really well too, but the first run is still a couple hundredths of a second quicker. After all of the riders in the 45 group had finished, I grabbed the top spot in the 45 division.

After the break, the riders in the 80-cubic-inch group got ready. When I got called up, my first pass isn't half bad, but not the quickest time of the group. I'll have to take a different path on my second pass and try to get a better time. On my second attempt, it didn't go so well. About three quarters of the way up, the front end got light and I couldn't stop from flipping the bike and breaking the handle bars. Dick Austin won the 80 group on The Big Inch, but I still picked up a fourth AMA Championship trophy for the winning time in the 45 expert division.

***** ***** *****

It's been over a year ago since Papa talked to Judy about our family history for her school report, but since then, Papa has had a third stroke, and this last one was especially bad. After the first two, Papa used to squeeze a rubber ball to strengthen his hands and grip because the strokes made him lose strength. But now, most of the right side of his body is basically paralyzed.

Mama is 65-years old and she's doing the best she can to take care of him, but she's still working at the Del Monte cannery, so doing so much has been tough on her. For Papa, he feels helpless in his condition, and it hurts his pride that people have to do everything for him since he can't really do things for himself anymore. Folks from the old country are proud, and they never want to be a burden to their families. They would rather be put out to pasture.

On the night before Thanksgiving, I got a late night call from my brother Danny. Any late night call usually means bad news of some sort. He said that sometime after midnight, Mama had heard the sound of a shotgun out in the garden, and she called him to come over. I'm sure that Mama had a good idea what had happened, but hoped that it wasn't true. Danny said that Papa had somehow gotten the shotgun from above the back door, crawled with it into the back yard, and shot himself.

✲✲✲✲✲ ✲✲✲✲✲ ✲✲✲✲✲

George "Bobo" Sepulvada started racing last year, and he's gotten to be a fast rider on his 500cc single-cylinder Matchless. Bobo is winning some heats and being competitive in the mains, but you can only do so much on a Matchless. Bobo knew as much, but it's a matter of saving enough dough to afford a race bike. He had been talking about it for a while, and one day he and his Dad came into the dealership with cash and the 74-inch Harley he won in the raffle two years ago and ordered a new WR.

These days you can order a 45-cubic-inch WR straight from the Harley Davidson catalog for any type of racing. You select how the bike is set up from the tires, to gas tank size and gearing, and once the order is mailed to the factory, in four to six weeks, the bike will be shipped right to our dealership. Like most of the WRs that get ordered, Bobo's is bare bones flat track model in black, three gears hand-shifted, no lights, and no brakes. It's ready to race upon arrival.

Tom is always trying to think up new ways to improve his bikes, and, when he's doing his backwards whistling, you know that he is onto something. Lately he's been whistling a lot, and he just completed a couple new sets of cams for the upcoming season which everyone has high hopes for. Once the bike gets put back together, Larry's WR is guaranteed to be even faster for 1951, but last season's success will be tough to top.

Though Tom handles everything on the bike, in Class C events, you have to own the bike(s) you race, so the WR is in Larry's name. He and Tom have a contract stating if Larry wants to "sell" the bike, he has to sell it to Tom for one dollar. Riding a Sifton-tuned Harley greatly increases your chances of winning, so Larry is fine with the 50/50 split, and Tom also covers Al's work in the pits out of his own pocket.

The blue bike is set up for the mile tracks, but Larry will still use his own bike for half-miles and less. Tom maintains Larry's bike too, so it's not lacking power, but it doesn't have the power of the blue bike. For shorter tracks like Belmont you don't need as much punch because the rear tire breaks free too easy if you gun it, and it doesn't have the long straights where more power is needed. For the upcoming season the guys decided to give Larry's WR a new paint job in the standard Harley colors of orange and black.

***** ***** *****

It has been five weeks since Bobo ordered his WR, and it just arrived at the Palo Alto dealership. When Bobo came by to pick it up, he was itching to get the bike on the track, but the motor needs to be broken-in before he pushes it wide open during a race. Bobo lives about a dozen miles away in Redwood City, so he just rode home along the orchard roads to put some miles on the motor. But he's also riding without brakes, so the only way to slow the bike down is by downshifting and dragging your feet, so hopefully he doesn't get going too fast.

During the season, Belmont practices are on the afternoon of the evening races, but the Sunday ahead of Belmont's season opener they have open track time for practicing, and Bobo took his bike there to get in some laps. This is the first day that he's ridden the WR on a track and during time trials, from what I heard, Bobo looked like a natural and turned the fastest lap time of the day, 17.65 seconds. Within a couple minutes of riding the WR, I'm sure that Bobo didn't miss his old Matchless.

I was at a hill climb that day so I wasn't at the track, but when I came in to work Tuesday morning, I saw Bobo's mangled bike inside the trailer behind the shop. My first thought is I wonder which hospital he ended up in, but once the guys showed up for work they said that Bobo only got banged up a little in the excitement. I guess Bobo was doing some broad sliding during practice and basically screwing around when he got a little out of control and flipped the WR end over end. He managed to break the handlebars and dent the tank, but in two days we had the bike patched up, and although Bobo is a little sore, he's set for the season opener.

Opening Night

Opening night at Belmont is always fun because besides the racing, we run into old friends that we haven't seen since last season. Most of the 2000 or so customers that show up each Friday night are regulars, and they tend to sit in the same seats with the same people, so you know where to look if you want to find someone. Outside of that, on opening night, it's always interesting to watch the new crop of riders and see if any of them really stand out. With Belmont being a progressive track, the fastest riders go into the main event regardless of class, so a novice could be up against seasoned professionals, and that's when you can really see who the good riders are.

For tonight's season opener, Bobo is here along with Larry who is proudly sporting the #1 plate. Last Sunday during open practice, Bobo proved that he's a fast rider, but he didn't keep the bike in tight and rode too high on the track to get a good lap time. You can't get away with many mistakes out here. On Friday night there could be over 100 riders trying to qualify, so if you slip up, someone else makes the cut instead. Bobo is still learning as a rider, and that's part of the process: you learn what you did right and did wrong, and try to improve each time out.

During one of the heats, a new rider caught our eye. He's on a dark red Triumph with number 98x on his plate, and although he looked a little raw, he's a hard charger on the track. He passed everyone into and out of the corners, but down the straights, the Harley's pass him up. Tom said to me, "That's the one to watch." I've always trusted Tom's evaluation of talent, so if he said the kid is good, I believe him.

For the final race of the night, the 16 fastest riders got out on the track for the start and besides Larry, the kid with #98 made it too. The riders are lined up in two rows of six and once the flag dropped, Larry quickly got out front. Larry looks to have things under control, but his main challenger is #98 who is not far from Larry's rear tire as they are going into corners. Number 98 is a new guy this year, but the "X" after his number makes him from Southern California (compared to Y and Z for northern California riders). I know that Jimmy Phillips out of San Diego used to have #98 before switching to #8, so this kid has Jimmy's old number.

Number 98 got deep into the corners, which rookies usually can't pull off, and he might have been as fast as Larry, but once Larry pulled out of the corner and got back on the groove, his bike had too much steam for #98 to keep up with. The groove is wide enough for only one set of tires, so if you want to pass someone you have to go outside of the groove's hard surface, so your bike needs plenty of power to go on the looser dirt and make ground.

Number 98 tried to pass off the groove a couple times near the end, but Larry took the checkered flag with #98 coming in two bike lengths behind. It's a great start for Larry with his #1 plate and the next race coming up in Napa on Sunday.

Napa isn't a half-mile track, it's closer to 3/8s with shorter straights and the track itself isn't very good. The soil is a combination of sand and dirt, and even when they water down the dirt before the races begin, the soil still dries out too quickly. Larry easily qualified on the Napa track, and when the main event started, he got out front quickly and stayed there to take the checkered flag, so he's two for two to start the season. An interesting thing is that once again #98 came in second behind Larry. Number 98 is still a novice, but he had to race up with the experts, so even though he's young, he's got to be a talented rider to keep up with Larry.

We heard that the kid with the 98 plate is Joe Leonard out of San Diego. He was racing in the Aztec Motorcycle Club at some field meets when Frank Servetti, who owns the San Francisco Triumph dealership, saw him racing at Carroll Speedway on a BSA Popper. Servetti must have been impressed with the kid, because he offered to sponsor Leonard and provide a bike if he came north to race for him. So Leonard moved to San Francisco about a month ago, and the Triumph that he's been riding is Chuck Masterson's old bike.

New Facility

I've been at the High Street location for one year now and things are going well. I feel comfortable with the amount of traffic we're receiving, so we moved the dealership into a much bigger new building on El Camino. The new shop has a service area nearly three times the size of the old one, and we have a much bigger showroom floor, which means I'll need to order a few more bikes from the factory.

Some other changes are happening with the move: Al went back to the San Jose dealership, which was expected because he came to Palo Alto to help me out, and I appreciated it. With Al leaving, I got ahold of Art Holler to take his place, and then Bobby Boyd left and Jimmy Weiss came on board as my second mechanic.

The next Friday night at Belmont, Larry is one of the riders that qualified for the final event. We are watching as the main event began, and in the early part of the race, as Larry is coming out of the second corner, he got sent to the dirt, and it looks like he must have gotten shook up. The black flag came out to get the riders off of the track, and soon the ambulance drove out to pick up Larry. Once they came off of the track we got word that his left leg was broken.

When I talked to Larry later, he said that he wasn't exactly sure why he went down. The track is at sea level, and when the tide comes in, it gets slicker as the night progresses, so that may have played a part in the crash. But he's familiar with the track conditions and he should have been able to deal with it. All Larry can do now is focus on recovering, and should have enough time to make it back on the track late in the season. For now, though, he'll be home in bed for a couple weeks while his leg heals.

Pacific Coast Championship

This weekend is the Pacific Coast Championship races in Tulare, and I'm going along with Bobo to pit for him and provide any pointers he might need on riding the track. As we were shooting the breeze on the drive, I asked about his nickname. "Well, my brother John is one year older than me, and when I was just a baby he couldn't say "brother", it came out Bobo. He kept calling me that, and soon relatives and friends started calling me Bobo, and the name stuck."

After we arrived in Tulare and the races for the novice division started, Bobo looked unstoppable, and he basically led from start to finish and became the novice division Pacific Coast Champion of 1951. To show how good Bobo was in the dirt, for the short six-lap race, he lapped two guys on his way to the win. Next up is the amateur main event, and we watched as Joe Leonard rode his Triumph to a win and became the amateur division Pacific Coast Champion. After Bobo's Pacific Coast win, I started sponsoring him and began providing him with tires and gas, so he'll wear the Palo Alto Harley Davidson sweater at events.

We've kept an eye on Joe Leonard, and although he's young age-wise, he is focused on being a successful racer. After a few weeks of racing in the Bay Area, and hearing good things about Tom Sifton's tuning, he knew that hooking up with Tom would be a good move. Triumphs aren't known as good flat track bikes, and Indian Scouts are typically the fastest bikes on the track, but if you're riding a Sifton-tuned Harley on a mile track, that trumps all others.

Bobo, Chuck Masterson, and Joe have struck up a friendship, and as they were riding in Redwood City one day Joe asked Bobo if he could get him a ride on a Harley. Joe knew that Bobo is friends with Tom, so he hoped that Bobo could provide the in for him. Bobo said that it was worth a shot, so they rode down to the Sifton dealership.

Tom saw them walking into the dealership and asked, "What are you boys up to today?"

Bobo started, "Well Tom, this is Joe Leonard and he wanted to talk to you."

"Sure I know Joe, what can I help you with?"

Joe said, "Mr. Sifton, I was wondering if you might need another rider for your team."

"I don't really need any other pilots, but Headricks does. With him having a broken leg, his personal WR is available. If you're interested, we'll supply the motor, but you'll have to split any earnings 50/50 with Larry and his family. I don't want any money out of it."

"Sure Mr. Sifton, that's fine with me."

"Keep in mind that this is just until Larry comes back, so I don't want you to get your hopes up that this is long term. Larry should be able to make it back before the end of the season, so you might be out of a ride when he does."

"Sure I understand." Joe replied. Even if this is temporary, this is too big of an opportunity for him to pass up.

Tom said, "Drop back by on Tuesday and we'll get his bike set up for you."

"Thanks Mr. Sifton."

Now Joe had to break the news to Frank Servetti. Although Joe came up to ride for Servetti, it's not like they have a contract or anything. When Joe told him that he was switching to Sifton, Servetti wasn't happy, but he understood.

They will need to make some adjustments to Larry's WR to get it ready for Joe. With Larry being about four inches shorter, and close to 35 pounds lighter than Joe, the main thing is that the gearing will have to be changed. Tom didn't let on then, but because of Joe's bigger build, he wasn't convinced that Joe can win on a mile track, but we'll see how that plays out.

Stockton Mile

After every race, the motor is pulled out and the top end is gone through. If anything like pistons or valves has too much wear, they get replaced, while new rings are put in on each tear-down. Usually after three or four races, new pistons are put in, but for national championship events, we always put in new pistons and rebuild the bottom end. Larry is feeling better and he's been coming by the dealership with his leg in a cast to help Joe get the bike ready.

Joe will be on Larry's bike at the Stockton mile, so we will see how he does against the smaller racers. It's always competitive between racers, and especially if they are on different makes such as Indian, Harley, and the British bikes like Triumph and BSA. Guys are protective of their bikes of choice, and at Stockton, the Triumph riders are needling Joe for switching to the enemy.

As the race began, things didn't go well for Joe out on the track, and he was never able to compete. Joe has to be wondering himself if he did the right thing by switching to Harley. To add insult to injury, Ed Kretz Jr. took the checkered flag on a Triumph. We figured that something is wrong with the bike because we know how good of a rider Joe is. When he came into the pits he complained how the bike lacked power.

We took the bike back to the shop and started checking it over and found that the top motor mounts are loose. Larry and Joe had put in the new rebuilt motor into the frame two days before, and somehow they must have gotten sidetracked during the install and didn't go back and tighten the bolts. Without the motor bolted solidly to the frame, the motor shifted when Joe gave it power the full amount of torque couldn't transfer to the rear wheel. This is an easy fix, and we'll see how the next race goes, but it shouldn't have happened to start with.

The next race is the Bay Meadows mile (June 1951) and it's a national championship race like last year, but as with all flat track nationals, only the pro division is a championship and not the amateur and novice divisions. The day ahead of the race, Tom and Joe went up to the track in San Mateo to do some practice laps and make sure that the bike is running good. They don't want any mistakes like they had last time.

One of the racers prepping for the race today is Paul Goldsmith and he is a seasoned veteran and friends with Tom. The two of them are talking the pit area and Tom says, "Goldie, can you show my rider how to go around this thing. I'd like him to see how a pro does it."

"Sure Tom, I can do that."

Shortly after, Joe got out on the track behind Goldsmith for a few laps, and Joe is right on his rear tire the whole way. After a couple laps, Joe had enough of going slow and went shooting around him and laid it on for a few laps. When they came in off the track, Goldsmith walked over to Tom and said, "He doesn't need to learn anything from me." A little later someone remarked how Joe will be something once he turns pro, that's when Goldsmith found out that Joe is an amateur and just 19. Goldie thought that Joe is already a pro, and he couldn't believe the kid is already this good.

The next day, practically everyone we know is at the San Mateo track to watch Joe race. After the first outing at Stockton, if Joe didn't do well, both he and Tom would look awfully bad. Joe is chomping at the bit and before the race he's still hearing it from the Triumph guys, but he held his tongue and didn't get caught up in the talk.

Once the flag dropped, the boys got humbled real quick as Joe crushed everyone and won by a straight. Joe winning the 20-lap race was never in doubt and that put an end to the talk from the Triumph riders. Just to make Joe's win a little sweeter, in second place is Ed Kretz Jr., the guy that he had lost to in Stockton. Now we got ready for the expert class.

Kenny recently got enough points to become an expert, and he made the cut. Now he'll be up against some of the best riders in the country like Roy Andres, Paul Albrecht, and Jimmy Chann. Kenny is a good rider and with the light blue bike, he should be in the thick of things. During the 20-lap race, Kenny stunned the crowd to win his first National Championship.

Outside of Kenny's win, the second biggest shock of the day might be that Burt Brundedge, who is a big boy and probably tops 200 pounds, managed to come in second on a Triumph. He's probably 50 pounds heavier than the next heaviest rider, and that extra weight really slows a bike down. Burt also won on a Triumph, which isn't known as a good race bike for a mile track, but he is riding for Johnson Motors out of the Los Angeles area, and those guys build fast bikes.

With Joe winning the amateur event and Kenny winning in the expert group, it's been a good day for riders on Sifton-tuned bikes. One other surprising thing is that when we compared the lap times for the day, Joe's time is faster than Kenny's in the experts, and he's not even riding Tom's fastest bike.

They don't have a novice class for nationals so Bobo wasn't there, but he is doing well racing for me. After winning a trophy dash at Belmont against some top experts a few weeks ago, he followed it up with a win at the Salinas half-mile, and soon, after when the monthly American Motorcyclist magazine came out, it ranked Bobo as one of the top novice riders in the country.

Street Crash

Larry is proving to be a slow healer and his leg isn't close to 100% yet, but he's working again and riding a motorcycle to work. It's going to be a month or so before he'll be recovered enough to race, but he still might make a race or two before the season ends. About a month after Larry started working again at the San Jose dealership, he hadn't arrived for work like usual so they figured that he must be out sick.

As I heard later at the Palo Alto dealership, about a half hour after opening, a customer came into the shop and said that Larry had been hit by a car over on Second Street, and they were taking him to the hospital. I guess that Larry was riding on his way to work when an old man in a sedan didn't see Larry to the left of him and took a hard left in front of Larry. He instinctively laid down the bike, but in hitting the hard pavement he managed to break his left leg once again, just in a different place.

When I went to the hospital after work, Myrt is already there with Dot, and Sleepy is asleep in the nearby bed. As I walked into the room, Dot stood up and hugged me with tears in her eyes. "Dot, I'm so sorry." This is hardest on his family, but it's sad for everyone because we all like Sleepy. Not a bad word could be said about him.

Although his crash isn't as devastating as the one that happened to Al Rudy a year earlier, in both cases it was the left leg that got the brunt of the damage. The doctors said that Larry's front leg bone (tibia) is shattered in numerous places, but he'll be able to walk again. We were afraid to ask if he would be able to race again.

I stayed with Dot and Myrt most of the evening and, as we sat there talking, I thought as I looked over at my friend in the hospital bed, this is first time that I've ever seen Sleepy actually sleeping. As we got more information from the doctors, they said that because the bones are so broken up, his left leg will be a couple inches shorter than the right and he won't be able to put much pressure on his left leg without it causing discomfort. After a hugely successful year that took my friend to the top of the flat track world, it sounds like it's over. What a crying shame.

With fate stepping in, an opportunity opened up and Joe came on as Tom's full-time rider. He'll ride Larry's orange and black WR for the rest of the season, and Tom will build a new motor for him ahead of next season. Tom's equipment is better than anyone else's out there, and with Kenny's win at Bay Meadows and Joe's obvious talent, Tom is going to have them both head back east to compete in the Springfield Mile.

After sending in the required paperwork and being accepted Al, Kenny, and Joe made the long drive to Springfield. The day of the race we stuck around late at the shop because we were hoping for a phone call on the race results. Finally Al called to say that Joe came out on top in the amateur group, and although Kenny didn't win in the expert group, he came in a respectable second behind Bobby Hill. So it didn't turn out to be two first place finishes liked we hoped, but it was pretty damn close.

When Kenny came by the Palo Alto shop after the trip, I asked,

"Kenny, how did you do in Springfield?"

He replied sheepishly, "Second."

"Second? That doesn't count."

"Hey, I was close to winning, but a couple laps to go, the bolt holding the primary chain guard fell off along with my foot peg, so I had to ride with my leg out and away from the open sprocket so I wouldn't be pulled in."

***** ***** *****

Joe is not a mechanic, but he needs a regular job, so Tom has him delivering parts and working around the shop as a handy man. The problem is that Joe is on the lazy side, and we found him sleeping at work on more than one occasion. Joe kidded, "I guess I'm not meant to work unless it's out on the track." There might be some truth to that because that's where he does his best work, but so far he doesn't have two nickels to rub together. Even if you're winning races as an amateur or a novice, it doesn't pay much. It's not until you start winning as an expert that the money is good. The top expert riders might make $100 racing four days a week, while most working stiffs are making half that at regular 8 to 5 jobs. When I was racing four nights a week after the war, I made enough each season that I could afford to buy a new car each year.

It's a good thing that Joe and Larry get along so well, because Larry invites Joe over to his house for dinner all the time. Dot's a great cook and Joe often says so, but Joe is really still a kid, and his parents are glad that Larry and Dot, along with Tom and Stella, and Myrt and me look out for him.

Although Joe races for Tom out of the San Jose dealership, my Palo Alto dealership isn't far away and it's closer to the Belmont track, so with motorcycle racing there every Friday night during the summer, Joe spends a lot of Friday's at my shop. He's asked my advice about riding at Belmont a time or two, but he soon had the track figured out. If I were to guess, I think Joe comes around the shop to hear my old race stories more than anything.

***** ***** *****

Each summer we try to take a family vacation to Big Sur. The jagged coast line that starts from Carmel going south is a beautiful place to spend time in. The night before we left, we loaded up the Oldsmobile with our food and camping gear, and the next morning we got the kids into the car half-asleep and made the two and a half hour drive. While the kids and I enjoy camping, Myrt doesn't care that much for it, but she goes along so we can be together as a family.

We arrived at the Pfeiffer campground and proceeded to set up our big canvas tent. The tent is always a chore. It took a half hour before we could move our stuff into it. We'll be staying here for four nights, so we'll have time to unwind. One of the things that I like about going to Big Sur is that I get to fish for mountain trout, and I always bring along a couple bamboo poles for the kids just in case they want to fish too. That's the plan for tomorrow, but today we'll probably walk over to a nearby spring feed pond so that the kids can play in the water, and then later I'll cook hamburgers and some corn on the cob for dinner.

As we set around playing cards that evening, Judy asked me,

"Are you going fishing tomorrow?"

"Yep, bright and early."

"Can you wake me up too? I want to go."

"All right, don't take long to get ready and no complaining about how early it is." Judy is a lot of fun when we go camping and besides her liking to catch fish, she likes to clean them too.

The next morning as the sun came up, I added kindling to the still warm embers and got the fire going to brew some coffee and relax with a cup during the peaceful morning. I let Judy sleep in a little, and when I woke her up, I covered her up in a blanket so that she could keep warm. I got all of our fishing equipment together, and then we walked about a quarter-mile upstream.

By the creek, we climbed down a short slope to a nice spot by a tree for us to sit down. I grabbed one of the bamboo poles, put a line and hook on it with a rubber worm, and gave it to Judy. Then I set up my fishing pole, put a juicy worm on the hook and got down to business. Judy sat by me with her line in the water, but after 20 minutes of no excitement, she lay down with the blanket wrapped around her and fell asleep.

New KR Model

Also this year, Harley came out with a new 45-cubic-inch (750cc) racing model called the KR. The new KR is replacing the WR, which came out in 1937, and it's set up to compete with the lighter and smaller British bikes. Both the WR and KR models are 750cc side valve motors, but the new bike looks a lot different from the old WR. The KR is a smaller framed bike with telescopic front forks instead of the springer-style front end, and it has twin shock absorbers on the rear. The other improvement is that the new model has a foot shift and hand clutch setup instead of the old hand-shift/foot-clutch arrangement.

Once we got one of the new KRs at the shop, we all did laps around the block. It seems like the KR is a dud compared to our WRs because it doesn't have as much horsepower as Tom's and it's heavier too. The WR is a three-speed and the KR is a four-speed, so the bigger transmission adds more weight, but the KR's transmission is housed in the rear of the engine case and not separate like the WR. Since the case has to be bigger to house it, more weight is added. On the plus side, having the engine and transmission in a single unit provides more low-end torque, but the real test will be how the KR does on the mile tracks.

About the time we were getting the next year's models, Joe and Paul Albrecht left on a racing circuit late in the season that is going through Houston, Shreveport, and Texarkana. Albrecht is a good guy for Joe to go with because he's a great rider and someone Joe can watch and learn from. I went up against Albrecht a couple times in my last year of racing, and he's always a contender, so they should get some wins on the trip.

It's a tough circuit down south and, to add to the unpleasantness, it's usually humid and hot as hell. I was surprised to hear that about a week and a half after they left, Paul and Joe returned early because Joe had gotten hurt in a crash. I went by to check up on Joe early one evening at the YMCA where he's been staying. The YMCA on Third and Santa Clara is a good place for a single guy, and it only costs $2.50 a week (or 50 cents a day) for a bunk in the barracks style room. Besides being cheap, the other good thing is that it has both an indoor pool and an indoor wooden running track that Joe can use to stay in shape and help keep the weight off.

After parking my Harley, I went inside and found Joe where he is bunked.

"How's the leg, Guiseppe?"

"Hey Santo, it's been better."

Joe is sitting in a chair with his leg up on the mattress as he bent forward to shake hands. "How's Myrt?"

"Good." I said as I sat down on a nearby bed. "She says to come by for dinner once you're okay. So what the hell happened?"

"Well, Paul and I were at the Texarkana half mile, which is a crappy track that's more of a rounded off triangle than an oval. Many of those southern tracks have crash barriers that are made of barbed wire stretched between metal fence posts, plus they have wooden planks intertwined in the barbed wire to add strength. At Texarkana, most of the metal posts holding the crash barriers are bent over from previous crashes. I'm surprised that it was even an AMA-sponsored event because they had no concept of safety down there."

"With this being late in the year, the sun is at a low angle and, when I was coming out of turn one into turn two the sun is directly in my eyes.
I thought things were okay, but I got bumped, and the next thing I knew I went tumbling towards the outer fence and got tangled in barb wire which sliced me up, but my leg took the worst of it. What I didn't realize is that I had a sliver of metal under the skin by my right shin."

As he said this, he lifted his pants leg to show me a long cut on his shin. "My leg hurt like hell, but I just ignored it until the lower half of my leg started swelling up. Paul was still racing, and I didn't want to stop him from making money. But as my leg got worse, Paul convinced me that I had a problem and needed to get to a doctor. Well, I wasn't going to have some hillbilly doctor in Arkansas working on me, so I got a shot for the pain, and Paul drove for two days straight to get us back to San Jose as my leg was throbbing the whole way."

"When I got to a San Jose doctor, he used a scalpel to cut a five inch slice in my leg and green puss came out, but thankfully the intense pain I felt went away nearly at the same time. My leg was so infected that the doctor said in another 2 or 3 days I probably would have lost it to gangrene. The doctor put some powder on my leg, wrapped it and said to come back in a week, or if it looks okay don't come back, so here I am."

"So the leg feels okay now?"

"Sure. I'm just trying to stay off it. I'll be ready to race in a week or so."

That's Joe, upbeat as usual, even though he could have lost his leg if he had screwed around much longer.

***** ***** *****

A couple weeks after I visited Joe at the YMCA, he came into the dealership and said that he and Diane (Gilbert) had gotten married over the weekend. They've been dating for a little while, but this is the first time that I had heard anything mentioned about marriage. (Nov 24, 1951) After getting her parents' approval, Joe and Diane tied the knot at the Reno courthouse with her sister Ellen and her husband Herb serving as witnesses.

Herb Bosch works for Tom at the San Jose dealership and he's a top mechanic. Herb does well in hill climbs and in enduros, but at close to 300 pounds, he's a big boy, so track races aren't for him. We've known Diane for several years, she is two years older than Sammy, and as a teenager she used to come to some of the races with Ellen and Herb. At first, when we heard that Joe and Diane got married, we kind of wondered if they had to, but they are just young and impulsive like a lot of people at their age. Hopefully married life won't slow Joe down on the track, but we'll have to wait until next season to find that out.

***** ***** *****

The following weekend, Tom and I made a quick trip up to Lewiston, Idaho, for the National Hill Climb Championship. Although most nationals are late in season and use the current point rankings to select which riders to invite, the Lewiston National is in May and uses the rankings from the previous year. Several riders from the West Coast are here, and many of these I have been up against before.

It's hard to say if I needed better bikes, or it just wasn't my day, but I came in second in both divisions. I thought I had come prepared, but this is the first time that I've ever gone to a National Championship and didn't walk away with a first place trophy. I lost to Windy in 45-cubic-inch division and to Roy Burke in 80-inch division. Roy is a BSA dealer in Oregon, but he rode on a borrowed Harley. I know that BSAs aren't set up for hills, but it's funny that a BSA dealer is using a Harley to compete.

Meanwhile Dick Austin is still using the old police bike that Tom built and, after winning a National at Corvallis, he used the bike at Friant Dam to top the hill in 4.26 seconds, beating the 4.6 second record time that I had set five years ago on my spaghetti-framed Class-A climber.

Local Racers

Charlie West is a local guy and a good racer, but an even better builder, and he started working at the dealership a couple months ago. Charlie has been racing both motorcycles and open cockpit jalopies since the late 1940s, and he's known to build fast motors. Charlie had his own shop for car repairs, but he specialized in building motors for the guys that race at the Santa Clara fairgrounds. Once Charlie got the offer to work for Tom, he closed his shop and became Tom's assembler for racing motors.

Tom is a genius at designing cams, head patterns, and other improvements, but Charlie is the right guy to put it all together. He'll have everything aligned correctly with the proper clearances, and he'll make sure that the motor is perfectly tuned and balanced. Charlie is meticulous, and you can eat off his motors before they are put together. So Charlie is a big addition to the Sifton team, and when you have two or three guys that are racing nearly every Friday and Sunday for about seven months of the year, you need someone full time just for rebuilding race motors.

Shortly into the 1952 season, Bobo earned a rare hat trick at Belmont. During time trials Bobo had the fastest time of the day which put him into the trophy dash with the day's four fastest riders. In the short four-lap race, Bobo beat all of the other hot shots. Then, after winning his heat, he was put on the outside back row for the 15-lap main race. Even with having to start in the back, Bobo crossed the stripe first and, by winning the three events, earned the hat trick.

Joe raced for Tom in the second half of last year and did really well. And now, this season, he's giving Kenny a run for his money as Tom's top rider. Belmont is our local track and, as Joe began beating his teammate there on a regular basis, that didn't go over too well with Kenny. Kenny soon started telling people that Tom gave Joe the better bike and that's why Joe's been beating him. Before long word got around to Tom about the things being said and he called Kenny into his office. The discussion got a little heated, with Tom basically telling Kenny that if he didn't like things the way things were, he could leave, so that's what Kenny did.

With Tom down a rider, Charlie started riding for the Sifton team, but he continued to ride his own bike, so he's more of an independent. As far as the accusation that Tom was giving Joe the best stuff, Joe is just a better rider. If you give Joe a bike that's anywhere close to what everyone else is riding, he's going to win the race. With all of the success from Tom's team of local riders, they got the nickname "the San Jose Bunch." Now when any of Tom's riders show up at a track, the other riders know that they are at a disadvantage before the race even starts.

***** ***** *****

The Modesto hill climb is at Ospital Canyon on Easter weekend and it's a top climb each year. Like some of the other hills, this has a big ditch running across the path about three-fourths of the way up. If you are going too fast when you hit the ditch, you might get bounced off your bike, but if you are going too slow, you'll lose traction and won't make it far up the hill.

On my first run, I made the small jump across the ditch and kept both traction and momentum going and posted a good time, but I was the second fastest rider so far. On my second pass, I was going faster, and I jumped the ditch pretty much as planned, but the back end lifted too much off the ground, and once the tire chains reconnected, things got ugly. The bike bounced at least four feet off the ground, and I lost my hold of the handle bars so I'm several feet off of the seat. For a split second, I seemed to stop in mid-air, but when I came back to earth, something grabbed my leg, and I knew that I was in trouble. My left leather pants leg is caught in the spinning chain, and I can't do anything.

When I slammed back on the bike, I bent the handle bars downward so that the dead man's switch didn't work. Another bad thing is that instead of landing on my seat, I came down behind the short rear fender, so I am literally sitting on the spinning (horizontal) chains covering the rear tire and those spinning tire chains aren't gentle. I managed to kill the motor and come to a halt, and then the bike and I fell over. The hill crew rushed over to help, and it took some effort to get me free from the chain.

My pants leg is shredded, and my leg looks like hamburger, plus it feels like someone took a blow-torch to my bare skin. On top of that, my butt feels like it has been chewed on by a pair of junkyard dogs.

I made it to the ambulance to get looked over. Once they saw my leg, they had me hold it up so that they could pour merthiolate over it to clean the wound. Once they started pouring, pain shot through my body. It took a minute to recover from the shock, and they had me stand up inside the ambulance and pull down what was left of my pants and shorts.

Then I had to bend over so they could pour merthiolate on my shredded butt. For some reason they had the back doors of the ambulance open, so the curious people that like to look inside to see what is going on got an eyeful. As they poured the liquid, it felt like fire and I damn near passed out. I've never felt pain like that in my life and I doubt that I'll be able to sit for a week.

***** ***** *****

Tulare has a night race in September, and Larry is coming along with Bobo and Joe to pit. Tulare is a dangerous track, and at night it's especially so. The flood lights that illuminate the track are on tall posts near the middle of the track, and while it's bright on the straights, it's dark in the corners. A six-foot wooden fence going around the outside of the track has the fence posts on the inside of the wall instead of outside, so you don't want to clip one of those because it would be like hitting a tree. To make things worse, just yesterday they had horse races, and the half-mile track is in terrible shape. It's a cushioned track with a couple inches of loose soil, but the cushion was too much for the horses, and their hooves created ruts near the outside of the track from where they had run.

Guys from different areas have their own styles, and while most of our local guys go wide down the straights and then cut back in the corners, the riders from down south like staying close the outside most of the time. On the third lap of Bobo's qualifying heat, one of the Southern California guys riding further out got caught in a horse rut and kissed the outside fence which laid him out on the track. Bobo narrowly missed the rider as he went down, but three other riders got caught up in the crash. By the time the black flag came out to stop the race, four guys were laying on the backstretch, two of them dead and two others badly injured.

As a racer you know this is a dangerous sport, and once your number is called, your time is up. But most seasoned riders think a certain way, and when they are confronted with a loss of one of their own out on the track, they pay their respects, block it out, and get ready for the restart.

Chapter 3 / Drag Race

Guys always drop by the dealership, and it's kind of a social scene, but some of their wives don't like their husbands spending so much time here. It's not like we are drinking or causing trouble, we're just talking about motorcycles and telling stories. I don't think that the wives care much for me because I'm in the center of it all, but I can't help it that I'm popular.

Folks like to brag about their bikes, which is fine, but sometimes they can get under my skin. Roger Hardcastle is a young guy that hangs around the shop, and besides being a hill climber, he also races drag bikes and does pretty well at it. Roger likes to talk about how much horsepower his drag bike has compared to our hill climb bikes. I get along with Roger, and I know that he's just trying to rile me up, but one day I took the bait.

"Roger, I'll switch my hill climber into a drag bike and spank your bike anytime you want, just say when." That really stopped the conversation for the guys standing around.

"Come on Sam, your bike can't beat mine on the strip."

"I think it can, and money talks and bullshit walks. Let me get my bike ready and find someone to pilot it, then we'll see who has the better bike."

"Okay Sam, how much?" He replied.

"Fifty bucks."

"You're on."

I said, "Give me two weeks to get my bike ready, and we'll meet to settle this."

My hill climber is already maxed out with the best of everything Tom has, so I'm not worried about power. The main thing is changing the gearing and massive sprocket to something for a quarter mile of high-end speed instead of gearing it for 400 feet of low-end torque.

I switched the bikes current transmission (hill climbers only need one gear), to a three-speed unit. Outside of a few other minor changes, like picking up a rear racing slick, the bike is close to ready, and all I need now is a rider. I know plenty of racers, but drag strips are a different world, so I contacted Red Cummings, and he agreed to pilot the bike. Red has drag bike experience, plus I'm sure he doesn't weight more than 100 pounds, so he's a good choice for the bike.

Near the border of Redwood City and San Carlos they have a pair of old, abandoned runways that they have drag races on, so we will meet there to see who comes out on top. I hauled the bike up to the runways on race day behind Myrt's 1950 Oldsmobile Holiday 88. When I made it there, they are also having drag race competitions for cars on the second runway and anyone can sign up for it. I plan to be here most of the afternoon, so I went and entered Myrt's car in the drag competition. A couple years ago when I bought the Oldsmobile, it was one of the hottest cars you could buy off the showroom floor. In fact, that year modified Oldsmobile 88s won six of nine NASCAR Grand Nationals.

This is the first time that I'll be racing with four wheels instead of two, so I don't really have high hopes, I'll just see what the 88 can do. I won't go toe-to-toe against someone, instead it will be a solo run with the best time in the stock eight-cylinder class being declared the winner. I always run high octane gasoline in the Oldsmobile, and I gave it a tune-up recently, so it's running good. After an hour or so of watching the action on both of the former air strips, they called me to get the Oldsmobile lined up for my single pass.

The Olds is in gear and I have one foot on the brake and the other on the gas brake-torqueing the motor. As the green light flashed, I took off down the pavement. The Olds performed great and topped 92 mph in 15.6 seconds for the quarter mile as I crossed the stripe. I ended up winning the stock division and even received a small 1st place trophy for my efforts.

It's getting close to time for Red's race, so I went over to the other runway and waited with Red and the bike. When it is time to get ready, I helped Red get his gear cinched up and pushed the idling bike over to the waiting area. Then Red rode my converted hill-climber out on the pavement and lined up against Hardcastle at the starting line. As the first yellow light lit up, they revved the motors, as the second yellow light went by and the green light flashed, they took off like bullets and disappeared down the runway. It was a close race, but Red beat Hardcastle by a couple hundredths of a second, and that ended his bragging at the dealership.

I know that Joe is over at Snows Go Cart tracks across the highway, so after I loaded the bike, I went by to rib Joe a little on my win in the family car. Cart racing is really popular, so much so that we're even selling carts at the dealership and Snows is a busy hang out for go cart racers. Cart racing pretty much started with 4-stroke singles bought at Sears and progressed to specialized shops building 100cc 2-stroke carts that go 80 mph on the track. Some higher-end set-ups have dual motors which can push the cart to 100 mph, and when you're sitting less than a foot off the ground in one of those things, it feels like you're driving a rocket.

I saw Joe over at the track. "What are you up to Moke?"

"Riding carts, goofing around."

I'm setting him up now. "Win anything?"

"No, it's just a bunch of kids."

"Look what I just picked up," I said as I showed him my new trophy.

"Where did you get that?"

"I entered a drag race across the street and won it in the Oldsmobile." Joe couldn't believe that I just showed up and won a trophy racing Myrt's car.

"Well," I smiled and said, "I guess we can't all win."

***** ***** *****

Tuesday morning Joe came into the shop all geared up. "Hey Sam. After I talked to you at Snows, I ended up winning a trophy, but you're not going to believe the story. After you left, I went back on the track, but my dual-motor died and I had to ride one of their single cylinders. Out on the track I had the pedal jammed to the floor and was passing guys left and right, but I couldn't get around this one guy. You can't really see the other driver when he's wearing a helmet, but he was a little guy and pretty good. Whenever I tried to make a move he would edge me out. On the last lap, I chopped over his front wheel going into a corner and got past him, but I think I came across a little desperate."

Joe continued, "Afterwards I was talking to a buddy when a kid that was probably 9 or 10 tugged on my shirt. The kid said, "Joe Leonard, that was a great race we had! My Dad used to race you over at Belmont."

The kid is grinning from ear to ear, and I'm thinking, this can't be true, this kid is the other driver I was up against? Here I was a grown man beating a ten-year old out on the track. I'm holding the little three-inch trophy that I won and said to him, "Here you go kid."

"Mr. Leonard you don't have to do that."

"No, I want to." The kid was happier than a dog with two dicks.

After he finished telling the story I said as serious as possible, "Moke, you win a trophy, you take it home." He laughed, shook his head, and walked back into the service area.

Bobo came into the shop one afternoon and said that he got his draft notice to serve in the Korean conflict. He says that he'll do a few weeks of boot camp in New Jersey, have a short furlough, and then he'll go overseas to do a two-year hitch. Now I'm left without a rider.

Return to San Jose

After running the Palo Alto dealership for three years, I sold the place to Herb Boesch and Bernie Bernheisel and returned to Tom's dealership to make the transition to owner. After a couple years of being on my own, I would have preferred moving to San Mateo to open a dealership out from under Tom's shadow, but Howard Overby owns a Harley Davidson dealership on Evans Avenue in San Carlos, and he has the territorial rights for the San Mateo area. At least the factory is glad to hear that I'll be the guy taking over the Sifton dealership, to hear them tell it, the Arena name, Harley Davidson, and San Jose are all intertwined.

Tom and I worked out a purchase agreement and it will take one year for me to pay it off and then I'll become the sole owner. Tom said that he'll let the inventory get low throughout the year so that it will be easier for me to cover the monthly payments once I take over. Herman Liebenberg, Al Fernandez, Lee McReynolds, and Charlie West are the current mechanics at the shop, and I think they are all planning on staying around. Also, Myrt is going to continue doing the books like she did at the Palo Alto dealership, so that's one less thing I have to worry about.

As far as guys racing out of the dealership, besides Joe, the other racer is Lee "Mac" McReynolds. Mac came on as a mechanic for Tom in 1951 and began riding for Tom this season. Mac started racing a little older than most, but he got up to speed quickly and won the Stockton Mile in the novice division. Charlie doesn't race much anymore; he focuses on building Joe's bikes. With Bobo going into the service, unless someone really catches my eye, I'll probably hold off on finding another rider.

After boot camp, Bobo got his two-week furlough to visit home, and he wants to get in one last race at Belmont before shipping out. We set up a WR from the shop and got it ready for Bobo, but as Friday rolled around, the race got rained out. San Luis Obispo is having a T.T. race on Sunday, so we'll get Bobo set up for a T.T. instead. That doesn't give us much time to change over from a flat track bike to something ready for a T.T. race, but we'll switch out the rear tire to something with a little more grab and add a rear brake to the bike.

For the Sunday race at San Luis Obispo, things were clicking for Bobo and he pulled out a first place finish. It's a good send off for Bobo because he's shipping out in a couple days for Germany where he's going to be stationed.

Cams Are King

As Tom got out from the daily duties of running a dealership, he devoted more of his time to tuning and making improvements on the motors. While he made some improvements to the KRs when the first models came out (Sept. 1951), he's going to focus on really improving the 750cc motor when things slow down this winter. When Everett Brashear won the Sturgis five-mile national late last year, it was the KR's first national win, but they have a lot of room for improvement, and Indians are still the bikes to beat. Bobby Hill and Bill Tuman are the top Indians riders: Hill won the Springfield Mile the past two years while Tuman won the Bay Meadows National this season.

Tom isn't a big talker, and when he's whistling under his breath to no song in particular, you know the wheels in his mind are spinning. Tom can be in his white undershirt in front of the lathe grinding metal for hours as the sparks are flying, and for him it's enjoyable. He designs his cams with larger lobs that push the valves open longer to take in more gas and create more power. But he and Tim Withum, who is like the Triumph version of Tom, have to build their own valve springs to handle the increased tension from being kept open longer.

When it's time to create a new cam, Tom provides the overall cam specifications to his vendor, and they manufacture and supply the 20-foot long metal blanks which are about two inches in diameter. The length of cams range from about three inches on the bigger bikes, to around a half-inch on the KRs. The KR's 45-cubic-inch motor has four cams made from two masters.

Starting with the narrow metal bar, Tom will cut off a piece and drill a hole in the center to hold the piece of metal in place while he works it over on the lathe. He'll grind off the excess metal and work the lobs to match the dimensions of the master. He will create two identical intake cams for the front and rear valves, and a set for the front and rear exhaust cams. After creating each "lob," they are pushed on a short shaft with a gear already on one end and welded into place. Once Tom has the cams made to his satisfaction, they are sent off to be hardened.

It's an exacting process to harden cams correctly. The metal must be heated to a specific temperature over a set time period, then the cams are placed in oil to cool, and the process is repeated until the metal gets to the right density. Rockwell is the hardness rating for metal, and while 60 Rockwell is hard and durable for motorcycle cams, 80 Rockwell is too brittle and more likely to break. So the guys at Santa Clara Hardening have to know what they're doing, or the cams can break apart under power in mid-race.

One day, Al is finishing work on a cam and walked away for a moment. While he was gone, Tom came around and proceeded to do a little extra work on the cam and somehow nicked it. When Al came back and saw what happened, he got a little worked up.

"What are you doing, you hamburger."

Tom looked at him. "You're calling me hamburger?"

"Well, the cam didn't need any more work, and now it's scrap metal."

After that, Tom started calling Al "Hamburger." For the next couple days it was hamburger this, and hamburger that. Soon the nickname caught on, and everyone from the shop guys to racers passing through town was calling him "Hamburger." So in a way he brought it upon himself.

Tom spent weeks designing and machining a new four-cam set for the motor. He had new pistons made, and he machined a new set of heads to match. Toms is friends with Louie Thomas who owns a motorcycle shop in Los Angeles and has a dynometer to measure horsepower and all of the different testing equipment needed. Tom worked it out to rent the dyno for two days and took two motors, with a combination of cams, pistons, heads, exhaust pipes (ranging from 32 to 37 inches), and all the parts he might need, and drove to Los Angeles.

During those two days Tom found the right combination to produce an extra two horses on the stock KR motor, bumping it up to 50 horses. With that horsepower edge, and the way that Joe rides, there's no telling what might happen this year in the win column.

After Tom made it back to the San Jose dealership, he built two race-ready KRs. When Tom needs to test his new modifications, the usual way is to take the bike out to Balsa Road. The road is long, flat, and out in the middle of nowhere with very little traffic, so it's a great place for test runs. I used to do it for Tom years ago, but Charlie and Joe are his test pilots nowadays.

The three of them went out early one morning to Balsa Road with the new KRs. As Charlie and Joe sat on their idling bikes, Tom took off in his hemi-powered Chrysler, and when it leveled off at 70 mph, Tom signaled out of the window for his riders to take off. This isn't a speed test; Tom wants them to get even with him and then roll the throttles to see how the bikes pull against his constant speed of 70 mph.

They probably went out to Balsa road a little too often because one morning the cops arrived and told Tom that people were complaining about the morning noise, so he needed to find somewhere else to test out his bikes. These bikes have short straight pipes coming off the motor, and when those RPMs go up, you can hear the sound over a mile away.

Gypsy Tour

When the Gypsy Tour restarted a couple years ago, they switched the event from the 4th of July weekend to the three-day Memorial weekend and added a T.T. race to the festivities. Even with the T.T. race, the weekend's high-point is still the 15-lap flat track race. This year some of the riders competing besides Joe will be Kenny, Charlie, and Gene Thiessen who will be racing one of the single-cylinder BSA Gold Stars that just came out. Last year, at the Gypsy Tour, Joe won both the T.T. and the half-mile race, so we all pretty much figure that he's going to win again this year, and the only question is who will come in second.

By the time the checkered flag waved, Joe came in first on his KR as expected, while in second place by nearly a straightaway is Kenny. But then, right after the race ended, Kenny went to the officials and protested. It took a while to figure what Kenny's beef is, but when a rider spun out during the race and the caution flag came out, everyone slowed down except Joe who got sideways coming out of the corner before slowing down. Kenny's protest is that he was ahead of Joe when the yellow flag came out, but Joe passed him instead of keeping his position. It was close, but it looked like Joe was already past Kenny by the time that the flag came out.

If it did happen, the race officials should have seen Joe move ahead of his position and the race would have been restarted with Joe in the back row. Even in a restart, Joe would have won again, so no one could believe that Kenny is making a fuss. Kenny tends to be a crybaby, and if he doesn't win, he has a ready excuse on why it wasn't his fault - that's just the way he is. Kenny is a good rider; it's just his mouth that gets him into trouble.

After a big discussion between the officials, the lead referee Aub (Aubrey) Isham, who is a really good guy and also a good hill climber that we all know, came over and talked to Joe. Aub said that he was sorry, but since it's a formal protest, and they aren't 100% sure if Joe passed Kenny or not when the flag came out, they had no choice but to disqualify him. With Joe disqualified, the second place rider, which is Kenny, was declared the winner. Joe knew that Aub is just doing his job, so he isn't upset with him, but Joe made a point of laughing at Kenny afterwards for complaining.

Protesting to the officials on Joe soured most of the guys on Kenny, and besides, Kenny is riding a Triumph for my bitter rival Phillie Cancilla. I grew up with Phillie's oldest brother Frankie and we're good friends, but I can't get along with Phillie. Most guys don't mind him, but we've gotten nose to nose before, although it's never come to throwing punches.

My problem with Phillie, besides the fact that I don't like Triumphs, is that he's notorious for building strokers when only stock cylinder bores are allowed. After one hill climb when Phillie's rider came in second, Phillie pushed the bike into his trailer and wouldn't let the stewards check it over. By refusing the inspection, everyone knew he was cheating and going to get caught. Everyone makes improvements to their bikes, but it's still done within the rules for Class C.

The day after the half-mile race is the T.T. event. They use the half-mile track as the basis for the T.T. race, but the racers travel in the opposite direction and take a turn into the nearby field for a small jump. Then the track curves a couple times before reaching a straight-away heading back to where they could open the bikes up. Joe is riding the 74-inch police bike that Tom built for Dick Austin nicknamed the "Big Inch" and it's been switched over for T.T. races. The bike is just plain blue and not much to look at, but when Tom builds a bike, looks aren't a concern, all that matters is how it performs.

The difference between this T.T. bike and Joe's usual race bikes, besides the bigger motor size and brakes, is that this one has floor boards. Tom added the boards so Joe wouldn't get the urge to put his feet down going into corners because this track isn't smooth and his feet could really get banged up if he put them down. It took Joe a while to get the hang of riding with both feet flat, but once he got comfortable, he had the boards lightly dragging ground as he slid through corners. As expected, Joe scraped the floor boards to a win for two years in a row.

***** ***** *****

Joe and Al are putting in a lot of miles of driving to national events, and they loaded up the trailer with a KR and spare parts and made their way east in mid-June. Joe proved to be the real deal by winning the inaugural Windber road race and Sturgis nationals before coming back to San Jose to get ready for the Bay Meadows mile.

The upcoming Bay Meadows National in San Mateo is gearing up to be a huge event with a tough crowd of riders. Guys like Bill Tuman and Bobby Hill will be there on their Indian Scouts, and they always put up a fight, but Hill has had the #1 plate for the past two years, so he's the man. Lots of riders will be there trying to make the cut, but only 16 will advance to the final.

When race day came, everyone is at Bay Meadows and the place is buzzing. Charlie has the bike running great, and although Joe is considered an underdog, a lot of people's hopes around here are riding on him. During the qualifying heats for the experts, Joe and Hill sailed through, and Joe has his laps down into the high 42-second range, so things are looking good for him.

Joe is focused even before they lined up, and by the time the 20-lap race ended, Joe won convincingly by a quarter lap over Al Gunter on a BSA single, while Bobby Hill on his Indian Scout came along in third. For all of the excitement building up to the race, it took just 14 minutes and 30 seconds to complete. After Joe's big win, all of us were happy as hell. Sammy even said that this was one of the happiest days of his life.

***** ***** *****

One evening the kids were out with their friends, and Myrt and I didn't have any plans for the evening, so we went to see "The Wild One" at the theatres. Myrt and I were there at the 1947 Hollister Gypsy tour that the movie is supposedly based upon, so we're interested in how they're going to show it. Marlon Brando and Lee Marvin portray leaders of rival biker gangs who take over a small town which leads to mayhem and eventually the death of an innocent citizen. During that three-day weekend nobody was killed, and most of the guys that actually got hurt were from racing at the half-mile track outside of town.

In the movie practically every bike is a British motorcycle, but at the actual event three-fourths of the motorcycles were Harley Davidson's. Triumph sponsored the movie which is the reason for nearly everyone riding Triumphs. Lee Marvin is one of the few that rode a Harley Davidson while Marlon Brando rode a 650cc Triumph Thunderbird. Triumph became my main competitor after Indian went out of business, so I'm not thrilled with all of the publicity they're getting.

But the main problem I have is that most of the riders were portrayed as thugs. The movie seemed to glamorize bad behavior but all of the riders I know are good people, so this is giving motorcycle riders an undeserved bad image. One of the interesting things is that in the color movie poster out in the lobby, Lee Marvin is wearing the yellow and black colors of the Palo Alto Yellow Jackets Motorcycle Club that I started. Overall, the movie is pretty silly and nothing like what actually happened in Hollister six years ago.

***** ***** *****

The Peoria T.T. road races are coming up, and the two previous times that Joe has shown up, he hasn't done well. Hopefully, the third time is a charm. The special thing about Peoria is that it's the only event with two national championship races happening on the same day for both 45 and 80-cubic inchers. Like most riders that show up at Peoria, Joe has a bike for both events. He brought a KR, with brakes and rear suspension instead of the rigid rear end, for the 45 inch group, and he also brought along The Big Inch for the 80-cubic-inch division.

Ahead of the races on the big day, some of the local riders couldn't believe that Joe has a smaller 74-cubic-inch bike when nearly everyone else brought the bigger 80-cubic-inch motors. Joe even had to deal with some knuckleheads telling him that he might as well pack it up because Sodie is going to win both races anyway. Roger "Sodie" Sodistrom is the local Harley Davidson dealer, and he's usually the big winner. He won one of the events in 1949, both classes in 1950, and one in 1952. Joe's hero Jimmy Phillips won both in 1951, so Sodie doesn't have a stranglehold on Peoria, but he's the one to watch out for.

The Peoria T.T. track is set in a canyon on what is basically a half-mile track, just with both left and right turns and a couple hills to qualify it as a T.T. race. The race begins on the half mile oval track, then off turn one is a small hill that you get airborne on, and by the time you get your bike straightened out, there is another jump. The second hill at Peoria is so high that it's a blind jump, and you can't see the other side at all. During time trials, Joe figured out how to jump on one side of the hill, turn the bike in midair, and land where he needed to be on the way down.

First up is the 45-cubic-inch group, and Joe's eager to silence the locals. After the past two years at Peoria, Joe got the hang of the track and by the time the 14 laps were over, Joe had put a straightaway on Sodie for the win. But Joe doesn't have time to enjoy it because the 80-cubic-inch division will be starting before long.

Winning both events is probably too much to ask for, but you must believe that you can win each time you get out on a track. When the 80-cubic-inch group finished, Sodie got the win and Joe came in third. But Joe got one national championship trophy at Peoria and that's a great accomplishment. Afterwards, Joe saw some of the guys that were giving him a hard time before the race loading up their bikes and Joe felt like rubbing a little salt into the wound so he yelled, "Don't you guys want to come and see the trophy that I couldn't win."

Even though Bill Tuman will have the #1 plate next season for winning Springfield, Joe has won four nationals at Bay Meadows, Sturgis, Peoria, and Windber, which is more than any other rider this year. The AMA announced that next season it will be a championship series consisting of 18 points paying races that will decide the winner, which means that no longer is the champion decided solely on winning the Springfield Mile. The series is mainly made up of flat track races, but it also includes road races such as Daytona and T.T. events at locations like Laconia and Peoria.

Poker Run

Myrt and I are going on a poker run this Sunday with some of the San Jose Dons. We try to have at least one of these each year because it's something fun that couples can do outside of our usual racing events. It's turning out to be a nice afternoon and 24 Dons, along with their wives or girlfriends, committed to ride, and we're meeting at the clubhouse at noon. Everyone showed up, and now we're just waiting for Eddie so we can get our maps and instructions. Fast Eddie, who's not fast at all, is dropping off cards at five different locations around town. We usually place them in city parks so that there's enough space for everyone's bikes.

As he rolled up, Eddie asked, "Everyone ready to go? Here are the written instructions on where the parks are located," he said as he handed out a sheet of paper to each couple. "In four out of the five parks, the cards are in a bag with each of the 24 cards individually wrapped in paper. At one of the parks, I put the cards out in a few different places just to make it a little interesting," he said as he laughed, "but the cards shouldn't be difficult to find.

Keep the cards wrapped until we meet back here later, then everyone can unwrap their cards and present their poker hands at the same time. Happy hunting!"

Everyone did a quick review of the map as Myrt and I got on my bike. As copilot, Myrt is in charge of directions as we got moving. It didn't take long for us to make all of the stops, and in a little less than an hour and a half, we had our five cards. The one spot where the cards weren't all in one bag was at the Rose Garden in Willow Glen. Eddie had set cards against rose bushes throughout the garden, so getting stuck by roses turned out to be the only problem.

When we met back at the clubhouse, four riders had already arrived, and 15 minutes later, everyone is back, so we unwrapped and laid down our cards. Myrt and I had a pair of nines which was good for a third place, but we're just having some fun. Fast Eddie has been cooking on the grill outside while we were running around, so by the time we made it back, he had burgers and sausages ready with sodas and beers on ice.

After many of the Dons' events, someone is cooking something for us like barbequed meat, beans, and garlic bread, so when the guys show up after a local event, there's something to eat. We have a great bunch of guys working at the shop, and with most of them in the Dons too, we see each other nearly every day with all of the racing events we attend. The Dons also have Christmas parties and Halloween costume parties at the clubhouse which are especially big hits, so most of the time we're like one big happy family.

***** ***** *****

Over the past year, I've finished paying off Tom, and I'm now the official owner of the San Jose Harley Davidson Dealership at 580 1st Street. Time has flown by since I first started working for Fred Merlow right out of high school, and it's been just over 20 years since Tom took over the dealership from Mr. Merlow in 1932. I'm happy with how things have turned out, even though my responsibility has increased ten-fold, and I've laid awake nights wondering if I can afford the payments on the inventory and building.

The first motorcycles that I sold since taking over are the 1954 models that started arriving in September of 1953. The basic FL Panhead model is $1000 and two additional packages are available; the standard solo group that costs $28.45, and the deluxe solo group goes for $83.30. Both packages have upgraded tires and rims, but the main difference between them is that the deluxe package has extensive chrome. Another new model is the K that goes for $865, and it has the new rear suspension with tube shocks, which is a big improvement in the ride.

Business at the dealership is looking good, and the Harley Davidson Company has just celebrated its 50th Anniversary. On the other hand, Indian Motorcycles have announced that they are closing their doors. Over the years I've ridden all kinds of motorcycles like a 1915 Thor, a belt driven Excelsior, even a Flying Merkel, and I can appreciate the improvements they bring to the industry. Although Indian calling it quits will help my business, I don't think that it's good that we're the only American motorcycle company left.

***** ***** *****

Years ago when we were first planning the Tin Hat Derby, we checked the farmer's almanac to find out the worst weather of the year, and today it's cold and overcast. I'm sure that many of these guys are wondering why they aren't still home in bed. Since Sammy turned 16 back in October, he's now old enough to enter the event, and he's looking forward to it.

All of the riders met at the clubhouse to sign in, and we have so many entrants that instead of one rider leaving at a time like before the war, two riders per row will be taking off a minute apart. After pulling our start numbers out of a bucket, I'm going to be nearly 20 rows after Sammy, so he'll have to figure things out on his own. Like most riders, Sammy and I have our schedules taped to our gas tanks covered in clear plastic, and by using that guide, plus our wrist watches and the bikes speedometer, that's about all you can do to help level out your speed.

You have to be a smart rider to win an endurance run, because it's not easy to average 24 mph, or roughly six miles every 15 minutes for 200 miles. If Sammy has problems, his fall-back plan is to follow the old-timers that have been in it before and pace off of them. He might lose points at a checkpoint or two, but he'll be closer to averaging 24 mph at the other checkpoints, and his overall point total should be in better shape than if he went it alone.

The trails are muddy, although not as bad as some years, but they'll get worse as the day drags on. Any small mud puddles will get churned into lakes of mud that can easily get you bogged down. Even with starting near the middle of the pack, I've avoided the worst of the trails, and my time has stayed pretty even.

At the halfway point in Boulder Creek, I saw Sammy and rode over by him.

I asked, "How are you doing so far?"

"Good. But my forearms are just a little tired."

"Well, at least we are halfway through. Did you have any problems on the trails?"

"I nearly slid out in the mud once, but I put my foot down into a foot of mud and kept upright."

I looked down to see that his boot is covered in drying mud going up to the middle of his shin. Sammy is near the end of his 30-minute break, so I'll see him later back at the clubhouse.

A few miles before the pavement starts again in Los Gatos, there is the notoriously bad fire trail leading into town. This stretch is maybe 100 yards long, but it's so steep that with the normal street tires used in Class C events, you mainly do a controlled slide down the hill. Some guys get off of their bikes and kind of walk it down the hill by holding the handlebars and sliding their feet, instead of riding down and risking going off of the side of the trail and really being screwed.

I guess that when it was Sammy's time to go down the hill, he lost control and both he and his bike slipped off the trail and down a 10 foot embankment into a narrow gulley. When they reached the bottom, the bike landed across Sammy's legs and pinned him underneath. As the other riders went by (at least the ones that saw him), they yelled down to make sure he was okay, but since they were on the clock, they kept going. It took Sammy about 20 minutes to wiggle free and push the bike back up to the trail before he could get going again.

With his time way off, Sammy figured that he had to ride wide open all the way until the last checkpoint by the clubhouse. Once Sammy hit the pavement of Los Gatos Boulevard, he cranked the throttle to make up time, at least up until the sirens started blaring, and the Los Gatos cops pulled him over. I showed up when Sammy is pleading his case, and since I knew one of the officers, I kept Sammy from being hauled off to the hoosegow. His time is shot to hell of course by the time we finished, and although I came out in the top 10, it wasn't the showing I hoped for. Herbie Boesch ended up winning it again, so this makes three wins for him which also matches Herman's total.

KR Frame

After bumping up the horsepower last winter, this winter Tom is setting his sights on building a lighter frame to bring down the KRs weight. Tom got to work and planned, designed, and built a more lightweight frame to replace the factory frame. It saves weight as intended, but maybe the most important thing he did is to bend the frame head slightly forward. With the front tire closer to the frame, it's easier to steer and requires less effort. Now the bike's handling is much improved, which will work out better on the flat tracks.

Using your own cam designs is one thing, but non-production frames aren't allowed in National Championship (Class C) events, so the Harley factory needed to be involved. Hank Syvertsen is the head of Harley's racing department and has been for 25 years, so Tom called him. Tom went over his frame modifications, and by the end of the conversation, they had plans to send a couple of their top riders to San Jose to try out Tom's frame.

Tom rented the Hollister half-mile track for the day and paid a crew to prepare it. The factory flew Chuck Basney and Bob Shirey in a Piper Cub to Hollister, and the pilot landed the plane in a level field by the track used for parking. Sammy is standing with me as we watched the Piper Cub land and pull around near the front entrance to the track. Tom had a short talk with Chuck and Bob before they put the KRs through some paces. When Chuck and Bob finished an hour or so later, they were impressed with the handling and said that they would relay their findings to the factory.

A few days later, the frame changes got the green light, and the factory needed to make copies so they could get them into production. We shipped one of the frames to Milwaukee and within a couple weeks, 25 duplicates were built matching Tom's frame. This is just one more example of Tom's engineering skill, and it shows why he's one of the best (if not the best), motorcycle builders in the country.

BSA Sweeps

When Indian folded, for the motorcycle dealers that wanted to stay in the business, they either went with Triumph or with BSA, both of which are the hot brands to have. Hap Alzina was a big wheel at Indian before they went under, and his dealership in Oakland that used to sell Indians switched over to selling BSAs. Hap is a great businessman and with his knowledge of the motorcycle industry, it wasn't before long he was put in charge of BSA's western territory.

Roland Pike is in charge of racing development at BSA, and his team has put together a new line-up of single-cylinder Gold Stars and twin-cylinder Shooting Stars. BSA is planning to unveil the new models at the Daytona 200, and Hap has put together a talented roster of riders including Bobby Hill, Dick Klamfoth, Al Gunter, and Kenny Eggers. With Hill winning Springfield in 1951 and 1952, and Klamfoth winning Daytona three times, Hap is stacking the deck.

We heard that our buddy Paul Goldsmith took an early lead, but by a dozen laps into it, Bobby Hill got out in front, and he's followed by Klamfoth. At the end of the 49-lap race, Hill took the checkered flag 30 seconds ahead of Klamfoth while Tommy McDermott finished third, Gunter fourth and Kenny fifth. This gave BSA not only its first win at Daytona, but a first top-five sweep. Hap Alzina couldn't have asked for anything better to promote the BSA brand.

None of Tom's riders went to Daytona this year. Instead, our focus is on the season's second national at Willow Springs. This is the inaugural event, and the 2.5 mile long track is located about an hour north of Los Angeles, more or less out in the middle of the desert. Sammy and I left for the race early that morning, a few hours before daybreak, and by the time we arrived at Willow Springs, the temperature has to be close to 90 degrees, and it isn't even noon yet. Both the riders and the motors will have to deal with the heat, and besides that, there was a car race a couple days earlier, and the track is in terrible shape.

Joe has bad allergies that cause his nose to run like a sieve. Joe jokes that the reason he has to be out front during races is so that his allergies won't be so bad. It's so windy and dusty here at Willow Springs that his allergies are as bad as it gets. He can't breathe through his nose, and using a handkerchief would be worthless after a couple uses, so Joe cleans out one nostril at a time by closing off one side and blowing. That ritual is how he picked up his nickname. Moco means snot in Mexican, and at first, we called him Moco Joe, but then it got shortened to Moke.

A couple hours before the racing began, Joe is out during practice when his KR's motor blew, and he doesn't have a replacement motor. AMA rules state that you can't use someone else's motor, but Joe is in a pinch, so he talked to Brad Andres about borrowing his extra. To be on the safe side, they decided to meet down the road. When they met to do the exchange, somehow the officials had gotten wind of the plan and showed up at the rendezvous, and Joe was disqualified. He wasn't going to race anyway without a motor, so it didn't really matter.

As the race started, things went along normal enough, but soon the heat started taking a toll on the new KR models, and they began breaking down. By three-fourths of the way into the race, 11 of the 12 Harleys are done for the day. All that the Harley mechanics could do is huddle around the pit area of the last remaining Harley to help anyway they could, but that KR finally broke down too.

Kenny Eggers has been riding a BSA for Hap Alzina, and after getting fifth at Daytona last month, he got out front in the reduced field to hold off Ed Kretz Sr. for the win and his second AMA championship trophy.

After we got Joe's KR back to the dealership, Tom tore apart the motor and found that the needle bearings were too small to handle the motors high RPMs, in addition to the soaring temperatures, and it caused the bearings to overheat and seize. To fix the problem, Tom designed new rod bearings with larger quarter-inch bearings instead of the current eight-inch size, which allows them to spin at half the revolutions so they won't generate as much heat.

Thankfully, Willow Springs is only the second national of the season, and sixteen nationals are still left to go. BSA won the first three races of the year, but after the KR motors got the larger camshaft bearings, things started turning around. Paul Goldsmith won the fourth national of the season at the Columbus half-mile, and the week after the Laconia road race in New Hampshire, Joe lead for every lap and broke the track record by almost three minutes. Joe didn't stop there and followed it up by winning the Wilmot road race in Wisconsin the following weekend.

The next time Joe came around the shop, he bragged to me about breaking the Laconia record by three minutes. "Yea I heard about it. That's something, but it's really nothing."

Joe is thrown by my response. "What do you mean?"

"Follow me." I led him to the back of the shop where a poster of the 1938 Oakland 200 race is hanging from the rafters.

"Tell me what it says." When Joe got to the part about me smashing the old record by 19 minutes and 20 seconds, I said, "Moke, when you get to a 20-minute record breaker, then maybe I'll be interested."

"Where did you get that printed up?"

"It's just a fact" I said as I walked away. I'm needling Joe, but in reality, he's knocking down records left and right, and he is just getting started.

***** ***** *****

The next national of the season is close to home at the Bay Meadows track, and with Joe winning the event last season, he's favored to win again this year. During time trials the day before, Lee "Mac" McReynolds had the fastest time out of all the amateurs. Mac has been doing a good job this year, and one of his wins was the amateur main event at Stockton two months ago. Wayne Bias, who is another San Jose rider, won the expert division at Stockton, so it's been good for the San Jose Bunch.

We arrived on Sunday and the racers have time to get in some hot laps, so Mac got out on the track to warm up and do a couple final laps before the races begin. As Mac is a few laps into it, he is just about to pass a rider on the inside, when Mac got cut off and had to go in low. When he did, he got off the groove and too close on the inside line as his left hand glanced off of one of the posts as he's going about 90 mph. Mac somehow managed to ride back into the pits, but his hand is severely damaged, and he'll soon be going to the hospital. That is really a shame, because with his time from yesterday, he had a great chance to win the amateur division today.

Once we got into the expert division's final event, Joe spun out and is dead last off the line, but he is making his way through the crowd. By lap five he's near the front, and it's coming down to a battle between Joe and Paul Goldsmith. Joe is holding off Goldie for the most part and he's maintaining the lead in front of the fifteen thousand fans. As they are coming around on the final backstretch, Joe managed to stay out front and won by barely a bike length over Goldie. Joe also broke his own 1953 track record by 20 seconds. Even though Charlie West is on an identical bike to Joe's, he came in third a little further back, but he is still ahead of Kenny Eggers on a BSA that came in fourth.

Mac came into work on Tuesday to show us his left hand. The collision with the post didn't break his fingers, it broke his knuckles. They had to drill into the bones at the ends of his fingers and put pins into them with little loops at the end. Through those loops they used banjo wire to tighten against a metal spider web on the back of his hand to keep his fingers straight. The contraption held everything in place, and it spread his hand out like a fan so that his knuckles could heal correctly, but that is going to take a couple months.

Chapter 4 / Springfield Mile

The 1954 Springfield Mile is on August 22, and Al and Joe are leaving a week early to make the drive. With the history of the Springfield Mile, it's still the biggest race out there, and the one that everyone wants to win, so top riders from all over the country will be there ready to compete.

As they made their way across the Midwest, the temperature has been steadily climbing, and when they arrived in Springfield, they found themselves in the midst of a week of 100-degree temperatures. On race day, the temperature is 103 degrees at the track and the humidity is horrible. Just being out in the sun saps your strength, and with time to kill before qualifying, Joe went to find a cool place to relax while Al stayed with the bike.

At the stadium, they have a tunnel going under the track leading to the infield, and it's probably 10-15 degrees cooler down there than above ground. They even have a couple cots along the sides of the tunnel for people affected by the heat. With no one around, Joe lay down to relax before his qualifying race came up. Joe is a big fan of napping, and knowing Joe, he was probably out carousing the night before, so it didn't take long before he fell asleep.

Forty riders get invited to Springfield, but only 14 riders make it into the big event. Qualifying consists of four 10-man heats with the first three riders in each heat advancing. The riders that came in 4, 5, and 6 in those four heats go into the 10 lap semifinal, with the top two making it into the main event for a total of 14 riders. But as always, first you have to qualify to advance.

As qualifying is about to start, Joe is missing, no one knows where he is, and things are getting frantic. Everyone is searching, and Al somehow located him sleeping in the tunnel and shook him awake. They made it through the crowd in time to get the bike started and lined up for the heat. When the qualifying race began, Joe is groggy from getting back into the heat after being snapped awake. For the first eight laps, Joe is in last place and things aren't looking good, but he woke up and made it into third place in the last two laps to qualify for the main event.

If Joe and Al went to Springfield and didn't qualify because Joe was sleeping, it would have been a very long trip to San Jose, and not a very pleasant homecoming from Tom.

When Joe got back to the pits, he started hearing it from everyone.

"Hey Joe, this racing stuff isn't getting in the way of your naps is it?"

Another guy said, "Good thing the nickname Sleepy is already taken."

Joe might have felt embarrassed, but laughed it off. "I qualified didn't I, what's the problem?" When it came time for the 25-lap main event, Joe is far from being asleep, and he's out to prove that his lackluster qualifying time was just a fluke.

Everyone is getting their bikes started and keeping their motors revved to prevent the plugs from fouling. Joe likes to close his eyes for a few moments before a race and plan things out in his mind. As he lined up at the starting line with the 13 other riders, Joe is all business. When the green flag dropped, Joe crushed everyone over the 25 laps and won the race by a straightaway over Bill Tuman. With his win on this big stage, Joe has officially arrived.

***** ***** *****

Sammy is in high school, and he's at the age when he needs transportation, so about six months ago I sold him a yellow 1942 Chevy coupe that I took in on trade. I got a good deal and only paid $50 for it, but as a businessman, I always try to make a profit on each transaction or I wouldn't stay in business very long, so I sold it to him for $100. It didn't take long to find out that it isn't a very good car and it soon started having problems and breaking down. Sammy has resorted to bringing the car into his high school's auto shop to keep it running.

Sammy has called me at work a couple times to have me bring the shop truck over and tow his car back to the dealership so the guys could get it running for him. The car has been in our service area so many times that on one slow day, the guys painted over the banana yellow color and gave the coupe a jet black paint job. But it is like putting lipstick on a pig, it might look better, but it still has the same problems.

***** ***** *****

At the Langhorne national in Pennsylvania, Everett Brashear took first in the expert main event, and Brad Andres is the winner in the amateur division. Everett is lucky that he's even around. Back in May he got into a crash at a night race in Alabama and ended up in a coma.

Everett was in a coma for a couple weeks, and when he woke up out of the blue, he couldn't remember what happened. They told him about how his bike was having problems during the race, and when he pulled off to the side of the track to check the bike over, he got hit by another rider. Everett had a broken arm and leg, but the head injury was the biggest concern. Only a couple people knew, but the crash also severed the optical nerve in his left eye, so he's blind in that eye. After Everett recovered and began feeling better, he started racing just three months after he awoke from his coma. Even more amazing is that he pulled off the win at Langhorne over Joe and Brad.

After the race, Everett along with Joe, Al, and Brad went out to celebrate. I guess they had a few too many beers to go along with a good meal before they got out on the highway to make the next race. Everett was driving a 1939 Cadillac and a trailer with all of their bikes and tools was being towed behind. As Everett was driving along about 90 mph at night they came to a "Y" in the road, one guy said to go left and someone else said right, but he ran out of road before making a decision and went straight. The car rolled a half-dozen times and somehow managed to land on its wheels and by some miracle none of the guys got hurt.

The Cadillac's roof had crumpled in, and the windshield along with most of the windows had busted out. After they got over the initial shock of the crash, they pushed the roof up so it didn't hit them in the head, hooked back up the trailer that had come off of the hitch and rolled to a stop, and drove on to the last national at the Hammond half-mile in Indiana.

Grand National Champion

When the 1954 season wrapped up, Joe had won eight of the 18 National events. One day in late August was especially impressive when he won both of the Peoria T.T. nationals, just like his hero Jimmy Phillips did in 1951. Interestingly, this year Jimmy came in second to Joe in both of these events at Peoria.

Joe had four national wins in a row at one point, so who was going to be the winner of the first ever series-determined championship was never in question. Joe was crowned the Grand National Champion by a landslide. Coming in second in the points total is our friend Paul Goldsmith, the same guy that Joe rode behind in practice at Bay Meadows three years ago.

Behind Joe's 76 points, and Goldsmith's 39 points, coming in third place with 31 points was Charlie West. Besides working on his own motors, Charlie is building Joe's motors too. Charlie is a good racer, but like the others, he has the misfortune of having to compete against Joe. Although Charlie wasn't able to win any nationals this year, he scored points in five nationals to push him to third in the overall rankings. The season might have started out rough for Harley Davidson because of the overheating problem the KRs had early in the season, but once the KR's got fixed, they came in first place for 13 out of the remaining 15 races.

Although Tom is no longer the dealership owner, he still works out of the shop since everything he needs is here, and Tom is trying to get more National Championships wins. Tom's profile jumped when Larry won the three one-mile championships in 1950. Then, as Joe became the first points-based champion, the Sifton name went to being known nationally.

Fairly often, out-of-state Harley racers make the pilgrimage to visit the shop, but they are less than impressed with the looks of the Sifton, and now Arena Dealership. It might not be a place of beauty, but guys can't dismiss the success that has come out of the shop. When riders stop in they often try to get Tom to build them a motor or two, but he only helps out a few that he trusts won't copy his cams.

All of the racers look up to Tom and respect him, so much so that he got the nickname "Great White Father." While it's partially for his head of thick white hair, it's mainly because of his engineering genius that can get more horses out of a Harley than anyone, and he's been at the top of his game for 20 years.

Last Tin Hat

It's a sad thing, but this year's Tin Hat Derby is going to be the last one. Over the years, most of the trails have closed as houses have been built into what used to be wilderness, and it's more difficult to get permission for a couple hundred motorcycles to ride on parts of the city streets than it once was. We've had 15 Tin Hats over the years, and I have ridden in all of them and look forward to them each year, but so-called progress can get in the way of traditions.

This year, well over 300 riders are participating. They are coming from all over the U.S. and as far as Canada to attend. The Tin Hat Derby is the longest one-day event in the country, and they'll be riding in the dark if they don't keep moving, so this year we're going to start four riders at a time. It's appropriate that the final year's weather is some of the worst that we've had in the last couple years. It's been raining for most of the past three weeks, and some trails should be rivers of mud, so making it through 200 miles on street tires will be a challenge.

By the time I got to the half-way point in Boulder Creek, I had passed too many stuck riders to count. I stopped once to help a buddy get his bike out of the mud, then I jumped back on my bike and raced ahead to find my row partner to get back on pace, but I can't do that for everyone. I'm sure that over the next few days a lot of guys will be coming back to pull their bikes out of the mud, and many of them will need help doing it.

As usual, it was a long day from dawn until dusk, and I'm worn down to a nub. After our last checkpoint near the clubhouse, we started to tally everyone's times. For my last Tin Hat, my goal like always is to come out on top, but it didn't happen. Bob Chaves did the best on averaging 24 mph over the 200 mile course and it gave him two Tin Hat Derby wins. This year he did it on a BSA, making him the only non-Harley rider to win it.

Upcoming Season

After Bobo got out of the service, he came by the dealership to catch up with the latest and to say that he's ready to get back out on the track. Bobo might be a little rusty after two years away, but I think he can still compete, even with the tougher competition, now that he's turning pro. Mac is riding a KR that I got for him, and with Bobo coming back, I'll get a KR for him too.

The Daytona 200 is coming up, and two weeks out from the race, I got a call from Dud Perkins saying that his rider Billy Meyers had gotten injured and he wanted Bobo to fill in. I don't have any problem with Bobo riding for Dud, so after talking to Bobo about it, he committed to ride for Dud. Joe and Al are making the trip to Daytona, so Bobo can catch a ride with them.

The thing I don't like is that Bobo hasn't ridden a motorcycle in two years, and he isn't close to being in racing shape, so he really shouldn't go. I know that he's trying to help Dud, but it's risky for Bobo. Riders aren't allowing practice laps at Daytona anymore, so once the race began, Bobo jumped right into going over 120 mph down the track with over a hundred other riders. It seems like San Jose riders never do well at Daytona, and by the end of the race, Bobo had clutch problems and Joe had his own mechanical problems, so neither of them finished.

For the 49-lap race, the victory went to Brad Andres, and this is his very first race as a professional. Brad is only 19 years old and his dad Leonard is a friend of ours. Leonard owns the San Diego Harley Davidson dealership, and the bike that Brad rode to victory is the same bike that Joe used last year to win eight nationals. We couldn't believe that Tom sold the bike after the success Joe had with it, but Tom is always about making money, so he sold it at the end of last season to Leonard Andres and built a new race-ready KR for Joe.

Belmont is the place to be every Friday night during the season for the two thousand or so spectators that show up. When they have higher profile races, it might draw four or five thousand fans. I've picked up a new KR for Bobo, and to put some miles on the motor, he rode it to Salinas and back in the dark with no brakes or lights. Another good thing is that Bobo has been trail riding and working out since he returned from Daytona, so he's had time to build up some physical strength for racing.

The season opener at Belmont is always exciting. The fans are happy that racing is back, and for the racers, it means the season is just beginning, and that's what many guys live for. In tonight's main event, Bobo, Joe, and Charlie all made the cut. By the end of 15-lap main event, Joe came in first, Charlie second, and Bobo came in third. Considering that about 100 riders or so try to make the main event cut each Friday, Bobo's finish after a two year lull up against Charlie and Joe showed that he still had it. If the Army didn't take Bobo for two years of his prime, he could have been a contender for the top rider in the country with the right equipment.

***** ***** *****

The next event is Gardena in Southern California. It's a cushioned track that's very fast, but it's also notorious for being dangerous. Like Belmont, Gardena has races every Friday night during the summer, so the locals have the advantage. Bobo and Joe made the trip south with Larry coming along to pit. The turnout is like a national event with top riders showing up such as Al Gunter, Don Hawley, Johnny Gibson, Tex Luce, and Chuck Basney ready to compete.

Bobo took some practice laps on the track, and when he brought the bike into the infield, the KR's motor is steaming. The gas tank seam has split and the gas is falling onto the hot motor and causing the problem. Larry found a gas tank to borrow from another pit crew, and he started switching the two tanks just before Bobo's heat is about to start. Bobo had about five minutes to spare when his bike got put back together. He didn't have any problems in his heat, thankfully, and placed second to qualify for the main event.

When it came time for the final, the riders lined up and they all have the goal of getting into the corner first. Once the flag dropped, it's a dash into the first turn, and after some jockeying for position, they came out of the second corner with some separation between riders. For the first couple laps there are several lead changes, but for most of the race it's Bobo right on the rear wheel of Johnny Gibson who has the lead. Bobo kept pushing, but he couldn't get past Gibson in time and he crossed the stripe in second with Al Gunter in third, while Joe had bike problems and came along in sixth place.

***** ***** *****

Tom must have recognized an opportunity in the BSA brand because he acquired the territorial rights to BSA dealerships in Santa Clara County. A couple of years ago when Gene Thiessen raced a single cylinder Gold Star at the 1953 Gypsy tour, it was most people's first time at seeing how fast the Gold Stars are. Ever curious, Tom got a hold of one of the single-cylinder motors soon after they came out so he could tear it down and see how it was put together.

After getting the territory rights, Tom located a building to rent on Alum Rock in east San Jose that would work out well for a small BSA dealership. Tom is putting up all of the money, but he's staying in the background as a silent partner, while Bob Chaves is going to run the dealership.

The Pacific Coast T.T. Championship at Riverside Speedway is an early season race and, although it isn't a national event, it's a popular 100-lap race and many top riders show up. Joe is the top dog now and he is sporting his new #1 plate. With the KR running strong, I'm sure that Joe is figuring on making some easy money today.

My old rival and good friend Ed Kretz Sr. also showed up ready to race. I've had many battles with Kretz over the years, and while he is better at road races, I was better on flat tracks. Kretz actually retired from racing seven or eight years ago to run his Triumph dealership, but he must have gotten the itch and came out of retirement to enter the competition. Triumph doesn't produce factory race bikes, so being a motorcycle guy, Kretz stripped down his own 650cc Triumph to ride. Kretz is in his early 40's, and he's packed on a few pounds since his old racing days, but he is still good enough to qualify and make the cut.

Joe did well and won his heat and the trophy dash, but when they looked over the times from earlier, Joe found out that Kretz's lap time for his heat is half of a second faster than his own. Once the main event stared, it isn't easy for Joe, and Kretz became the guy to beat. Joe is right behind him for much of the race and it came down to the last lap. As Joe tried to get past Kretz in the final corner, he took it too wide and ended up losing by half of a bike length.

When Joe came by the dealership a few days later, I had already heard about the race because I had called the sports writer at the Riverside Press to get the scoop. When the talk came around to the past weekend's race, I asked Joe who won.

"Ed Kretz."

"Which one, Junior or Senior?"

Moke knew where this was going.

"Senior," he reluctantly replied.

"Moke, you went down there and let Kretz beat you. He's an old man. You should have been racing him 20 years ago when he was good."

***** ***** *****

Myrt and I have been going to the Gypsy Tour since it restarted in 1951, but this year's Gypsy tour is set to be the last. We've had a lot of fun over the years, but as the event keeps drawing more people, and the crowds are getting rowdier, the city of Hollister decided that having the Gypsy Tour isn't worth the hassle anymore.

Sammy is old enough that we let him stay with his buddies at the track outside of town instead of getting a hotel room. Lots of guys sleep out at the Hollister track over the long weekend. The night time weather is great under the stars, plus it's doesn't cost anything. There's a picnic area off of turn one where they hang around and, when it's time to settle down, they can put their sleeping bags down in the grass or on the track itself.

One drawback about sleeping on the track is that you have to watch out for late night riders. Things are normally quiet, but after a few beers anything is possible. The next day Sammy told me how Gizmo was riding around the track late at night and kept getting closer on each lap to where Sammy and a couple friends were lying in their sleeping bags. After his last pass got too close for comfort, they rolled under the fence just to be on the safe side, and the next time that Gizmo came around the corner, he ran into the fence where they were just laying in their sleeping bags. Last year they were watching a guy doing laps at night when the headlight on his bike disappeared. They grabbed flashlights and went looking for him when they found a broken fence with the guy and his bike off in the bushes.

Besides the Gypsy Tour being over the long Memorial Day weekend, the Indianapolis 500 is also today, so guys are keeping track on that too. Billy "Vuky" Vukovich is racing in Indy today. He grew up in Fresno and many of the racers know him. Vuky had been racing midgets out of Fresno since after the war when he got the chance to drive in Indy.

For his first time at Indy in 1952, Vuky led nearly all of the way until he crashed. The following year he again led for most of the race and won it. When he won again in 1954, he was just the third driver to have back to back wins at the Indianapolis 500, so today he's trying for three wins in a row which no one has done before. The Calabrace brothers are childhood friends of his, so they are listening to the race on a radio, along with Harold Matthews who owns the Fresno Harley dealership, so we'll find out how he does.

It is late in the day, and I saw a couple guys that looked like they were crying. I wondered what was going on, then word got around that Vuky had died. He had a 17-second lead during the race, but he got into a chain-reaction three-car crash with slower drivers as he came around behind them and his car flipped multiple times. Later they announced the news over the loud speaker, which they usually don't do when a serious injury or death happens, but Vuky has a lot of friends around here.

***** ***** *****

Sammy is still having car problems with the 1942 Chevy, and the final straw is when he called from their hangout over at Mel's Diner on Santa Clara and 17th. Sammy is there with his girlfriend Anita and his buddies, so when his car wouldn't start in front of everyone, once again he isn't happy with me for selling him a lemon. After that, I gave him a 1950 Oldsmobile that I took in on trade, but within a few months we figured out that it's even more unreliable than the Chevy. I've been feeling bad about selling Sammy clunkers, so I went to talk to a buddy of mine that sells new and used cars.

I'm looking into getting a new Chevrolet, and after working on the price, I put down a deposit and placed an order for a 1955 Chevy Coupe with a V-8 and a three speed on the column. It's a basic model, no frills, no chrome, and the light green color is cheap to get. Since I covered the deposit, I let Sammy know that he is going to have to start making the monthly payments, so he'll work the parts counter on Saturdays to earn a paycheck.

Sleepy's Return

It's nearly the fourth anniversary of Sleepy's crash at Belmont, and he still hasn't gotten racing out of his system, so on the sly he and Chaves started putting together a bike at the BSA dealership for Larry. Chaves had recently taken in a one year-old 500cc BSA single on trade, so they are using that to build his race bike. Chaves is a great mechanic and while he handled the motor, Larry worked on stripping the bike of extra weight and getting it down to the bare bones.

It started out hush-hush, but it didn't take long for us to hear about their project. After a couple weeks, they had the bike ready to test out and both Chaves and Larry took it around the block a few times, and things are looking good. The upcoming Vallejo 3/8-mile race is less than two weeks out, so they will take it there and see how Larry does. When Larry got into the street crash, in addition to breaking his leg, his ankle sustained a lot of damage, so that will be a concern too as he goes into corners.

Sammy and I made the trip to Vallejo that day to watch Larry and Bobo on the track. As we're watching from the infield during practice, Larry got the bike out on the track and started doing a few mid-speed warm-up laps, and then he cranked the BSA up to race speed. The Vallejo three-eighths mile is a fast track and things seemed to be going fine, but somewhere around the seventh or eighth lap, Larry went into a hard slide and, as he put his foot down, you could tell that he had a problem almost immediately. Larry kept the bike upright, but his foot is dangling.

As he came off the track, Larry said that his ankle snapped. He has to be in pain, but he kept it in. The steel shoe lightly slides along the dirt and doesn't really catch on anything, so his ankle must be very fragile. We got him seated and the medic came over to attend to his ankle. As we were talking about how his comeback ended, you have got to love Sleepy when he said, "I just wanted to find out if I could still do it, and now I know." When they finished wrapping his ankle, Chaves took him to the hospital in Vallejo. We were all impressed that Sleepy got back in the dirt, and it's obvious that he still wishes he could race, but it just wasn't meant to be.

***** ***** *****

Before the season began, Tom built two motors for Leonard Andres and his son Brad, and things worked out pretty well. When the season wrapped up, Brad had won five nationals and earned the championship title. Everett also had five nationals, but because of the types of wins, Brad's points added up to be more. For Joe, it's been a disappointing season with only three national wins at Windber, Milwaukee, and Peoria in 45-cubic-inch division. He also had three second place finishes, but it's only good for a third-place finish in the point's standings.

Even though Tom built Brad's motors, and Tom is Joe's sponsor, there are no hard feelings between them, and Brad actually traveled a lot with Joe and Al this season. With most top-tier riders entering the same nationals, traveling together makes sense because they can share a lot of the costs. The racing schedule is grueling and life on the road isn't glamorous by any stretch. Nights are spent in sleeping bags under the stars or in the front or back seat, and you clean up in gas station bathrooms as you drive from place to place. You are with the same guy or two for 24 hours a day for weeks on end, most of that time in a car, so even a small annoyance can get on your nerves over time. When it comes down to it, you've got to love what you're doing to keep at it.

Tommy the Greek

Sammy has been working at the dealership over the summer, and when he saved enough money, we took his car to Oakland so that Tommy the Greek could pin-stripe it. Tommy is a local legend, and he has been pin-striping cars, trucks, and bikes for over thirty years. Tommy is quite a character, and he only does things first class. He buys a new Cadillac convertible each year, and when he shows up at Belmont on Friday night, he has a knockout chick on each arm, and when you see him the following Friday night, he'll have two new girls with him.

Tommy is a big fan of Joe's, and before the season started, he painted Joe's black helmet and black bike with chartreuse flames and pin-striped the flame outlines. When Joe is racing down the straights and lying flat on the tank, the flames on his helmet and bike look good together. Tommy knows most of the racers and he pin-stripes helmets and bikes for several of the guys.

Tommy is incredible at applying pinstripes. It is interesting to watch him work with a small brush and a little can of paint. He puts the stripes on so smoothly and perfectly, it looks like he just never makes a mistake. For Sammy's light green coupe, Tommy painted on two dark green stripes around the headlights and continued them down the sides of the car, and then he added the dark green stripes from the front to back on the roof too. Next, Tommy painted a white stripe in-between the dark green stripes, which made the contrast really stand out. I'm sure that before long, everyone will be able to recognize Sammy's car by just the pin-striping.

Sammy has wanted to try his hand at hill-climbing, so I took him out to a hill at Uvis Dam one afternoon with my 45-inch climber and the Big Inch. When I took over the dealership I got the old police bike as part of the inventory, and it's been a good bike to have around. I used it at a few hill climbs and did well with it, but I haven't had the chance to take it to a national yet. Even Joe got wins with the Big Inch at the Lodi T.T. and the Gypsy Tour's Hollister T.T. after we switched it over from a hill climber. The 74-inch bike is actually easy to ride, but it has lots of power so it will be a handful for Sammy. After we unloaded the bikes, Sammy first got on the 45 and made it to the top without any trouble.

When Sammy got on board the Big Inch at the bottom of the hill, I pointed out a spot about three-quarters of the way up where he needed to hit the kill button so he wouldn't overshoot the top. Besides that, my instructions for Sammy are simple, crank the throttle wide open, let out the clutch, and hang on for dear life. Sammy grabbed on to the handlebar grips that are covered in sticky tape which helps keep your hands from slipping when the power hits. Sammy fired up the bike, did as I said, and took off like a rocket. He made it to the top so quickly that he didn't have time to hit the kill button, and he shot over the ridge and out of sight. Myrt will give me hell if Sammy is hurt, but as he appeared at the top of the hill, I started laughing.

***** ***** *****

The San Jose Dons are still going strong after two decades, and we've been hovering around 60 members. We've cycled through many of our yearly Road Captains, but Myrt has been the treasurer for most of those twenty. We just moved into a new clubhouse after the Virginia Street house was condemned by the city. The house could have been condemned years ago. It was a dump twenty years ago when we first started renting it, but we had a lot of good times there over the years. It didn't earn the nickname "House of Corruption" for nothing. I know a few of the guys are having a hard time saying goodbye to Malatto's bar across from the old club house.

After renting for so long, we looked into buying a property and we found a house for sale on Columbia Avenue near downtown San Jose for $3500. When we figured out the numbers, it came out that we had a lower monthly payment than we had on the rental, but the new place is going to need some work. The house has a dirt basement and the plan is to dig out all of the dirt so that we can have our meetings downstairs and rent out the upstairs house to help cover the mortgage payments. The Dons chipped in on the work, and after a few months, we had all of the dirt hauled out and a cement floor poured in. We roughed in the walls with 2x4s, put up sheet rock, painted everything, and after we finished, the new place is a big improvement over the last clubhouse.

Stolen Cams

One day Dud Perkins called Tom and said that he wanted to buy a complete racing motor from him with a set of his A-cams. Tom's A-cams are used by Joe and just a couple other racers, and Tom isn't keen on just anyone having his cams. But Dud gave Tom his start in the business, and Dud is one of the oldest Harley dealership owners in the world, so Tom sold a motor to him with the condition that no one would take the bottom end of the motor apart.

Dud is always trying to suck up to the Davidsons, so shortly after he got ahold of Tom's motor, it was taken apart and the cams were sent to the factory. I would guess that someone at the factory had to know that the cams were coming, Hank Syvertsen has been the head of the racing department for over 20 years and he could have known, but for all I know it was Dud's idea to send the cams to the factory to be copied.

We have a spy working at the factory and when the cams arrived, Tom received a phone call. After Tom got off the phone he jumped into his car and made a beeline to Dud's dealership in San Francisco. When Tom got there he told Dud that the cams hadn't been hardened correctly and would break apart, so he needed them back and he would make a replacement set. After giving Tom the run-around, Dud fessed up that the cams were in Milwaukee.

Tom is furious about the deception. His cams are the foundation of his motor's success, but there isn't anything he can do. The factory has wanted Tom to pass on his cam secrets for years, but they were never willing to pay him what that knowledge is worth. But to shanghai his cams really crossed the line, and Tom cut off all ties with the factory.

***** ***** *****

Mr. William Kyne is the Bay Meadows owner and he recently passed away. And now his widow is only allowing horse racing at the track after this season. Mr. Kyne wasn't like most of the snooty horse track owners; he allowed car and motorcycle racing at his track, but now that is coming to a close. With Bay Meadows leaving motorcycles out in the cold, the AMA is scrambling to find a replacement location for a West Coast national, and they are in discussions about using the mile track at the Santa Clara Fairgrounds.

It's getting late in the season and Everett has two national wins. If he picks up another national, Joe's chances for another title will disappear. There are just seven nationals this year, and Joe has only one win at Bay Meadows, so everything hinges on the upcoming Peoria nationals. Besides dealing with Everett, Joe will be up against Brad Andres who is a road race specialist, and the Peoria T.T. is the kind of race he does well at. Brad had his first national win of the season a couple months ago at the Laconia road race, so he's just as anxious to win at Peoria to have a chance at being number one.

At Peoria, Joe set a new lap record of 30.31 seconds during time trials, so he's got speed in his favor. Once the 45-cubic-inch main event began, it's back and forth between Andres and Joe for the lead. Joe is out front most of the time, while Andres is staying right behind him. On the last lap though, Andres got a slingshot move past Joe and out front to win as Joe came in a close second.

Joe knew that he had to win today's 80-cubic-inch race, which is the last national of the season, to have any chance of winning the title now that both Andres and Everett have two wins.

In the 80-cubic-inch group, Joe pulled out the win in the 14-lap event with a time of 7 minutes and 16.8 seconds, which is just three seconds faster than Brad's winning time in the 45 inch group. Although a first place win gets the most points, second and third place finishes also earn points, so they are going to come into play. When the AMA added up the total points, Joe came out on top to grab his second championship title, and Andres was bumped to a close second in the overall rankings.

We got the word on Tuesday morning about a big crash at Gardena Speedway that killed Chuck Basney. Chuck was the Pacific Coast Flat Track Champion for many years, and I knew Chuck as a really good guy. Chuck was one of the riders that came out to test the KR frame changes that Tom had worked up. Brad Andres also got mixed up in the crash and suffered a broken leg and other injuries. They've had two short tracks near each other over the years in Southern California called Gardena Speedway, and both tracks have been dangerous places to race. Just a month earlier, another motorcycle rider died in a crash at Gardena.

***** ***** *****

With Sammy now competing in hill climbs, I started getting that competitive feeling and set out to build a new bike. The 55-cubic-inch Sportster XL had just come out, and I wanted to showcase the new model so people would get interested in it. One of the recent Sportsters to arrive at the dealership is a nice dark green, so that's what I'm using as my new hill climber. Although I will be competing against bigger bikes in the 80-cubic-inch class, I plan to get nearly as much horsepower out of the 55-cubic-inch motor as a 74, plus my bike will weigh less too, so I feel good about using it to compete.

I removed the heavy front fender, cut down the back fender, cut off most of the exhaust pipes, removed the lights, replaced the 4.5 gallon gas tank with a smaller version from the 125-S model Harley, and got to work on the motor.

Factory Racers

For the past five years Al Fernandez has been Joe's traveling companion and right-hand man at the tracks, but Al has decided to step aside. Al is a great pit man and he works just as hard as the riders out on the track. When Al is handling things, you know that Al will have your bike ready to race. Al started pitting for Sleepy in his big year of 1950 and after five years with Joe, he's had enough of the cross-country traveling and bad food, plus being gone so much is tough on a home life. Now with Al stepping aside, Charlie is going to be traveling and pitting for Joe, in addition to maintaining his bikes.

It used to be that most of the racers built their own bikes and did the repairs. They might have a buddy pitting for them on weekends, but it was mainly a one man operation. Into the 1950s, as the racing business really started growing and the purses grew with it, guys are traveling further to enter the high-end races, and they need a full-time mechanic to travel with them. Most of the current top guys are riding for the Harley factory because, besides a mechanic, they provide what is needed above all else, a steady supply of parts and motors. One or two of the factory favorites might even receive a small allowance to offset some of the travel expenses, but the factory is pretty tight with the purse strings.

One other big reason to ride for the factory is that there aren't many tuners near the level of Tom. But the horsepower edge that Tom's riders have enjoyed for over 20 years isn't the same as it once was after the factory copied his cams. When the new KR models came out, they were as fast as Tom's bikes, which isn't a coincidence.

Since selling the dealership, Tom has been sponsoring Joe out of his own pocket and after years of building race bikes and running a successful dealership, Tom can afford to slow down. As the 1956 season ended, the factory called on Joe about racing for them. Joe would never think of racing for anyone other than Tom, but after he and Tom talked it over, Joe accepted the factory offer. They'll provide him with a new KR and all of the equipment he needs, but no allowance to go with it. Charlie is included too, and he will continue to maintain Joe's bikes and travel with him, so overall things really won't change that much.

According to the terms of the agreement, Charlie can't race while pitting for Joe. They don't want to risk Charlie getting hurt and leaving Joe without a mechanic. Charlie is a key part to this; he is putting together great bikes, and the separation between the talent levels in the top three or four riders isn't much. Tom has taught Charlie all that he knows over the past few years, and Charlie has taken that knowledge to come up with his ways of improving the bikes.

Even though he's out of the picture, Tom isn't hurting for money, he always has things going on. Besides the cam business that he's running, Tom is expanding his business of providing motorcycle loans. Tom used to just provide loans for people he knew, but with British motorcycles gaining in popularity, he's providing money to new dealerships opening around the Bay area. Tom provides loans for flooring new bikes, and he finances the bikes that are sold to customers who don't pay cash. For individuals with so-so credit, he might still provide a loan, but they're offered at what could be considered mafia rates.

***** ***** *****

After the factory supplied a new black KR and a backup motor, Charlie got busy at his workshop off the road to Mount Hamilton. Charlie is big on making bikes lighter, and besides replacing parts with lighter aluminum, he also likes to drill holes in heat shields, grind down excess metal and welds - anything to reduce ounces. Charlie has the KR down in the 295 to 300 pound range, which really helps the horsepower-to-weight ratio.

Once Charlie finished with all of his changes over the winter, he painted a silver panel in the center of the black tank. When he brought the KR by the dealership, one of the guys joked that since this is the bikes maiden voyage, they should smash a beer bottle across the forks, but cooler heads prevailed. This winter we also got some exciting news from the AMA when they announced that the inaugural San Jose Mile is scheduled for July 21st, which is taking over for the departing Bay Meadows national.

Dealers Banquet

I'm attending the annual winter banquet in Milwaukee for Harley Davidson dealers, and each year a different dealership's owner is selected to sit next to Bill Davidson for the evening, and tonight I've been chosen. Bill Davidson is a great man and we've had many conversations over the years. Mr. Davidson also knows Tom very well and they both have mutual respect for each other. While the rest of the Davidson brothers aren't happy with Tom keeping his improvements to himself, Bill Davidson sticks up for Tom. As far as the fans, it's not a Sifton or a factory Harley, the winning bike is just a Harley, so the company still benefits from Tom's success.

Mr. Davidson and I have had several talks over the years and we get along fine, also I think that he appreciates the racing career that I've had. After dinner and all of the speeches, Bill and I were talking and the conversation veered to the current models. "Bill, you need to build a new model that grabs people's attention when they visit the showroom and they really want to buy it. I hear it all the time from people coming into the shop that they don't want the heavy street bikes anymore, they want smaller sporty bikes that still have plenty of power."

He is probably wondering where this is going. "Well Sam, what do you suggest?"

"You have the start of the bike already, the new Sportster, but it's too heavy. We need a streamlined version of it to interest customers. Something with a smaller gas tank, smaller fenders, and not all of the extra metal." I described the Sportster that I'm using on the hills and how I lighten it up to compete with the stronger bikes.

The Sportster XL that came out this year continues the heavy looking motorcycle that people associate with Harleys. As we talked, our conversation got a little heated, mainly because I don't think he realizes how much dealership owners need lighter but still powerful bikes to compete with Triumphs and BSAs. But, if I can't speak freely this evening to the President of the company that's also my livelihood, when can I?

We toned down our conversation, but Bill isn't sold that a market for the bike exists. He wanted me to talk with other dealers about a possible slimmed-down version of the Sportster and see if they would be interested. I talked to over thirty dealers during the evening, and by the end of the night, I had promise orders of nearly 400 units. Bill's eyes lit up when I told him how the dealers responded, but now it's up to him to get the model into production.

***** ***** *****

The season opener at Daytona is about here and Joe and Charlie are making the trip. Daytona hasn't been good to Joe the last couple times he was there, but hopefully this time will be different. On the Sunday of the race, for once, Joe didn't have any mechanical problems to ruin his efforts and he won the beach course race by averaging 98.5 mph over the 200 miles, winning by nearly a minute over the second place finisher. Joe received a winner's check for two thousand dollars, and per their agreement, he and Charlie split the purse 50/50.

The Modesto climb is the highest profile climb that we have in Northern California and it's a great hill to climb. I'm bringing two hill climbers, a KR and the 55-cubic-inch Sportster, while Sammy will use the Big Inch in the 80-cubic-inch class, and an older WR for the 45 group. Sammy and I left early on Easter Sunday morning as we trailered the bikes behind the Oldsmobile.

It's a strong group of riders that came to compete, but it turned out to be a great day for our family. I posted a time of 5.55 in the 80 expert, and a time of 6.16 in the 45 division, both times good for first place trophies. Sammy had a time of 5.22 in the 80 novice group, which earned him a first place trophy in just his second climb. It's much different from Sammy's first hill climb in Pacifica which became a giant mud pit, and neither of Sammy's attempts did well. They also announced that next year's Modesto climb is going to be a National Championship, so I'm really looking forward to it after today's success. Competing in nationals is the real test of talent, because only the top 12 expert and 12 novice riders in the sport are invited to compete, so it's the cream of the crop.

Chapter 5 / San Jose Mile

The rising star for Harley Davidson is Carroll Resweber. He just turned pro this year and is the one to keep an eye on. Resweber lives close to fellow Texan Everett Brashear and, when he was younger, he used to tag along with Everett who is a great rider to learn from. Resweber is a natural in the dirt, and with coaching from Everett, he has been tearing up the flat tracks.

After Joe won the Daytona 200, Resweber got the second national at the Columbus half-mile, and then Joe lapped the entire field for a win at the season's third national at Laconia on June 23. This is setting up for a battle between Joe and Resweber at the inaugural San Jose Mile on July 21st. We are excited that San Jose is going to have its own National Championship, and it's held at the fairgrounds, just a couple of miles down the road from the dealership.

All of the guys from the shop, everyone in the Dons, and members from nearly all of the bay area motorcycle clubs (Yellow Jackets, Apple City, and Tri-City) are at the fairgrounds, and you can feel the excitement in the air. With Joe having the #1 plate, and being that the race is practically in his back yard, Joe is the odds-on favorite to win.

Charlie has Joe's bike running strong, and Joe set the day's fastest lap time of 43.85 seconds. For his heat, Joe easily beat Everett and Eugene Thiessen. When it came time for the 25-lap championship race, Joe simply crushed the competition with an overall time of 18:29. Albert Gunter riding a BSA Gold Star came in second by half of a straightaway, but the closest battle was between Wayne Bias and Everett fighting over third place. Near the end of the race, Wayne got the edge and took third place while Everett came in fourth.

The San Jose Mile win gave Joe his 20th Grand National trophy and, at this point of his career, Joe is at another level compared to everyone else. This is a great win, and our town is now on the national map. After the events, I went home to pick up Myrt so that we can meet the rest of the Don's and their wives, or girlfriends, over at the clubhouse to celebrate Joe's big win.

***** ***** *****

Sammy and I have been entering all of the local hill climbs together, and today, we are heading to Scotts Valley. The Scotts Valley property is owned by my buddy Louie Margarettich, and the hill we're using today is practically straight up, so it's going to be a challenge for the riders.

After all of the novice riders in the 45 group made their two passes, none of them were able to make it to the top, so the winner is decided by distance. With Sammy making it the furthest up the hill, he took first in the novice group. After both passes were completed in the expert 45 inch group, once again we didn't have a rider make it to the top, but like Sammy, I won by making it the farthest distance.

During the open class for the novice riders, Sammy is the only novice rider that managed to cross the finish line. In the pro division, it isn't much better, just two riders made it to the top, and one of them is me, but I had a quicker time than Stan Schmidt to take the first place trophy. So for Sammy and me, we made a clean sweep at the event - four events and four trophies.

Sprouts Elder

We just got the news down at the shop that Sprouts Elder died. His wife recently passed away, and it must have been too difficult to go on without her, so my understanding is that he took his own life. After Sprouts retired from racing, he joined the California Highway Patrol. Sprouts has always been one of my heroes. I remember, as a kid, seeing him on the track and he was exciting as hell to watch sliding through the corners. I also remember about 20 years ago when he practically ran me over on the track. I still wince when I think about it. I remember asking Sprouts about his nickname, and he said that, as a kid, he raced horses, but he hit a growth spurt and squirted past six foot tall but stayed thin as a bean pole, so someone called him Sprouts, and the name stuck. Now that he's too tall to be a jockey, he made the switch over to motorcycles.

I heard that when Sprouts was young, he had a little trouble with a local girl, and instead of just leaving town, he left the country. I guess he wanted to see the world and made his way, along with his trusty Douglas motorcycle, to New Zealand. In New Zealand he watched the locals having bicycle races on quarter-mile wooden tracks with crowds of people watching. Sprouts somehow talked his way into a job of pacing the bicycles on the wooden track. He would bring the bicycles up to starting speed and then he'd tear away from the pack like a bullet.

After watching his motorcycle zoom around the track a couple times, the locals thought the hell with the bicycles, let's watch Sprouts. So Sprouts contacted a few racers from the States and they came down to New Zealand to check things out. After they switched to oval dirt tracks, they put on some races, and the races were a big hit. Sprouts later took the concept to Australia, and it took off there too. When I was racing in New Zealand they still talked about him."

***** ***** *****

This year the dealership is on track to sell over 50 new motorcycles, so business is doing well. When the new 1958 lineup came out in September, one of the new models is the 55-cubic-inch Sportster XLCH, the CH standing for Competition Hot. It's more or less a KR with a 55-cubic-inch motor that puts out 55 horsepower. This lightweight Sportster is the result of my conversation with Bill Davidson just last winter, and it's very similar to the Sportster hill climber that I built and have been using.

Most of the dealers that I talked to at the banquet about a lightweight Sportster told me not to get my hopes up because it wouldn't happen, but a few months ago, I was shocked when I heard they were actually building a bike on my suggestions.

When I saw the new model, I couldn't believe how stripped down it was, certainly more than I was expecting. The XLCH has no lights, short straight pipes, a chopped rear fender, and a small 2.25 gallon tank like what I have on my Sportster-based hill climber. They also bumped up the ponies by using larger valves and higher compression pistons, so it's a race bike ready for off-road competition. Something else the factory did, like many of us are already doing, is to use a magneto instead of a battery to help reduce the overall weight. It's a sporty bike, but the only problem I can see with the XLCH is that it might not sell many units since they aren't street legal. If they add lights and mufflers, it's bound to see an increase in sales for sure.

The first two XLCH models that the factory built were sent to the San Jose dealership, and they were addressed to Sammy and me. One of the bikes is red and white, and the other is black and white, and they are both really beautiful motorcycles. I also received a personal note along with the bikes stating, "For the California Crybabies" signed by Walter Davidson.

***** ***** *****

By the end of the season, Joe had four wins out of the eight national races to earn the national championship trophy. After winning the season opener at Daytona, Joe got on a three in a row win streak by taking the checkered flags at Laconia, San Jose, and Springfield. Resweber had the second most wins with his two half-mile nationals at Columbus Ohio and St. Paul Minnesota. So for back-to-back years (in 1956 and 1957), Joe kept the #1 plate and cemented his position as one of the top riders in the history of the sport.

Over the years, San Jose has had its share of talented riders, but after the 1957 season, Joe is the only racer still going strong. Sleepy, Rudy, and Chaves have been retired for a while now, and Charlie, Mac, and Kenny retired last year. Bobo decided to hang up his hot shoe as the 1957 season ended, only Wayne is on the fence whether to ride next year. Some of us are still competing on the hills, but it's not the glamour of the flat tracks.

It's interesting that Joe has only one championship with Tom, but now he's earned two championships with Charlie doing the tuning. When it comes down to it, Charlie doesn't get enough credit for what he's done. Most people outside of the shop probably think that Tom is still doing all the work for Joe. In the past, Tom was always busy designing and making new cams, which made a lot of riders successful, at the same time, he didn't have time to work on the small things, but Charlie has the time and patience to improve and fine-tune the bikes. Charlie can be a pain to deal with, his nickname isn't "Bulldog" for nothing, but he builds a fast motor, and that's what matters.

***** ***** *****

Myrt's 40th birthday is coming up this December 13th, and I have been working on her present for a few weeks now. I bought a German sidecar designed for a BMW motorcycle, and worked things over to get it to hook up properly with the new Sportster. The most difficult part was getting the linkage right so both the bike and the sidecar stay lined-up properly going around corners. Once I finished with the mechanical aspects, I painted the sidecar candy apple red with black pinstripes to match the Sportster, and they look great together, so I'm pretty happy about my work.

I brought it home on her birthday and parked it out in the driveway to surprise her. When I brought Myrt outside and showed her the candy apple red set-up, it isn't the response that I was hoping for. Myrt joked, "So I'm going to drive and you're riding in the tub?"

"That's not what I had in mind. Let's take it for a spin."

She looked at me and said, "Do I have to?"

"Come on, don't be a baby."

I coaxed her into riding around the neighborhood for a while, but I'm guessing that this will be the only time. Myrt appreciated the work that I did for her present, but she isn't going to ride in a side-car. After all of my hard work, I put the bike and side car on the showroom floor and it sold within a week.

Daytona 200

As winter turned into spring, the 10-race AMA national schedule for 1958 came out and Daytona, as usual, is first. Charlie and Joe made the cross-country trip to Florida, and when race day came around, we were anxious to hear the results. Charlie called to say that Joe won and completed the 49 laps 50 seconds faster than his last year's win by averaging 99.86, a new track record. A week earlier, our friend Paul Goldsmith won the Daytona 200 stock car race on the 4.1 mile beach course. Goldsmith became the only guy to win the Daytona Beach Road course in both a car and on a motorcycle with his Daytona win in 1953. With Joe winning the motorcycle race and Goldsmith winning the stock car event the same year, their paths had crossed once again.

Goldsmith is a good friend, and one day when he was in town, he dropped by the dealership. As we were shooting the breeze, he said how he had the 1955 Daytona in the bag, but screwed up.

"I was making good time and the bike was holding up well when they flashed the sign that I was up. So I'm sitting pretty, except that I had salt water and oil on my goggles and could hardly see. As I'm coming out of corner four to get back onto the beach, I went too wide and hit an outgoing wave at around 110 that I never did see. I hydroplaned a little on the water's surface, and then the bike got sideways and flipped while I got airborne and traveled another 25 feet before slamming into the water."

I nearly fell off my chair as he's telling his story because I'm laughing so hard. I've seen other guys taken out by waves and I can imagine how easily it can happen.

"I got the bike upright and tried to get it started, but the air filter had been torn off, so the motor was probably flooded in seawater and Andres went on to win it."

BSA Project

One spring day, we were surprised to see Tom pull up at the shop with a BSA Gold Star in his trailer. When asked about it, Tom said that he's going to build a BSA to compete on the mile track. We know that the 500cc single cylinder is a durable power plant, and Tom must have some ideas on how to squeeze more ponies out of the single cylinder. I have no doubt that he can do wonders with the BSA, but this is a big change for a die-hard Harley guy.

About the only knock against the BSA is that the pushrods tend to expand when the motor gets too hot which, in turn, throws off the valve timing and causes power lose. During long races, you can practically tell from the lap times that the BSAs were slowing down as the race went on. Tom will machine new push rods and rocker arms that should fix the problem. The biggest overall improvement will come from creating new cams, and Tom is anxious to get to work.

Even with his arthritis and knee problems, Tom spent hundreds of hours over several weeks standing in front of his lathe milling different cams for the BSA. After he created two sets of cams that he was happy with, he sent them out to be hardened.

***** ***** ******

Friday night at Belmont they're through three heats in the expert group, and we're watching Joe compete in the fourth heat that just got started. As Joe is coming back around on the front stretch, he's about a foot behind leader Donny Smith and they are going gangbusters. As Joe is getting ready to swing out, Donny's motor suddenly crapped out. Joe tried to quickly scoot to the side, but he clipped Donny's rear tire which sent Joe airborne and he landed shoulder first and tumbled several times.

As Joe pulled himself towards the outer fence, all of the riders missed him as they went past, all except Don "Deadly" Redley who rode over Joe's right knee. Everyone knows that Redley is nearly blind and should be wearing glasses if he's out on the track, but unless someone wants to make an official protest about it, he's free to race. They stopped the race, and the ambulance came out and picked up Joe.

Once they looked him over, they said that he's got a broken shoulder and a crushed knee. Joe is certainly out of the upcoming San Jose Mile, and he might done for good if his knee is too far gone. Joe was the favorite to repeat at the San Jose Mile, but now the field is wide open.

Tom contacted Everett a couple weeks ago and asked if he'd be interested in riding his BSA at the San Jose mile. Everett is a good guy and we've known him for years. All Everett wanted to know is when he needed to be in San Jose to get ready. Everett has over 10 National Championship wins in miles and half miles, so he's an oval track specialist and just what Tom needs. Among those wins are back-to-back Springfield Miles: the first in 1955 over Bobby Hill by a couple bike lengths, and in 1956, he edged out Charlie by a bike length.

Everett is a great mechanic himself and he came up a week early to help Tom get the bike ready. Once they handled the mechanics, they did the dyno testing at a machine shop a few blocks away from the BSA dealership. The single cylinder registered a nice bump in power because Tom found a way to squeeze 52 ponies (almost 53) out of the BSA, but the question is how that power translates to the dirt.

With Joe's bike now available, Charlie got ahold of Don Hawley, who is five foot six and tough as nails, to pilot it for the race. This is probably going to be Hawley's best chance of winning a national because Charlie has him on a great bike, but the competition is going to be solid.

San Jose Mile II

On the morning of the race, Everett got Tom's BSA out on a track for the first time. Several laps into it as Everett started pushing the bike, the Gold Star did well and things are looking good. We were a little unsure if everything would come together in time because British bikes have different temperaments than Indians or Harleys. British bikes like cool overcast days, not the warm weather of San Jose, so you have to get the jets adjusted correctly.

This is a huge national championship race, and as people started filing into the fairgrounds, it looks like it's going to be standing room only before long. During time trials things got interesting as Joe's single-lap speed record from last year got beat not once, but three times by Johnny Gibson, Carroll Resweber, and Everett. Among the 16 riders that qualified for the main event were Don Hawley, Brad Andres, Al Gunter, Resweber, and Everett.

Once the 25-lap main event began, so many lead changes took place that no one led for more than a lap or two at a time. When they were about 15 laps into it, there were times when you could have thrown a blanket over Hawley, Everett, Resweber, and Sammy Tanner because they are so close to each other. For Hawley and Resweber, they got out front a few times, but they both started fading down the stretch.

It became a battle of BSA Gold Stars between Everett and Sammy Tanner. We watched as Everett made a perfect exit out of the final turn to take a two-bike length win over Tanner at the flag, with Resweber and Hawley coming in third and fourth. Everett's winning time on the Gold Star came in 9.53 seconds faster than Joe's time from last year on the KR. Harley Davidsons might have took the top spots in last year's San Jose Mile, but with BSAs taking the top two spots this year, it shook up the racing world.

The Harley factory isn't happy with their third and fourth place finishes. They aren't happy that Everett switched from a Harley to riding a BSA, and they certainly aren't thrilled that it was Tom's BSA that came out on top. I'm sure that if the factory hadn't screwed him over on his cams, Tom wouldn't have gone through the effort to show them up. With his BSA Gold Star winning this national event, he proved that his engineering skills went beyond just Harleys.

This is probably Tom's last big project. He has a new house in the east foothills with a machine shop next door, and he's making good money from his cam business, so he's set. Not long after, Tom decided that he didn't have enough time for the BSA dealership, so he sold the business to Chaves who has been running it since the dealership opened.

Joe's Knee Problems

Joe is hobbling around the shop on crutches and his arm is in a sling, so he's not looking like the picture of health. When Joe got checked over at the hospital after the crash, the examining doctor said that his knee is too damaged to ever get back to normal, and his racing career is likely over. Seeing Joe this banged up around the shop, we're thinking that the doctor might be right, but we sure hope that he isn't.

His broken shoulder will take a while to heal, but his knee is the biggest concern. Although Joe could barely bend his knee after the crash, it's loosening up a little, and he's been trying to exercise and stretch it. Joe puts Sloan's liniment on his knee and rubs it into the skin in hopes that as the lotion heats up, it will get the blood flowing to help rehabilitate the knee. Injuries have ended the careers of many racers in their prime. Our friends Al Rudy and Larry just to name two, but neither Joe nor Larry is willing to accept that Joe's career is over.

As Joe's knee started to slightly improve, Larry came up with an idea on how to stretch it out even more. As Joe is laying face down on a cot in the shop, Larry sits on Joe's butt backwards, and slowly bends Joe's leg at the knee as far back as he can. This isn't too pleasant for Joe, and he's dealing with a lot of pain, but that's what it's going to take for him to make it back.

They've been bending Joe's knee daily, and the pain got bad enough that I heard Joe say, "You're killing me Sleepy. Are you some kind of masochist?"

Larry paused for a second. "Well, I never thought about it, but I might be."

Not being able to race, Joe didn't have any money coming in so Ted Smith gave him a job at Belmont driving the watering truck. Joe would probably be there on race nights anyway, so at least this way he can get paid to watch the races for a few months until he recovers. The track gets damp on its own when the evening tide comes in, so Joe doesn't need to water that often. The truck is mainly used to knock down the dust earlier in the afternoon. One benefit of Joe working at the track is that he's learning a lot on the texture of the track and how it changes through the evening, which should be helpful if he ever comes back.

Joe and Larry have been working on Joe's knee for several weeks, and Joe's knee can bend close to half way, but it isn't even close to normal. The way we see it, Joe just needs it to bend enough to get his foot on the peg.

Last Sunday, Sammy rode the old police bike at the Friant Dam hill-climb and topped the hill in 4.03 seconds. That time is quicker than Dick Austin's time from 1951, and it's over a half second quicker than my time a dozen years ago on the spaghetti-frame Class A hill climber. The old spaghetti frame may be sitting over against the wall in the service area with the motor and the rear tire gone collecting dust, but the Big Inch is still going strong after a half-dozen years.

***** ***** ******

Joe hasn't raced in three months, but when the Springfield mile came around, he felt good enough to make the trip back east. The week before Springfield is the Sturgis half-mile, which isn't a national this year, but Joe and Charlie stopped in to use it as a warm-up race. Joe qualified for the main without any troubles, but he came in second in the main event. Sturgis is only 10 laps start to finish, and takes less than two and a half minutes to decide the winner, but it's a good start for Joe after so much time off from racing.

When Joe showed up at the Springfield track a couple days ahead of the race, he is using a cane to walk and some riders protested that he isn't physically fit and shouldn't be allowed to race. But after a short conference, the officials cleared Joe. On race day, I guess his bum knee isn't too bad, because Joe went from having a possible career-ending injury three months earlier and using a cane to get to his bike, to winning Springfield just like the year before.

Modesto National

The 15th annual hill climb at Modesto is here, and this year it's a national championship. I've been climbing this hill since before the war, so I know it well. In fact, I've been looking forward to it being a championship event. But, the Modesto hill climb is going to be very competitive and the top ranked riders from all over the United States have been invited to the event. This year the whole family, including Judy's boyfriend Wes, are driving together to Modesto. Wes graduated from high school last year and Judy is graduating this year. They have been dating for a while, and they are making plans to marry in October.

Early on the day of the climb, Sammy and I loaded the trailer with our bikes and hooked it behind the Oldsmobile. Once everyone is ready, the five of us piled into the Oldsmobile for the couple hour drive to Modesto. When I built my Sportster-based hill climber last year, I had the only one around, but after the XLCH came out, several guys had the stripped-down Sportster at the climb.

First up is the novice division, and Sammy came in third place in the 45-cubic-inch group, with Gary Lindstrom having the best time of 5:78. For the 80-cubic-inch group, Sammy won on the Big Inch by posting a time of 5:48, which gave Sammy his first National Championship.

For the expert group, I beat the competition in both divisions to earn trophies. In the 45-cubic-inch class, I posted a 6:24 compared to second place finisher Floyd Payne's time of 8:16. In the 80-cubic-inch (open) class, I registered a 6:10 time, which barely edged out Aub Isham who had a time of 6:11. I have won both divisions on the same day in the past, but this is the first time I did it at a National Championship event, so I'm really happy with how things worked out and the Arena family had quite a day. On the way home, Sammy had fun telling me that if I was in the novice division, I would have been runner up in both divisions.

After those two national wins, I decided that it's time for me to retire from competition. I've had a lot of fun over the years, but getting ready for hill climbs on Sundays isn't as enjoyable as it used to be. I've been racing for 25 years on nearly every type of surface (except ice), and I feel that I'm going out on top with over

100 trophies and six Hill Climb National Championships to my name.

As the 1958 AMA national championship season is coming to an end, and it's down to Joe and Resweber battling it out for the #1 plate. Even with repeating his wins at Daytona and Springfield, Joe came in second place behind Resweber. When the final points tally came out, Joe lost to Resweber by only one point!

It's been a few months since we had the national in Modesto, and today is Judy's wedding day. On this day of October 4th, Judy and Wes (Charles Wesley Webb) were pronounced man and wife at the Westminster Presbyterian Church of San Jose. It's a beautiful Saturday afternoon, and Myrt and I couldn't be any happier. For their honeymoon, Judy and Wes are staying at Holman's Ranch in Carmel Valley, which has bungalows throughout the property and horse stables for guests to use; it's also said to be once owned by Charlie Chaplin.

Back to the Present

As Sam is telling me about Judy's wedding, we saw his neighbor John coming up the back way. There's a cement waterway that goes along the side of the hill behind their houses, and it's actually a quicker way to get back and forth than by using the sidewalk out front. After crossing Sam's property line, the waterway takes you past a giant cactus, and how Sam got the cactus is an interesting story by itself.

Sam enjoys growing different types of plants, and he always wanted to grow a cactus from a clipping that would bloom white flowers. As he was out riding a bicycle one day, Sam saw a big cactus in a field not far from his house with beautiful white flowers, exactly the type of cactus that he's wanted to try and grow.

After enlisting John's help one evening, they drove over near the field about dusk and parked the car. After hopping a fence, they crossed a six-foot-wide creek by jumping on a rock midstream to get over to the cactus. They hacked off a couple small thorny pads and put them into thick burlap bags they brought along so they wouldn't get stuck. About that time they heard dogs barking, and soon someone started shouting, so they took off running back to the car. John made it across the creek first, but when Sam tried to jump on the rock in the middle of the stream holding the bag, he came up short and fell on his butt into the water screaming and cussing. The water was maybe half a foot deep, but Sam was completely soaked. John nearly died laughing, but Sam got up, and they made it back to the car and sped away without being caught.

After passing the back yard cactus, which is now over eight feet tall, you walk up wooden steps past Sam's olive and fig trees on the south slope, until you arrive at the deck where we are sitting.

I shouted, "There's John!" John has a bottle of red with him, although it looks to be only about a third of the way full. He usually brings over a leftover bottle from one of his parties, but it's always better than what we're drinking. I bring over a bottle or two each Saturday that I show up, but it's on the cheap side.

Thankfully John brings the good stuff. If he brought over some of the wine that he made out in his garage, we might need our stomachs pumped.

John asked, "What are you guys talking about?"

"Sam was telling me how when he retired from racing in 1958, he had over 100 trophies and six AMA National Championship wins."

"Wow Sam, I'm lucky to live next door to you." John likes to harass him. He says it helps keep Sam young.

Sam said, "Remember the first time you came over? You stopped by on your bicycle and said that you were thinking about buying the house next door and wanted to meet the neighbors. After a couple hours and several glasses of wine, you had to call Donna to come pick you up because you were drunk."

Sam is laughing by now. "When you were loading your bicycle into the station wagon getting ready to leave, I asked, well did I pass?"

As Sam is laughing, John smiled and said, "You passed, but just barely."

Sam Arena – 1948 Modesto

#20 Bob Chaves, #66 Al Rudy, #79 Sam, #13 Bernie Bernhiesel
(photo by D.R. Edmond)

Al Rudy and Sam Arena – 1948 or 1949

Sam Arena – 1948 Covo or 1949 Vogel (photo by Clarence Colwell)

Al Rudy Benefit – Belmont 1949

Tom Sifton, Al Rudy, Sam Arena

**Bob Chaves and Larry Headricks – 1950 Belmont
(photo by D. R. Edmonds)**

Larry Headrick – 1951 Belmont (photo by Pat Corner)

114

**Sam and George Sepulvuda – 1951 Tulare
(Pacific Coast Championship)**

#43 George Sepulvuda and #98 Joe Leonard – 1952 Gypsy Tour

#3 Paul Goldsmith, #98 Joe Leonard, and #31 Charlie West

Tom Sifton (kneeling) Working on Joe's KR

Sam Arena – Scotts Valley 1955

Lee McReynolds – Friant Dam 1955

Sammy Tanner, #25 Everett Brashear, Carroll Resweber
1958 San Jose Mile

Diane Leonard with Joe's National Championship Trophies

Epilog

The Big Day

It's been several weeks since my last visit, but I'm stopping by Sam and Myrt's this afternoon. When I arrived at their hillside home, I came in through the side gate, as usual, and by the sounds of it, Sam is on the deck listening to a San Francisco Giants baseball game. It's always good to let your presence known, especially for someone whose hearing has been damaged from years of motorcycle racing. Those old bikes had two exhaust pipes that were usually only about two or three feet long coming straight off the motor, and when those bikes were running wide open, it's like a Metallica concert, so it's no wonder his hearing is shot.

Sam used to have a little dog named Fonzi that would announce guests, but he passed away a few years ago. Fonzi was a terrier and maltese mix that lived until an old age of 17. Fonzi got bit on the nose by a rattlesnake a few years back along the hill, so it's surprising that Fonzi lived that long. Once a rattlesnake sinks their fangs into a dog that small, the odds aren't too good for surviving, but he was tough like his owner and recovered. It's funny, but that little dog and Sam made a good couple. I'm sure that Fonzi helped to mellow out Sam through the years.

I shouted, "Sam!"

"Tyler!" He yelled back.

"How are the Giants doing?"

"Bunch of bums." That's a typical Sam response.

"It sounds like we might have some excitement today."

"Yep, I'm going to try and start the hill climber after a while. John and Ray are in town, so they should be dropping by, and Sammy is already inside with Myrt."

After I put a bottle of Merlot and a wedge of cheese on the short metal table, I said to Sam, "This cheese should be pretty tasty, it's been aging in a cave for three years."

Sam replied, "It's probably got bat guano on it."

"It's got to be good then. Let me go inside and say hello to Myrt and grab a glass of water."

I opened the back slider and walked into the kitchen where I can see Myrt on the lower level sitting on the couch talking to Sammy.

"Hey Guys. What's going on?"

"Just eating a little soup and talking to Sammy."

Soup is the main staple for Myrt, so it's no wonder she's thin as a rail. I think her breakfast is just a couple bananas.

Sammy asked, "How are you doing Tyler?"

"Doing fine. I'm just looking forward to your Dad starting the old hill climber."

"Hey Myrt, I've got a question for you, whatever happened to Sam's flat track shoe?"

"Sam sold it a couple years ago when he was cleaning out closets. He sold all kinds of things like old Harley Davidson sweaters, jackets, his old helmets, even the motorized bicycle he built for Sammy. I wish he hadn't sold his shoe though. I'd really like to get it back."

After a short chat, I went back outside and settled into a chair across the table from Sam and poured a glass of wine from a bottle that's sitting out. As I relaxed, looking out over the Santa Clara valley, I feel fortunate coming by on Saturdays to spend time with Sam and Myrt.

"Sam, what's the latest?"

"I started a new batch of wine. John and I went to Kerrigan winery and got some must."

"What the hell is must?"

"It's the leftover grape skins and seeds used to make the juice. Both of us have a five-gallon jug fermenting, mine is in the guest bedroom."

"Well, I hope John's turns out better this time."

Sam laughed. "I told him not to leave it out in his garage for too long, but he doesn't listen."

After I had a few sips of wine, and a nice slice of cave-aged cheese, I said, "It seems like 1958 was a big year: you won two National Championships, Judy got married, and it was the last year of the San Jose Mile for a long time."

"The San Jose Mile turned into the Sacramento Mile because Sacramento had a much bigger grandstand to handle more paying customers. The venue might have changed, but the same guys just drove the extra two hours northeast to Sacramento. For the first year race in 1959, Joe banged handlebars with Don Hawley, and Joe went tumbling on the first lap or two. Carroll Resweber ended up winning."

"I hear Carroll Resweber was really good."

Sam replied, "He was. After Joe's back-to-back championships in 1956 and 1957, Resweber became the guy to beat. Resweber held the number one plate for four straight years, and in three of those four seasons, Joe came in second."

"By the mid-50s most of the top riders were racing factory bikes, so horsepower was fairly even, but a big advantage for Resweber is that he's a horse jockey's size and weighed maybe 120 pounds. Compare that to Joe, who had to diet to get to 165 pounds, and that really makes a difference. Joe once made it down to 155, but he was just skin and bones. For riders on the KRs at the time, 12 pounds equaled one horsepower, so Joe gave up two or three horses to the smaller riders. On shorter tracks it doesn't matter as much, but it's huge on a mile track. After that, your talent has to make up the difference."

"In 1961, Joe won three nationals so he could have raced longer, but by then, he was already transitioning to cars. Resweber was on his way to winning a fifth title in 1962 when he had a career ending crash on a dusty track back east. Resweber never raced again, but he probably would have won the number one plate for a couple more years if it wasn't for the crash."

"What was Sammy doing at that time? Was he hill climbing or racing?"

"Sammy and Gary Lindstrom, the son of my hill climbing rival Windy, were dominating on the hills. Gary is a small kid, it looked like he could barely hold on to the bike for the climbs, but for the two years him and Sammy won about everything in the novice and amateur divisions."

"Sammy turned pro in 1960 and went to the national hill climb championship in Lewiston, Idaho with the Big Inch. Back when Sammy won the amateur division at Modesto, folks didn't really pay attention, but now that he's competing as an expert, guys were curious to check out what kind of bike he had. Most of the climbers had bikes that were all painted and chromed, so when Sammy unloaded his decade old plain black bike, people laughed at it. But when Sammy won the 80 cubic inch division that day and earned his second National Championship trophy, and first as a pro, they weren't laughing anymore."

"By the early 1960s, most of the hill climbs moved north to Oregon, and as the hill climbs in Northern California died out, the Big Inch sat in the back of the shop collecting dust. For the climbs they did have in California, chains were out, and Harley XLRs (900cc) with regular tires were the way to go."

"They started having drag climbs with two riders going against each other, and one of the main drag climbs was a state championship on a 600-foot hill at Bass Lake near Yosemite. The hill was kind of wavy and long, not as steep as the old hill climbs, but the speeds were faster. It was a double elimination event, and if you kept winning or didn't lose more than once, you kept racing. So unlike typical hill climbs where two timed rides are the norm, you might ride a dozen times to get to the final matchup. Myrt and

I went with Sammy in 1961 to watch him compete, and he won the State Championship trophy."

"When we went to Bass Lake with Sammy the following year, I brought along an XLR and entered too. As the day went along, both Sammy and I kept winning and by the last race of the day, only two riders were left gunning for the trophy, Sammy and me. I was just shy of 50 at the time, so I wasn't the rider that I was in my youth, but I've never raced without giving my all. For the final race we had our bikes ready at the starting line, and when the flag waved, both of us cranked the throttles and took off up the hill, but Sammy edged me for the win. First he beat my Friant Hill time, then my Modesto time, now this. Once we were stopped at the top of the hill and shut off the bikes I told him, "You don't respect your elders, damn punk kid."

"The next year was the final drag climb at Bass Lake, and I skipped bringing a bike. But for three years in a row Sammy won the event. Sammy was also flat track racing, and one time he was getting ready to go on a circuit through the Midwest when he met his future wife Sharon, just a few weeks before the trip. Sharon is easy on the eyes and Sammy was smitten. So when the time came for the tour he didn't want to go, but he went anyway because he felt obligated."

"So how did Joe manage to go from bikes to racing cars? I'd think that it would be difficult to do."

"Joe switched to cars on the suggestion of Paul Goldsmith. Goldsmith went from motorcycles to cars back in the mid-50s, and he thought Joe could do the same. Goldsmith probably convinced Joe by telling him that he could eat all the food he wanted, which is music to the ears of motorcycle racers that must always watch their weight."

"Joe started racing jalopies and then modifieds, although he still raced motorcycles on occasion. His last two motorcycle races were at the Sacramento Mile and he was riding a Triumph for Tim Whithum. In the 1962 race, Joe was leading when he got a flat tire. In 1963, he was leading by a straightaway half-way through the race when his oil line ruptured, and that was it for him racing motorcycles."

"In 1965, Joe was in his first Indianapolis 500 driving a rear-engine Halibrand Ford, but an oil leak forced him out of the race. He still came in 6th in the standings that year, which is good, but he was up against Mario Andretti for many of those races. In 1968 he drove a turbine-powered Lotus at Indy, which is basically a jet motor strapped to four wheels. The motor idled at 50% and only had one speed, so Joe always had to use the brakes to slow the car down. Joe led for most of the race and it looked like he was going to win, but with nine laps to go, the turbine quit with a broken fuel pump shaft and the car rolled to a stop."

"In the mid-1960s, we moved to a new dealership at 2921 Monterey Road with a greatly expanded showroom and service bays. Gone were the days of standing in the service area around the wood heater in the middle of winter because it was the only heat in the whole place. It was a top-flight place, and Sammy started managing the dealership full time. By then, guys drifted away, and Tom didn't come around much, but the overall number of Harley racers were down too. The 1950s might have been Harley's golden years, but by the late 1960s those high times were ending, and the company wasn't selling many units. Besides Harleys, Sammy had the idea to start selling Kawasaki motorcycles which were still fairly new to the United States."

"The Kawasaki factory put on a contest for an all-expenses paid trip to Tahiti for the top 25 dealers in the United States. Our shop quickly became one of the top sellers in the nation, and we were one of the dealers that won a trip. Sammy was too busy with the shop to go, so Myrt and I went instead. Our good friends Sleepy and Dot wanted to go too, so they came along by paying their way to Tahiti. Myrt has always been very nervous about flying, so we had to get her a little tipsy in the airport bar before we got her onto the plane for the long flight."

"One day, Sleepy and I went to a motorcycle park that they had in Tahiti. Once we started twisting the throttle, Larry was chasing me all over and I thought he was going to get killed out there." As Sam was laughing the sliding glass door opened and Myrt came out with a bowl of meatballs that she had cooked.

I asked, "Is this for us?"

"Sure is."

I smiled and said, "Boy Sam, you have a great wife."

"I think I'll keep her."

Myrt just looked at him, then looked at me, and rolled her eyes.

"Hey Myrt, how did you like Tahiti?"

"Tahiti was beautiful and it had the clearest blue waters I've ever seen. We also visited Bora Bora which was even more beautiful. We had a wonderful time with our friends Larry and Dot. Before our trip to Tahiti, the last time we went outside of the country was for our honeymoon to England."

I said, "Very nice."

Myrt smiled. "Well, I'm going back inside to watch Emeril."

I asked, "Do you ever make any of Emeril's dishes?"

"No," she chuckled, "I just like watching him do it."

Then Myrt went back inside and left us to enjoy her homemade meatballs.

After a meatball or two I asked Sam, "Your view is so great. When did you two move here?"

"We had been living in our house on Puerto Vallarta for ten years when Myrt said she wanted a new house. I told her that we would move only if we paid cash." (Author's note: I remember talking to Myrt about buying this house, and she told me that she was the one who said they would move only if they paid cash, not Sam. Sam has been known to do a little revisionist history now and then.) "I knew that Myrt had been putting a little money aside, and within two years she had put together enough money for us to go looking."

"We found a new subdivision in Almaden Valley that was just being developed with wonderful views of the Santa Clara Valley, and it was only going to have about 30 houses total. Except for three already purchased, the developers said that we could choose any of the building lots on either side of the street. So Myrt and I stood on the different hillside lots, looking out on the views of the valley from the back yard, we didn't want the hillside views on the other side of the street, and we choose this spot. We picked one of their floor plans which priced out to be $49,500 for the house, $300 for the chimney, plus a charge of $1500 which they said was for the view. We moved into our new house on Thanksgiving Day in 1971, and had our first family Christmas party a month later."

"I still showed up to work daily, but Sammy was really the guy running the place. When I sold the dealership to Sammy, he ran it for 10 years before selling the business when the Harley Davidson Company was really at its lowest. With all of my free time, I started playing golf a couple days a week and I used to play some old racers like Everett Brashear when he came to town. Everett is a really good golfer, and I wasn't too bad for taking it up so late in life. But as I got older, I kept getting worse until I finally gave up on it. Another hobby I started after I retired was making jewelry. I bought a rock tumbler and some semi-precious stones and started experimenting. Before long I could do the complete process of making a cast for my designs, melting bronze or silver to pour into the cast, and create rings and medallions. I've made several nice pieces for Myrt over the years."

I said, "Don't forget your most important hobby - making wine!"

Sam laughed a little. "My Dad made wine when I was growing up, so I learned some from him. Then my brothers Danny and Joe made wine, and I've read a few books on it. Hopefully what John and I just made turns out well, at least mine," he said with a chuckle.

As I scooped some garlic from Myrt's mixture of olive oil, white wine vinegar, olives, and garlic from the bowl on the table, I said, "Besides your wine, I like that you grow garlic in your garden."

Sam added, "I grew the oregano that's dried and sprinkled in there too. I didn't cure any olives this year, all of the olives that I've seen around here have dark dimples on them. That means they have little white worms in them."

"I'm guessing that you saw Joe race cars in his heyday?"

"I saw him race at the 1971 California 500 in Ontario. Joe invited me, Sammy, and Judy's husband Wes to come and spend some time together over the weekend. I usually turn down invitations, but with Sammy and Wes coming along, we accepted and drove there to see him."

"The night before the race, Joe and his wife Dianne took us out to dinner. We went to a nice steak restaurant and sat at a long table with A.J. Foyt, Cale Yarborough, Al and Bobby Unser, plus James Garner and Steve McQueen. McQueen had just completed the racing movie "Le Mans," and I think he was the highest paid actor in Hollywood at the time. He was the Grand Marshall for the California 500 that year. James Garner wasn't so well known yet, and he must have had a thing for Joe's wife and spent half the night talking with her. Dianne is French Canadian with dark hair and fair skin, a very pretty girl. Things only got better when Joe won the next day. Later he said that the reason he won is because I was there," Sam smiled.

I said, "What a wonderful thing for Joe to say."

"Joe became a great driver, and he won consecutive USAC national titles in 1971 and 1972. He's the only person to ever win both a motorcycle championship and an automobile championship, and the kicker is that he had back-to-back championships in both."

I could hardly believe it. "Wow, how awesome is that!"

"When did Joe stop racing cars?"

"That was three years after his win at the California 500 when he crashed at the same track. Joe was close to the lead, when his front left tire blew which sent his car into the inside cement barrier at 160 mph. The front of the car was so crushed that they couldn't pull him from the open cockpit, so they had to cut the car apart. Joe said his biggest worry was that sparks from the cutting tools might ignite fuel around the car and he would have been helpless to escape."

"Joe's left ankle was so damaged that the doctors wanted to cut his foot off, but he wouldn't let them. I guess he hoped that surgery would eventually fix his foot, but it never did. If Joe would have let them remove it and gotten a prosthetic foot, he would have walked better and might have still been able to race, he just needed to be able to push in the clutch without problems. But as it was, Joe needed a cane to help walk, and with a fused ankle the Indy officials wouldn't clear him, so his racing career came to an end. But today he still drives a turbocharged Ford Probe around town like a bat out of hell."

Sam added, "I only had a couple broken bones from racing. I got tore up more when I crashed my 10-speed bicycle a couple years ago. As racers we might get banged up a little, but we still want to compete. I'm sure that given the chance, Joe would get out on the track again."

I smiled and said, "I love hearing these old stories."

"There are a thousand of them from the old days. One day a bunch of us guys were riding to Hollister during the winter and everyone was wearing heavy coats. Joe was drafting Charlie West, because he had a stronger bike, and Joe tucked up under Charlie's elbow as they were moving at a pretty good clip. Joe didn't know that when he got in close, his brake lever got caught in Charlie's coat sleeve and when they moved apart, Joe got pulled off his bike going maybe 100 mph. Joe went tumbling ass over elbows and ended up hitting his head on a guard rail, it's not like anyone wore helmets just riding around."

"His crash cut short our Sunday ride, so I said, "You ruined my day, Moke."

"Well how do you think I feel?"

Joe rode on the back of my bike on the way home, and he was talking like a seven year old, which meant that he really got his bell rung. Joe had a bald spot from where the pavement tore off a chunk of his scalp, and it took a while before hair started growing there again. Over his years of motorcycle racing, Joe had three concussions and only one of them was on the track, but all three times he ended up at our house recovering. Myrt would call Diane, and she'd ask, "What happened this time?"

"It's funny that Joe is really two years younger than everyone thinks. As a kid his dad wouldn't sign papers to let him race at 16, so Joe lied and said that he was born two years earlier in 1932, so that would make him 18, and he could enter competitions."

Sam started laughing, "My favorite story to harass Joe with is when he lost to the previously retired Ed Kretz at the Pacific Coast TT Championship. This was just after Joe had just gotten his #1 plate. Kretz was a tough motorcycle racer, and in the 1940s, he earned the title
"Iron Man," so losing to a racer like him isn't far-fetched."

Just then, the sliding glass door opened, and Sammy came out on the deck to join us.

"What's going on out here?"

I said, "Just hearing some old stories. Sam says that back in the early 1960s, you were getting ready to go flat track racing through the Midwest, but you didn't want to leave because you had just met Sharon."

He started laughing. "I met Sharon (Serradell) about three weeks before Charlie West, Alan Kaiser, Ron Boyarsky, and me were going to Sturgis and Springfield. Ron was one of the top amateurs in the country and Charlie was building his bikes. After I had a couple dates with Sharon, I didn't want to go, but the trip was planned out. When I got back, Sharon and I picked up where we left off and three months later we married."

"You move fast!"

Sammy asked his Dad, "Did you tell Tyler about when the guys went to Sturgis and stayed with the mayor?"

Sam said, "Joe, Charlie, and Al were going to the Sturgis Half Mile, and the mayor of Sturgis had invited them to stay at his house when they came into town, so they took him up on the offer. The guys borrowed an old trailer, that I had built in the 1930s, to haul their bikes. The tires on the trailer were pretty much shot, but they didn't have any other option. To show how broke they were, by Salt Lake City they had to start siphoning gas from cars just to make it to Sturgis."

"On the way to Sturgis is Deadwood, which is a good place to stop in for gas or food before continuing on. I think that the town was maybe a few blocks long, and half of that distance was just bars. On the second floor above the stores on Main Street, you could go around to the back and up the stairs to where the brothels were. I think that the first time the guys stopped in Deadwood, it was just for a pit stop, but they ended up staying for three days."

"So they made it to Sturgis and the half-mile, and on their final day in town, the mayor was out doing official business when one of the guys came across two new tires on six-lug rims out in the mayor's garage that would fit on the trailer. Six lug rims were pretty difficult to find, and since the current tires weren't going to last much longer, they "borrowed" the tires on their way out of town. I guess they thought that they wouldn't be going back to Sturgis again, but Joe ran into the mayor a year or three later and got an earful."

I said, "These stories are great. I thought the story about the factory stealing Tom's cams was crazy. I'm surprised a law suit or something didn't happen because of it."

"Bill Davidson was a straight shooter and respected Tom, so when he found out he tried to stop it, but it was too late. Once word got around on the underhanded way they got Tom's cams, Dud's reputation took a hit, at least from those who knew about it. But it just shows the lengths that people would go through to get a set of Tom's prized cams. Although the factory said that they didn't copy his cams, later on they paid Tom several thousand dollars to make amends."

"So you were involved with the Gypsy Tour when they had all of the problems in Hollister?"

"It wasn't nearly as bad as what they made it out to be. Even the local police said the bikers did more harm to themselves than they did to the town."

I said, "I've seen that old photo of a drunken biker on a Harley with beer bottles all around him."

"That whole thing was set up; it wasn't even his bike. That guy was a preacher's son, and he had just stumbled out of a bar, and the photographers talked him into getting on the bike. Then they gathered up all of the empty beer bottles lying around and started taking pictures. How they exaggerated that one incident, and especially that photo when it appeared in LIFE magazine, started the change from good people in motorcycle clubs out having fun on the weekends, to the images of lowlifes riding around and causing trouble."

"In the late 1960s and 1970s, when guys in the Hells Angels came into the dealership, I had them to leave their leather jackets outside. I didn't want them coming into the shop and scaring some Mom who was there to buy a motorcycle for her kid. Sometimes one of them might say that they'll go to another Harley dealership where they didn't have to take off their jackets, I'd tell them to go ahead. I guess they respected me because they would leave their jackets outside."

"I have a question. Is there anything in your life that you wanted to do, but weren't able to?"

He thought for a second, "I really wanted to get at least one National Championship on the track, but the biggest thing is that I never went to Trabia to see where my parents were born. That's something I really wanted to do with Myrt, but it never happened."

As I refilled my wine glass, I thought, if I make it into old age, I hope that people will come by my house for a glass of wine and tell a few stories, but you have to be the brunt of jokes on occasion. One Saturday, when Sam, John, Ray, and myself were on the deck, I asked Sam,

"If you went camping with some buddies and woke up in the morning with vaseline smeared on the inside your thighs, would you tell anyone?"

Sam quickly replied, "No!"

"Do you want to go camping?"

We nearly died from laughing as Sam sat there stone-faced. That became a long running joke over the years.

About then the back slider opened, and Ray came outside to join us. "Hey guys."

"Ray, pull up a chair. How's the koi pond?"

"Great. Yesterday I had to spend a few hours thinning out the water plants that were taking over. You'll have to come over and see this big albino koi that I have."

Everyone got the idea for starting a koi pond from Sam's little gold fish pond. Sam's pond could hold 15 or 20 gallons, and then John had an elaborate in-ground version built that holds around 2500 gallons complete with a small water fall. For Ray, after his kids moved out, their swimming pool wasn't being used anymore, so he converted it into a huge koi "pond," and now he's got dozens of koi. They say that fish grow according to the size of their enclosure, and he's got some koi the size of catfish that keep getting bigger. When he feeds them, it's amazing how the water just churns as the koi are fighting and sliding over each other to get to the food.

We started joking that it's after 5, so John should be by pretty soon, and not five minutes later we saw him coming up the back steps. "Speaking of John, there he is."

"Hey neighbors."

With John living right next door, he has all kinds of insight into Sam's ways, and some of them are pretty funny. One story John told me is how early on a Saturday morning, as he was looking outside from his second story window, he saw Sam in his garden stealing corn! The funny thing was that Sam had his arms so full of corn already, that he couldn't hold it all and kept dropping ears. Then every time he reached down to pick one up, he would drop another. It got to be so funny that John woke up Donna so she could watch. Sam was cussing with each dropped ear, and it just kept getting funnier as Sam made his way up the back path to his house.

John pulled up a chair and settled in by pouring a glass of wine.

"Hey Sam, are you going to start up the bike today?"

"I'm going to try. The guy that sold me the motor guaranteed that it would work. It has gas and the motor has spark, so it should fire up." Then he said, "Since everyone is here, why don't we grab a glass of wine and go out to the garage."

We followed Sam through the open slider and headed for the garage. As we passed Myrt sitting on the sofa, I asked "You coming out with us?"

"No, I'm sure I'll be able to hear from here," she said smiling.

Out in the garage, the spaghetti frame bike is up on an old metal milk crate, all chromed and shiny, looking like it has been waiting for us. I remember years ago when it was just a red frame hanging on a big nail on the garage wall. Now she's a beautiful motorcycle.

Looking around the garage, I see the two long shelves running high along the wall with dozens of dusty trophies, many of them are broken from earthquakes that knocked them off the shelves over the years. On another wall are the two large posters from his racing days: one is about his National Championship hill climb at Dubuque Iowa in 1949, and the other is the 1938 Oakland 200 victory where Sam looks beyond exhausted, but happy with his win.

Sam undid the trickle charger from the battery, and we got the bike off of the floor stand. Sam got on the bike and after several kick-start attempts, the hill climber roared to life. We had the garage door open, but the sound inside the garage is still deafening. The whole house is shaking as Sam revved the motor. For him it must have felt, and probably sounded, like old times. I wondered if memories from the hill climb at Friant Dam forty years ago aboard this bike came to his mind, or maybe he is thinking of another favorite climb.

The bike has come around full-circle. From a record-breaking hill climber, to little more than just a frame, and now it has been restored to a complete bike. I thought to myself, what a cool moment to be part of. I remember what Sam once said to me as we were sitting out on the deck one Saturday, "If I had to do it all over again, I would do it all the same way."

That's the way life should be for all of us. I'll drink to that.

For my buddy Sam, thanks for the fun Saturday afternoons, the red wine, and the stories.

1938 Oakland 200 – Poster in Sam's Garage

1949 Dubuque Iowa – Poster in Sam's Garage

Sam and Myrt's 50th Aniversary (1986)

Acknowledgements

I'd like to thank all of the racers, mechanics, and family members that talked to me over the years. This great bunch of folks include: George "Bobo" Sepulveda, Joe Leonard, Al Fernandez, Lee "Mac" McReynolds, Everett Brashear, Norm Smith, Paul Goldsmith, Chris Rudy, and Judy Arena who helped with stories outside of racing. Also, many thanks to Raphy Alden for doing a quick review and edit on this book on short notice.

I'd like to credit to the AMA hall of fame website (http://www.motorcyclemuseum.org/halloffame/) which was very helpful in getting various dates correct. Another help was the AMA Pro Flat Track Series Guide which listed the Grand National race winners beginning in 1954, which again, was very helpful in getting races in the correct order from 60 years ago.

Finally, a huge thanks goes to Sam "Sammy" Arena. Sammy answered too many phone calls to count over the years, and he provided a wealth of information that I couldn't have gotten anywhere else.

Photos

In the compilation of photos, I've gathered them from various sources. A few were from the internet, but most of them were from Arena family members. Some of these known photographers include: D.R. "Doc" Edmonds, Clarence Colwell out of San Francisco, Mike Musura, Don Emde, and Pat Corner out of Daly City. Also, Roy Frates took videos during the 1940s might have also taken some still photos.

Every effort has been made to trace the copyright holders of the photos, and I apologize if any sources inadvertently remain unacknowledged or wrongly acknowledged. Any information that will help to trace copyright holders, or correct details, will be gratefully appreciated.

Sam Arena's National Championships

80-cubic-inch Hill Climb in Milpitas, CA – 1947
45-cubic-inch Hill Climb in Milpitas, CA – 1948
80-cubic-inch Hill Climb in Dubuque, Iowa – 1949
45-cubic-inch Hill Climb in Eugene, Oregon – 1950
45-cubic-inch and 80-cubic-inch Hill Climb in Modesto, CA – 1958

Made in the USA
Middletown, DE
15 June 2017